# Glory Unveiled

An inspiring journey towards spiritual maturity
through the wondrous story of metamorphosis

By Christine Cartwright

British Library Cataloguing in Publication Data available
ISBN  978-0-9562528-0-7

Cover Design by Kathryn Chedgzoy (www.kathryn.chedgzoy.co.uk)
Intext Design by Kathryn Chedgzoy and Alan Batchelor
Photographs by Jay Cossey, Bob Moul and William Zittrich
Printed in the United Kingdom, in association with Deanprint Limited.

To my beloved family and friends

for your encouragement in the Lord

# Contents

# Introduction

# A vision given; a life changed

*Faith is a journey, but there are definite moments when truth propels a person from one state of being to another. I can name several defining moments in my life. I wonder if you can do the same. Heather Gemmen*

In August, 1999, the vision of the butterfly was spoken over my life for the first time. Although I had been a Christian for years, I was just beginning an earnest quest to be changed into the likeness of Christ to bring glory to him. Failing to see the beauty and value holiness brings to life, I knew I did not desire it as I should. I faced a daily struggle to comprehend my purpose on earth and an overwhelming desire for a passion in life.

At this time, a friend unexpectedly spoke into my life. In her words:

*"All the things that have been put into you, everything from when you were very young, are going to come out; maybe you feel they are not coming out enough ... but they will. You will bring restoration to those who need it; you will bring healing to people. I see a butterfly with wonderful colours and jewels with the colours red and green, shimmering brightly."*

The words were very beautiful but I did not really understand the significance of such a vision, so I wrote the words in the back of my journal and did not share the vision with anyone else. For five years the words lay unspoken, though not forgotten.

By summer, 2004, I had passed through a period of disobedience to the Lord and was praying with a friend for forgiveness and a fresh start. She suddenly declared that she had a picture for me but she was unsure of its relevance. She was seeing a butterfly. I confirmed to her that the Lord had indeed spoken to me in this way before. However, this time, the vision came with a cautionary note; I had not become the butterfly I was destined to be but was still a little worm, a caterpillar.

Upon her departure, I sat in stunned silence, shocked that the Almighty God would speak to me twice in the same way. I knew then that I had to discover the full meaning of the vision. But where should I start? I knew that I had never read anything about butterflies in the Bible but, in desperation, I opened my Bible up at random. The page fell open on Isaiah 41 : 14. To my utter amazement, I saw already clearly underlined in my Bible: *"Do not be afraid, O worm Jacob, O little Israel, for I myself will help you,"* declares the Lord, your Redeemer, the Holy One of Israel.

My heart flooded with thankfulness to the Lord. He recognised my wormlike state but he was encouraging me from the outset that he would take me by my right hand and lead me towards my true destiny – the butterfly. It would take years before I was to grasp fully the magnitude of that verse.

The following story is the culmination of several years of the Lord speaking into my life through my researching the butterfly.

# Why share the vision?

*"We proclaim Him, admonishing every man and teaching every man with all wisdom, so that we may present every man complete in Christ. For this purpose also I labour, striving according to His power, which mightily works within me."*
*Colossians 1 : 28,29 (NASB)*

My purpose in sharing this vision with you is not to present a dry set of clever analogies between creation and spirituality, although creation does marvellously speak of the Lord and his wisdom. I share because I believe the story of the butterfly is one picture through which God wills *"to make known the riches of the glory of this mystery ... Christ in you – the hope of glory".* (Colossians 1 : 27) I was living like a worm when I was called to be a butterfly. How deceived I had been! I would far rather be a new creation in Christ – a butterfly – than live in the old nature, a wormlike creature. Holiness was not about dullness. Quite the opposite! It was about fulfilled destiny, beauty, purpose and vision.

I want to help you to attain *"to all the wealth that comes from the full assurance of understanding, resulting in a true knowledge of God's mystery, that is Christ Himself in whom are hidden all the treasures of wisdom and knowledge".* (Colossians 2 : 3,4) (NASB) In short, I believe God wants to open your eyes to the treasure within you so you are more likely to be excited about finding it in your own life and then sharing it with others!

This book is to bring hope for change and reason for perseverance when growth and the Lord's cleansing work in your life is painful and slow and, above all, to give to each one of you the promise of vision and purpose. My prayer is that the lessons and warnings which are to be found through the study of the life cycle of the butterfly will indeed give you "the wealth of assurance" in the mighty and gloriously-loving God you serve, riches from which you can draw when difficult times come.

No earthly story completely symbolizes an eternal truth ... Only as types and allegories help us to apply truth to our lives, and as they agree with all other Scripture, are they valid revelation. The ultimate purpose of all revelation must be to transform us into the image of Christ.

Fuchsia Pickett

As you follow the story of the Creator-God taking wormlike creatures, the lowly things of this world, and transforming them into winged insects of great beauty and wonder, may your heart be inspired to share this special message with friends who have not yet heard of the loving grace and awesome life-changing power of the Lord Jesus. Everyone, even children, can relate to the story of the butterfly.

## Comment on the analogies drawn and scientific research

It must be recognised that I am in no way a scientist and I have not written this book as a scientific paper. There are thousands of species of butterflies and all behave in different ways and have different life cycles. As I give the various analogies, I do not claim that all points are true of all butterflies. Though the credibility of the analogy does hang on its accurate reflection of what happens in reality, it is the spiritual lesson I seek to convey rather than an exact correspondence between science and spirituality.

The analogies are also separate of themselves; for example – one could use the life cycle of the butterfly to portray the process of an unbeliever coming to know the Lord. However, it is equally effective in portraying the believer's on-going process of moving towards spiritual maturity, through various phases of ministry, relationships and the development of spiritual gifts.

# Thanks and Acknowledgements

I have, to the best of my ability, sought to ensure that the scientific and biological references are accurate. I wish to thank Prof. Lincoln Brower of Sweet Briar College, VA for his contribution to the scientific editing of Chapter 8. All references from my internet research can be found in the endnotes.

Mr. Jay Cossey, field photographer for the University of Guelp, Ontario generously gave me his kind permission to use his beautiful photography. If you wish to see more of his work, please visit his website www.PhotographsFromNature.com. For the generous permission to use their photographs, my thanks and credit also go to: Mr. Bob Moul (www.pbase.com/rcm1840) and Dr. William Zittrich. (www.geocities.com/wyllz/id299.htm)

I extend heartfelt thanks to my parents for their unswerving support and prayers, and especially to my father, Mr. G. D. Cartwright, for his patient editing of the text. I am also indebted to Kathryn Chedgzoy and to Mr. Alan Batchelor for their great generosity in designing the cover and typesetting the text and photographs in preparation for printing. Special thanks must go to Mrs. Janet Hughes for proofreading the final draft and to Mrs. Pamela Matheson for her time and encouragement as my mentor whilst writing this book.

I could not have completed this work without the kind support and encouragement of my church leaders, friends and family. I appreciate all those who proofread the text and gave their comments. For all those who, through their generosity, made this project possible, I ask the Lord's richest blessings.

Finally, I wish to thank Sharon Brown and Nicola Gollings who, in obedience to the Lord and in faithful use of their God-given gifts, gave me the butterfly vision. I hope this book will encourage you and others to continue to use your spiritual gifts.

*"You say, "I am rich; I have acquired wealth and do not need a thing." But you do not realise that you are wretched, pitiful, poor, blind and naked. I counsel you to buy from me gold refined in the fire, so that you can become rich; and white clothes to wear, so that you can cover your shameful nakedness; and salve to put on your eyes, so that you can see. Those whom I love I rebuke and discipline. So be earnest, and repent. Here I am! I stand at the door and knock. If anyone hears my voice and opens the door, I will come in and eat with him, and he with me."*
*Revelation 3 : 17-20*

# The Story in a Nutshell

*"In him you were also circumcised, in the putting off of the sinful nature, not with a circumcision done by the hands of men but with the circumcision done by Christ, having been buried with him in baptism and raised with him through your faith in the power of God, who raised him from the dead."*
*Colossians 2 : 11,12*

The caterpillar represents the old nature that Christ takes and transforms into a new creation. The near-blind caterpillar lives a self-centred lifestyle. It has a ferocious hunger, shedding its skins up to four times in order to grow. As it reaches the time to become a butterfly, it must give up its entire body, entombing itself in its final pupal skin. Before this 'death to self' takes place, the caterpillar rids itself of all the dirt (frass) within its body. Then it surrenders itself to the watery grave within the chrysalis to begin the process of metamorphosis. As the caterpillar breaks down, the chrysalis fills with a fluid and, from the caterpillar's former nature, the Lord God creates a new creature in the darkness and secrecy of the chrysalis. The DNA of the butterfly is within the caterpillar but, in order to become its true identity, it first has to die to self. So, too, we are called to confess our sins. We are purified through repentance. Having been symbolically buried with him in baptism, we arise new creations in the Lord. Indeed, there is no resurrection without a death.

As the new butterfly emerges from the chrysalis, it initially looks rather stunted. It has to wait whilst blood pumps into its wings to expand them and then let them dry in the sun. The new butterfly becomes a 'sun–worshipper' as it is cold-blooded. It must frequently bask in the sunlight to retain its energy for flight and purpose. If it falls into shady places for extended periods of time, it becomes inert and so very vulnerable to enemies. It may eventually die from cold. This speaks of our need to stay in the light of the Lord's will for our lives and live as 'son–worshippers.' The butterfly, unlike the caterpillar, lives a life of service as well as bringing beauty and joy to the world around it. It pollinates flowers and lays eggs to bring around the next generation of 'sun-worshippers'. Life is usually very short but full of purpose, beauty, meaning, flight and vision.

Amazing Grace

Amazing Grace – How sweet the sound
That sav'd a wretch like me!
I once was lost but now am found,
Was blind, but now I see.

'Twas grace that taught my heart to fear,
And grace my fears reliev'd;
How precious did that grace appear,
The hour I first believ'd!

Thro' many dangers, toils and snares,
I have already come;
'Tis grace has brought me safe thus far,
And grace will lead me home.

The Lord has promis'd good to me,
His word my hope secures;
He will my shield and portion be,
As long as life endures.

Yes, when this flesh and heart shall fail,
And mortal life shall cease;
I shall possess, within the veil,
A life of joy and peace.

The earth shall soon dissolve like snow,
The sun forbear to shine;
But God, who call'd me here below,
Will be forever mine.

John Newton
(1725-1807)

# Chapter 1

# The Start of Life
## The Importance of our Origins

*"All the days ordained for me were written in your book before one of them came to be."*
*Psalm 139 : 16*

Life is a miraculous gift. Spiritual life is an even greater gift!

A caterpillar's life, beginning from its days as a tiny egg, is a creative marvel. However, there is even more of a wonder to be discovered within the genes packed inside the pinhead-sized egg. Every caterpillar is born with the potential to become a new creation - a beautiful butterfly. None of them is destined to remain a plain worm. They have a God-given future filled with beauty, flight, vision and purpose.

The story of the caterpillar becoming a butterfly is one we know even from childhood. As such, it has perhaps become so familiar to us that we have lost the wonder of the miraculous change that occurs. Imagine if you had never seen a caterpillar before and then, for the first time, witnessed the transformation! The nature of our modern lives has probably left us with a similarly jaded view of life, taking for granted the everyday functioning of our bodies and the beauty of nature. We often fail to see the miracles that happen all around us each day. However, when we stop to reflect, our lives here on earth are a miraculous testament to an amazing Creator. The fact that we were born and have life is a miracle in itself. Yet, as in the life of the caterpillar, there is even more to our lives than meets the eye. There is a glorious wonder waiting to be unveiled in our lives too. Each individual is born with a destiny to be so much more than a mere mortal. Man is made in the image of God and, as such, is an everlasting being. God, who sustains our every breath, has planted within us the capacity to know him and "be born again". No matter how our life starts, the state of our health, or the length of our days, life is a miraculous gift and has an eternal purpose. No-one is a mistake. We can all be used by our awesome Creator to bring forth his glory from our lives. Recognising this treasure within is the start of our journey to the miracle of spiritual metamorphosis - the wonder of becoming, day by day, a new creation in Christ.

"I have come that they may have life, and have it to the full."

John 10 : 10b

A near-blind, ugly-looking, earthbound caterpillar cannot begin to imagine what a marvel it must be to live as a butterfly because its current wormlike state is so far removed from the glory of a butterfly. Similarly, the Bible tells us that we, too, first need to begin with a step of faith. We commit ourselves to God with the conviction that, through our spiritual growth, we shall be as comprehensively changed as the caterpillar is to become the butterfly. The belief in the greater value and joy of the 'winged life' of spiritual maturity is essential to our beginning and persevering through the journey of faith from immaturity to maturity.

No butterflies are born; only caterpillars. There is an unavoidable process through which each caterpillar must go. Similarly we, too, are faced with a life of seasons and learning curves - spiritual growth; stripping away; changes and metamorphosis! Life, from the vulnerability of the tiny egg to the days as a butterfly, is fraught with many dangers, under constant threat from enemies and disease. Yet every caterpillar should be a joy to behold for within its frame lies the life of another beautiful butterfly, no matter how short its lifespan. Life will be hard for us too but the miracle lies before us to be seized – the miracle that we are here at all ..

...... and with the opportunity to know God

.......... and to be spiritually born again

.......... and to find our destiny in him

............ and to live with him forever!

Will you look at the caterpillar's life story and believe it for your own life? Will you, in faith, begin your own journey of spiritual metamorphosis? It all starts with the realisation that this life-changing gift of personally knowing God depends upon a personal choice. The Lord makes known his desire for a relationship with us but we must make an active decision to begin the process of developing the faith, obedience and surrender that leads to transformation. Throughout this book, we shall look at this process, with its many questions and ups and downs, to see how we can ensure that we reach the miracle of metamorphosis and live the fulfilled life Jesus came to give.

# The Start of Life

*"For I know the plans I have for you," declares the Lord, "plans to prosper you and not to harm you, plans to give you hope and a future." Jeremiah 29 : 11*

The start of life can be the source of many difficult questions for some. I recognise that in beginning here, I shall potentially, if you will pardon the pun, open the proverbial can of worms. However, the mistake of leaving issues from our origins and earliest days unaddressed, can cause tragic malfunctions in both our physical and spiritual growth, as we shall see later.

The journey of life starts in so many different places and in so many different ways. This should not surprise us. As we look at the natural world around us, we see evidence of this over and over again. The Creator loves diversity and with diversity comes a richness, beauty and depth to life.

Within any kind of species, not all begin life in the same environment. So it is with the butterfly. It is estimated that, as the second largest species group of insects, there are tens of thousands of different types of butterflies and moths, with up to one hundred thousand still to be formally identified. Their lives begin in many different habitats of the world. They can be found almost everywhere, except in the polar regions! The eggs laid by these thousands of species of butterfly, although all tiny, come in quite different shapes and colours. Some are round; some are grooved or pitted, whilst others are smooth. Many butterfly species, such as the Red Admiral or the Comma, will lay only one egg. Other species will lay clusters of eggs - the Peacock laying as many as five hundred eggs in one batch. The genes held within these diverse eggs will bring forth butterflies of a myriad of colours, design and wingspan. Some will live months, others weeks and some only a matter of days. The butterfly egg is, of course, stage one in a caterpillar's life.

The one thing that most caterpillars have in common is a birthplace carefully selected by the mother butterfly. All butterflies will try to lay their eggs where the emerging caterpillar will immediately find its food plant - its source of strength, future identity markings and means of survival. For example, a Monarch will only lay its eggs on milkweed. The consumption of milkweed provides not only nourishment but also the toxins which will make the caterpillar, and later the butterfly, poisonous to birds and other predators - an important part of their defence mechanisms. The butterfly will also retain, within the cells of its wing scales, colour pigments derived from plants eaten at the caterpillar stage, giving the butterfly some of its unique colours. These colours can be used for startling predators, often warning them of the unpalatable taste of the butterfly. They are also used in attracting mates.

Evidently, the choice of birthplace is extremely important to the development of the caterpillar and even to the future of the butterfly. Likewise, our origins, our genes, and our childhood play an important part in the person we become. We have no control over it. Like the caterpillar's parent butterfly, our Father in heaven decides where we begin life. God determines where every man should live. Subsequently, we all come from very different backgrounds, countries and family situations. Through the wonder of our DNA, we have a variety of personalities, gifts and talents, as well as varying weaknesses and defects.

The apparent 'unfairness' in the huge variation of our backgrounds, and our start in life, can cause us to question the wisdom and the love of the Lord. Sometimes it is easy to doubt that the Lord is in control of our history. Many people struggle because they cannot understand why the Lord allowed their life to begin in a certain family or in a certain environment. However, Psalm 139 tells us that, amazingly, all our days are ordained for us before one of them came to be. This includes where God placed us from birth. He knew where he wanted you to 'hatch' and which life experiences you would undergo in your maturing process. He makes no mistakes; he knew the 'plant' upon which you would be born and your subsequent 'food source'. He knew from whence he would call you and which 'colours and effective defence mechanisms' you would retain as a result. He knows every detail, and he will use your personality and experiences to enhance your relationship with him and your ministry.

Brother Andrew, in his book, "The Calling", talks of his childhood in Holland, growing up under Nazi occupation. Sometimes his family were so desperate, they ate tulip bulbs cut up into small slices so as to last them for days. Yet he writes: *"Looking back, I see how God used every one of those events to prepare me for his service. The dire conditions we lived under during the war helped me to identify with the hardships many Christian families face in repressive countries. And there are many other ways God prepared me. It's important that we do not despise our own life experiences. We can look back and know that God will use them all for his service."*

Too often, we are tempted to think that life should be uniform - that we should all have the same opportunities in life. However, if this were the case, there would be no variation; no wonder in uniqueness or extraordinary talent – just as the thrilling beauty of butterflies would be lost if all butterflies had been given the same colours and design! Could it be that we even worry about things that are not actually a problem for the people concerned? What do I mean by that? Growing up in England and privileged with an excellent education, I felt so blessed that I struggled to accept the fact that God did not allow everyone to begin life in the same way. However, as an adult, I now appreciate that a South American tribesman, for instance, looking on at my world, would undoubtedly shudder at the thought of living in the structured, grey streets of an English town. He loves the hot, tropical forest around him with its beautiful flowers, birds and animals. My upbringing and education gave me the opportunity to become a high-school teacher, to speak different languages, to enjoy studying and writing and to desire to tell others what the Lord has taught me. However, I would not have the faintest idea how to conserve the rainforest or look after tropical plants and animals. My landlady will tell you I even have trouble remembering to water the plants. The Lord has given us all different opportunities and skills for his wonderful purposes.

A professor might look at a person with limited academic ability and question why God could not have blessed them both with the same intelligence. He might fail to appreciate that the person concerned is a craftsman of great skill, able to carve beautiful wooden artefacts. This skill brings the craftsman great joy and fulfilment. He might never go to university or become rich but he suffers no frustration over not being created sporty or academic. Even the understanding of what constitutes a good education varies from country to country. One may measure 'an education' in terms of academic achievement which leads to a job with a good salary. Elsewhere, an education might only be worth its salt if it teaches you to appreciate life in a much deeper sense – how to care for a family; how to grow your own food; how to maintain skills essential to life in that environment.

Clearly, there are situations that provoke huge challenges to our faith, causing us to ask "If God were a God of love ......?" We can begin to question if there is a point at which life no longer seems a miracle, where God's wisdom in granting life is doubtful. Is life a blessing if you have to live in poverty? Is life worth living if you are abused? Is life a gift if you are handicapped? We need to question the spirit behind such ideas. It is certainly not of God. It has very dark consequences. The Nazi policy of eliminating all handicapped people, believing their lives to have no purpose or value, is just one shocking example of such a mentality. Some, in the light of such tragedies, even go as far as to say that the world is so wicked that they hesitate to bring a child into it, no matter how privileged a start in life they were able to provide. But, what are we truly saying if we question God who allows life to continue even in its fallen state?

Proverbs, chapter 8, is a great source of wisdom and comfort to me in these dark questions. Our omniscient creator-God, knowing the end from the beginning, could see all of human history ahead of time – the relentless battle between good and evil and the innumerable victims of the conflict. Nevertheless, in the mysterious references in the book of Proverbs, chapter 8 : 22-31, divine wisdom personified rejoices over the creation of planet earth and takes special delight in the sons of men. He rejoiced even though he

"When he marked out the foundations of the earth, then I was beside him, as a master workman and I was daily His delight, rejoicing always before him, rejoicing in the world, His earth, and having my delight in the sons of men."
Proverbs 8 : 29b -31 (NASB)

knew he would suffer disappointment and grief almost from the very start of creation. God's foreknowledge of the potential consequences of man's free will did not stop him creating. Furthermore, he has persevered with his creation through all of history because he saw 'the big picture'. He saw the fulfilled destinies - those who would persevere and grow into a relationship with him and, one day, be with him for eternity. If God, in his infinite wisdom, so values his relationship with us as to be worth the pain and tribulation, should we not also regard that relationship as the one thing, above all others, that makes life worth living? There must be something more profound than our current circumstances to use as the basis of our evaluation of life. The value of life cannot be based on our background, our health, our education, our success or our relationships. If it were, God would have seen that not all men would be blessed in these ways and would surely have decided against creating life. What's more, life's value must not be cancelled out even by the horrendous experiences some people encounter. Indeed, if life is only of value once we consider God has blessed us adequately, why are some of the most privileged of people found amongst the most unhappy and unsatisfied? They have missed the point. The value of life lies within our opportunity to know God and so become a new creation qualified to spend eternity with him.

This is so far removed from our twenty-first century secular way of thinking that we need to renew our minds and our attitudes. I do not write these words glibly. I know that, as a person who has not experienced a troubled start to life, or crushing experiences of ill-health, abuse, tragedy or poverty, I might well be criticised for over-simplifying what is a very deep issue. However, I feel that there is no greater gift to hold out to those who have suffered than the assurance that their life's greatest value still holds true. To deny the existence, or the goodness, of God in the face of life's mysterious trials only makes matters worse for, indeed, it makes everything we endure absolutely meaningless. Job, in his suffering, asked God, *"Why is life given to a man whose way is hidden, whom God has hedged in?"* (Job 3 : 23) But God was in control and had a purpose. Job later confessed that, in questioning the wisdom of God, he *"spoke of things (he) did not understand, things too wonderful for (him) to know."* (Job 42 : 3b)

There are some questions we shall never be able to answer. So what shall we do in the meantime? Feeling angry that you were not born in a more privileged environment, or not blessed with the skills others possess, is damaging to one's personality. Rather than battle with inequality, let us look instead at the opportunities and potential in the miracle of life we have been given. Let us appreciate how our different backgrounds and experiences in life bring together a human race of such different cultures, skills, beauty and variety. Our 'colours and varying shapes'- personalities and subsequent gifts for ministry - issue from the broad variety of 'egg shapes' and 'hatching grounds'. Would we really want to alter that diversity?

# The Start of Spiritual Life

*"When Israel was a child, I loved him, and out of Egypt I called my son." Hosea 11 : 1*

Why did I address the physical start of life before looking at the spiritual start of life? As we have discussed, each of us has a different upbringing and family history which determines many things about our future as adults. Without question, our physical start to life also affects the start of our spiritual journey of faith. For some people it will prove to be a major stumbling block. Unless we can accept the loving sovereignty of God, we will not turn to him to make true the greatest value of our lives. Each one who reads this will have a completely different story to tell. One thing is sure - the Lord makes no mistakes. We live in a fallen world but all things are under his control and work together for the good of those who love him. The Lord calls us out of our backgrounds and our experiences in order to follow him.

Every season has a God-ordained purpose which Satan will try his utmost to thwart. This is never more true than at the start of life. He knows 'the time in the egg' can determine the health and survival of the future caterpillar. At the outset of our spiritual journeys to pursue righteousness, there is the potential within each of our lives to bring about the Lord's purposes in this world. Satan, aware of that, will do all in his power to minimize, or destroy, that potential. Mature believers must appreciate the importance of protecting 'the egg stage' in those who are on the threshold of new birth.

# Vulnerable time

Caterpillar eggs are extremely vulnerable. Both predators and parasites will use the caterpillar's life to their own ends. This horror struck home to me when I read that caterpillars, as early as the egg stage, can be hijacked and infiltrated by species such as flies and wasps! The caterpillar then passes through the various stages, apparently as normal. They grow as caterpillars and shed skins but, all the while, they are being eaten from the inside out and will eventually be killed. In some cases, the parasite even goes into the chrysalis. But what comes out? Instead of a beautiful, harmless butterfly emerging to live with purpose, a parasitoid wasp or fly emerges!

Have you seen the equivalent happen in the lives of those around you? Early on in their spiritual walk, bitterness is allowed to creep in like a parasite, as questions, hurts or disappointments from the past are left unaddressed. All seems well, maybe for some years. Eventually, that bitterness, like the parasite, takes its toll. The persons concerned fail to mature spiritually as expected and are incapable of living life to the full, with the joy of the Lord as their strength. Instead, they are stunted in their spiritual walks, sapped of all their energy by some underlying issue of unforgiveness or anger, either towards God or towards others.

Resentment about the 'species', or the environment into which we were born, or events which took place as we grew up, must be dealt with. Otherwise we leave ourselves open to a 'parasite', which will drain vital life from us and rob us of the 'winged life'. It is a veritable tragedy, a life wasted, when Satan prevents us from finding the Lord's purpose for our lives simply by fixing all our attention on our personal grievances. Is it possible that you are vulnerable to such a parasite? How can you protect yourself? As you begin your spiritual journey to metamorphosis, ensure that you are starting in an attitude of worship and gratitude for what you are, and for the God-given promise that he has a wonderful plan for your life. Too often we look at others and wish we had started somewhere else, or in different circumstances. Now, just for a moment, let us imagine ourselves to be butterflies. The Monarch would not have the food source to become a beautiful orange and black butterfly if it did not begin life as a caterpillar feeding on a poisonous milkweed plant in North America. The hot, sticky, Brazilian rainforest may be inhospitable to many butterflies but not to the beautiful, iridescent, blue Morpho. In colder climes, it would perish. Each butterfly is suited to its particular environment for the purposes God has ordained for them. Furthermore, God uses its initial circumstances to heighten its colourful beauty.

# The importance of our origins

As we have seen earlier, another way to protect ourselves from infiltrating 'parasites' is to know our spiritual origins - created in the image of God - and to glean from them as much as we can about our destiny. A caterpillar's life would be so limited, if not wasted, if it never realised its potential to become a butterfly. It would lead a life crawling in the undergrowth, almost blind, often ugly or plain-looking, with a self-centred, self-gratifying nature. It would always be hungry, yet never satisfied, never fulfilling its true identity and destiny. The time on the wing would be lost. Likewise, any failure on our part to recognise our God-given potential could have even more serious results.

Satan squandered his unique opportunity to live out his glorious destiny. In the light of his loss and punishment, we see more clearly the motives of Satan to rob us of our destiny – our place as the beloved of God, those ordained to be guardians of this world. He will do anything to ensure that we forfeit our spiritual birthright. Having blinded the minds of unbelievers, he will do his utmost to undermine the believers' confidence in

God's promises and purposes. Once we have set out on the road to spiritual maturity, Satan will still exploit every hardship to make us lose heart. He will use events, circumstances and erratic emotions to provoke us to question the existence of a bigger picture with a Sovereign Creator in control of the great epic of our world's history. Perhaps his most subtle way of doing this is to make us question our origins, for they determine our identity and give us many clues as to our destiny. Satan knows that if we are deceived or confused about our origins, he can persuade us to use only our present circumstances to evaluate ourselves and our future prospects.

Let us look again at the caterpillar and imagine, for the sake of the analogy, that the caterpillar can see and think. To discover it came from an egg would only give the caterpillar limited information. To know about its true identity, purpose and future prospects, the caterpillar would really need to know who put the egg there! If it saw a butterfly lay the same eggs as those from which it crawled, and could understand the significance of this, what a difference that would make to its entire life, and to how it perceived the time as a wormlike creature. It would be able to comprehend that its current state is only one stage towards becoming something far superior. Knowing this, it would press on purposefully through the journey of eating to grow, facing all its enemies and even, eventually, facing death to self in the chrysalis. The whole process would be experienced differently because of its wider understanding of its true identity and preordained future.

> "In the beginning was the Word, and the Word was with God, and the Word was God. He was with God in the beginning. Through him all things were made; without him nothing was made that has been made. In him was life, and that life was the light of men. The light shines in the darkness, but the darkness has not understood it."
>
> John 1 : 1-5

The same is true of us. Our origins are always significant. It is not enough to simply know we came from a fertilised egg which grew inside a womb. We need to know who put us there! Ask someone who does not know their mother or father, or both, and you will find that they have a strong opinion about whether, or not, they wish to know their background. Many would like to know who their parents were, and from whence they came, believing that this would help them to know who they truly are, and would explain their characteristics, reactions, desires and fears. However, there are others who would not like to know for fear that they might discover something they would rather not discover. Both positions confirm that knowledge of our origins affects our understanding of both our present circumstances and our future prospects.

I emphasise this apparently obvious point because I believe it has a much greater bearing upon our lives, especially, our spiritual lives, than we might at first realize. Man has a general need to know his origins and, thereby, to find a guide to the meaning of life, a purpose and an explanation for many mysteries. Just look at the huge sums of money spent every year on research into the origins of the universe and, most recently, on the high-profile, research project in Geneva based on the assumption that our beautiful, highly complex universe accidentally came into being as a result of a random explosion of gases. However, as in the case of the caterpillar, I believe that it is not enough to discover the 'outer shell' of our origins, for this still only tells us about our current state. We need to know who put us here. That all-important discovery will illuminate the pathway of our daily development and provide the motivation to *"press on to take hold of that for which Christ took hold of (us)."* (Philippians 3 : 12b) We discover a Creator who can answer questions about his purpose for creation, his feelings towards us and what kind of relationship he desires to have with us.

As Christians we should be very serious about understanding our origins. The thrill of discovering that we are the beloved sons and daughters of a father-God, who has a plan, not just for the world in general, but for our individual lives in particular, is nothing less than awesome. It is sufficient to overcome our natural reluctance to surrender unconditionally our lives into his hands. Thereafter, nothing in life can claim to be of greater importance than deepening our relationship with our heavenly Father and learning more of his perfect plan for our lives. This is why there is such a ferocious spiritual battle over the issue of creation/evolution, and the integrity of the book of Genesis. I believe that the Lord knew we would need to understand our origins. Have you ever considered that we are the only part of the created order whose creation is actually described? We were so important that God – Father, Son and Holy Spirit - actually discussed our creation. God did not speak man into existence but took the trouble to form him out of the dust of the ground. Life was then imparted to the body by God breathing into man's nostrils and so man, created in the image of God, became a living soul – a soul capable of communion with God; a soul capable of receiving the gift of everlasting life; a soul which survives the corruption of the body. God's spirit is eternal. This is absolutely crucial. We are not just the latest stage of a random evolutionary process. Our souls will live forever - either in God's presence, or out of it. That is why the journey we make through this life matters so much. We were set apart from the beginning, made in God's likeness, given authority and purpose as part of our relationship with God. I personally believe it is an insult to insinuate that God would be so indifferent to his creation as to allow it to 'develop' through a random process of chance and mutation. If you wanted to create something of beauty, would you not lovingly preside over every detail and stamp your identity on it clearly? When one wishes to accomplish something of value, it requires an ordered process of thoughtful design. Within the sacred trust of human parenthood, no loving mother or father would dream of leaving a baby to fend for itself with the assumption that the evolutionary process would guarantee its survival and development. They would preside over every detail of that child's life, from infancy through adolescence and beyond, all with a view to ensuring

> 'It was I who taught Ephraim to walk, taking them by the arms; but they did not realise it was I who healed them. I led them with cords of human kindness, with ties of love; I lifted the yoke from their neck and bent down to feed them.'
>
> Hosea 11 : 3, 4

> Then God said, "Let us make man in our image, in our likeness..."
>
> Genesis 1 : 26a

the child's welfare, as well as seeing their potential realised. The way we are designed and created gives us an important perception and understanding of our Creator.

For this reason, the Lord tells those who are serious about growing up through pursuing righteousness, to look back to the quarry from which we were hewn. This does not refer to the physical quarry from which we were hewn (i.e. our parents) but, rather, the spiritual quarry, the everlasting Rock, our mighty God. The Lord knew it would be vital for us to understand the all-important significance of our spiritual heritage. Otherwise, how could we aim to become something we never realized we had the capacity to attain? How could we pursue righteousness if we did not understand the nature of righteousness? How could we become Christlike if we didn't know what Christ was like? We must look back to our spiritual origins - to our Creator. We all need to know who our Father really is and, thereby, know ourselves and what we have been created to enjoy and to do for our Lord.

"Listen to me, you who pursue righteousness and who seek the Lord: look to the rock from which you were cut and to the quarry from which you were hewn."

Isaiah 51 : 1

Such knowledge is basic and fundamental, paving the way to a life of service to the glory of God.

For those who have not had a particularly desirable start to life, this will be especially noteworthy. Do not allow Satan to ensnare you with issues regarding your background. Even though our families are important, our spiritual heritage is far more so. Look back to your spiritual quarry. The Lord knows you intimately. He knew you before you were even formed in the womb. What's more, he has a plan for your life – a plan for good and not for evil (Jeremiah 29 : 11).

# Don't sell your birthright for a mess of potage

In Scripture, the subject of birthright is highly significant. It held the key to privilege, status, authority and, ultimately, inheritance. Through every stage of a man's life birthright determined his prospects.

Satan, therefore, will always try to undermine the value of our spiritual birthright in order to persuade us to surrender it for the sake of gratifying immediate desires. There is a story in the Old Testament of a man called Esau. Despising his birthright, he sold it to his brother, Jacob, for a bowl of lentil stew. Exhausted and hungry after a hunting expedition, Esau asked his brother for a bowl of broth. Jacob obliged on condition that Esau gave him his birthright.(see Genesis 25 : 29-34) Only later did Esau realize, with remorse, the gravity of his carnality.

We may look at this story and think that Esau must have been a fool. However, let us consider how many times we have ignored the value of our birthright as sons and daughters of the Most High God. How often have we been prepared to grieve the Holy Spirit in order to satisfy the desires of this life, which deceptively present themselves to us as having far more value than an invisible inheritance in heaven? Desires and ambitions which become higher priorities than pursuing a life of total abandonment to the Lord are 'parasitical'. The only way to prevent ourselves from being hijacked by these 'parasites' is to know the true value of our birthright. In analogical terms - we are part of the species "Lepidoptera" – our destiny is not to remain as caterpillars but to be butterflies. The here and now is not the "be all and end all" – we are on a journey with a glorious destiny. We must not be persuaded that our present circumstances are all we are ever going to experience. Banish the thought of grabbing what we can, while we can. As individuals made in the image of God, we are part of an incredible drama. Right from the beginning of Genesis we see that God had a plan – sometimes called "Redemption's story". Even after the fall, expelled from the Garden of Eden, Adam and Eve were assured they had a destiny. God promised that Eve would bear children and that, in due time, one born of woman would crush Satan's head. That promise was fulfilled when Jesus came into this world to destroy the works of the Devil. Redemption's story is ongoing. Even if Satan tries to persuade us that Genesis is just a myth, and this world only exists as we experience it in the here and now, we are still the Lord's beloved creation and he continues his work in our lives. The actions we take, or anyone else takes, for that matter, do have consequences. We must press on to maturity. Why? Because only in maturity can we fulfil our Creator's long-term objective. The caterpillar, representing the immature stage, is incapable of reproducing. The butterfly, representing the mature stage, can and does reproduce. Satan would love to stop the line of those who will one day inherit the earth and reign with Christ. Therefore, there will be a battle over our lives. If our lives can be destroyed, or hijacked, as early as 'the egg stage', Satan will be all the more pleased. This is why the Lord is urging us to look back to our spiritual origins and realize that our true identity is our spiritual identity; our true birthright is our spiritual birthright of being made in the image of God, to the glory of God (Ephesians 1). He chose you from before the beginning of time. The Lord God Almighty is your father and is interested in every detail of your life. He reads your heart even as you read this book. The heart and mind of God, and his desire and purposes for this world and the next, is the very Rock from which you were hewn.

# A battle for your mind

Knowing who we are, in the sight of God, helps us to understand who we are before other men. What's more, this knowledge also helps to protect us from Satan when he attacks us, questioning our spiritual birthright and identity. If he does not succeed in persuading us to doubt 'the bigger picture', he will try instead to undermine the value of our personal role within it. He will attack the area in which we are most vulnerable. This might be through health problems, emotional traumas, mental illness, loneliness, inability to get over mistakes in the past, family problems, relationship breakdowns, abuse, shattered dreams or even an apparently unsuccessful ministry. However, when forewarned, we can be forearmed.

Whilst working in an AIDS camp in the Bahamas, I came across a young man who had been a paraplegic all his life. If anyone had reason to be bitter, he had. He lay in a filthy wooden shack all day long. His less than desirable meals were shoved onto the end of his bed and he ate them, face down in the plate. He rarely had any visitors. Yet, when I sat and talked with him, he said that every day was a gift. He was happy to be alive. In the lonely, dark Caribbean evenings, he told me the Lord came to sit and talk with him. He glorified God and was cheerful even in his dire circumstances. He valued his life. He had overcome his life-long handicap and the miserable conditions in which he lived. He had persevered against the potential 'parasites and predators' and found the greater miracle. He knew God personally and had discovered the secret of eternal life. He understood that there would be a glorious end to his life and he would one day be with the Lord. Therefore, he could only be described as an overcomer. Because he was living the 'winged life,' his life displayed a beautiful purpose - God's glory was unveiled in his life.

Let us compare this to the life of a person who has everything and yet, due to ignorance of Satan's schemes, squanders it through indifference, bad choices or self abuse. Which is more of a tragedy? The life with many handicaps and yet at peace through knowing God, or the one who began life in enviable circumstances, yet never realised he had a 'butterfly life' within? Privilege does not automatically equate to blessing, nor does our start in life necessarily determine our future. American writer, Joyce Meyer, for example, has overcome difficult circumstances to lead a life now that blesses those around her. She suffered abuse of various kinds in her childhood and, in escaping it as an adolescent, experienced further horrors. Through a determined choice to deal with her past and leave it behind her, she has walked forward in a spirit of praise, believing that God has a plan for her life. She now ministers to people all around the world. It must have taken enormous courage and faith but Joyce Meyer now has an amazing testimony to the glory we bring to God as overcomers.

Take note of the start of life experienced by our dear Lord himself. Initially, he was conceived out of wedlock. He was born in the rather squalid surroundings of a stable and then became a refugee within days of his birth because of a threat to his life. He remained so in the land of Egypt until he was a small child. Even on his return, he did not live in fine houses but was trained as the apprentice of his carpenter-father. He spent most of his life in obscurity. Yet, he knew his true identity; he knew his real Father and that determined the course of his life, and his victorious triumph over death.

## Let us press on to maturity

Your life will become a greater miracle the day you realize that whilst you may have been born 'looking like a worm,' you have a beautiful destiny within you. Your upbringing, circumstances and subsequent choices in life, set you on a path, I believe, towards the Lord and the good works which he has prepared for you. These works are particularly suited to your nature, your required climate and, most importantly, to reaching the needs of your environment. We all have the potential to be 'butterflies' – to bless; to heal; to restore; and to begin a new generation of 'caterpillars'! Your choice to embrace the genes and surroundings you were given will make all the difference. You can, of course, choose to harbour resentment that you feel as insignificant as a caterpillar and, in your bitterness, refuse to commit yourself to God to be transformed. Do you see the irony of that?

Maybe this is the time for you to look to *'the quarry from which you were hewn'*; to stop wishing you were something else, or someone else, and look instead, with eager anticipation, to the beautiful colours, design and strengths you have been given within the 'species' from which God brought you forth. He waits for you. He waits for you to 'hatch', so to speak. He waits for your journey of faith to start. He waits for you to recognize your destiny and to trust him to take you through the process to maturity. Each stage presents a choice. God never forces us towards our destiny. If there is one thing to be learned as we follow the caterpillar through its life cycle, it is that God uses a process in life. We need to accept and learn from each stage. When you are at the very start of your journey, you may feel insignificant, either as an individual in society or, perhaps, even in your church. Maybe you feel that no-one notices you! Take heart from the caterpillar egg. There are numerous ways by which a butterfly can minimize the chances of its eggs being eaten. Eggs are often cryptically-coloured to blend in with their surroundings; they are also usually laid in places (e.g. the underside of the leaf or in bark crevices) where they are not easily visible. Protection comes from their very plain beginning. Similarly, our 'camouflage' of anonymity guards us from the unwanted attention of 'predators.'

As you grow from one stage of maturity to the next, the Lord will wait for you to reach points at which you are increasingly aware of the longing in your heart to know him at a deeper level. That longing is evidence of the Holy Spirit working in your heart and will lead to surrender each time in order 'to grow into a new skin'. Through each new stage, your faith in Christ will develop. It will no longer be based on tradition, routine, head knowledge, or upholding the values that your parents have instilled into you. Instead, your faith will flow from your hope in a God you have come to know intimately and to trust. Finally, it will lead to surrendering even your very self because you know whom you *"have believed"* and you are *"convinced that he is able to guard what (you) have entrusted to him until that day."* (2 Timothy 1 : 12b) The assurance of his perfect love will lead to commitment without fear. (1 John 4 : 18) Having spent time developing an intimate relationship with the Lord, your desire to share and your ability to share your knowledge with others will be greatly enhanced!

All of this lies within 'the egg'- your spiritual origins - just as the genes which determined our development lay within our very first embryonic cells. Spiritually, we are God's children made in his image. We are children of light, not of darkness; we are not meant to stay as near-blind 'caterpillars' in the dark; we were created to be 'son-worshipping butterflies', rejoicing in the light.

Take time to stop and consider 'the egg'. Marvel at the miracle of everlasting life that is contained therein and may the recognition of your rich inheritance help you to persevere throughout the journey!

O Jesus Christ, grow Thou in me,
And all things else recede;
My heart be daily nearer Thee,
From sin be daily freed.

Each day let Thy supporting might
My weakness still embrace;
My darkness vanish in Thy light,
Thy life my death efface.

In Thy bright beams which on me fall,
Fade every evil thought;
That I am nothing, Thou art all,
I would be daily taught.

More of Thy glory let me see,
Thou Holy, Wise, and True;
I would Thy living image be,
In joy and sorrow too.

Fill me with gladness from above,
Hold me by strength divine;
Lord, let the glow of Thy great love
Through all my being shine.

Make this poor self grow less and less,
Be Thou my life and aim;
Oh, make me daily through Thy grace
More meet to bear Thy name.

Johann C Lavater
(1741 - 1801)

# Chapter 2

# The First Instars
## Small Beginnings

*"There is a time for everything, and a season for every activity under heaven: a time to be born and a time to die...." Ecclesiastes 3 : 1,2*

The incubation period of the tiny eggs is usually a few days but, in some species, the eggs may not hatch for eight to nine months. Such a pause in growth is known as diapause and is usually a response to unfavourable environmental conditions, such as cold temperatures or lack of food for the caterpillar. They survive such obstacles by remaining dormant, emerging when conditions become suitable again.

The Creator knows when it is the right time for us to begin our journey of faith and many other conditions around us play a part in determining when we finally give our lives to the Lord. From the very start of our spiritual lives, it is important to note that God brings all things to pass in season. He ordains various periods of growth. If we try to bypass any of these stages, we miss the God-ordained purpose for them. There is wisdom in accepting that immaturity is a stage through which we must all pass. Time is needed to mature. The caterpillar's life is separated into different stages called "instars." It starts each new instar as it reaches the optimum size for its old skin and sheds it to reveal a new one. Each instar represents a period of growth and various developing features of the caterpillar. There are different purposes, as well as challenges, to each stage of its life. Let us consider the first-instar caterpillar. It has many lessons to teach about preparation for the days ahead of us, as well as how to make the most from times of development.

## Eat to grow

When the eggs hatch, the emerging caterpillars are only a few millimetres long. They instinctively know that it is most crucial that they start eating in order to grow. Caterpillars are known to be eating machines. As a result, caterpillars have the fastest growth rate of any animal. It is stated that if a normal seven pound human baby were to grow at the same rate as a Monarch larva, the baby, in just one month, would be the size of a London double-decker bus and weigh tonnes. They have only a matter of weeks until they must be ready to face metamorphosis. Consequently, they spend that time eating to prepare themselves for one of the most amazing transformations in all nature. A caterpillar has to eat all the food it will need for its life as a butterfly for then it will drink only fluids, predominantly nectar, rather than eating.

The caterpillar's first meal is often its former egg-shell, which provides an initial source of nutrients. The framework of our start in life, no matter its shape, can also be the source of important 'nutrients' for our development. Our digestion and assimilation of these primordial 'nutrients' are the prerequisite to a mature spiritual life.

When the baby caterpillar is so small, it is vital that it focuses its attention on feeding to gain the energy it needs to become a butterfly. This self-centred eating pattern has often earned the poor caterpillar the reputation of being a pest. Upon reflection, however, we must acknowledge that the caterpillar's insatiable appetite is God-ordained. Just as we do not condemn a small baby for crying out night and day for food, so we should recognise that a voracious appetite for the Word of God in the early stages of our spiritual growth is a healthy and desirable sign. A baby has no notion of being selfish, or of having a relationship with its mother based only on its needs. It is only conscious of hunger and, even then, without any comprehension of why it is hungry. For many months, a baby will not even be aware of the concept of growth but this does not make its hunger pangs any less real. The basic instinct of survival ensures growth through feeding.

The Word of God is a source of growth and life to us. Jesus said,

*"Man does not live on bread alone, but on every word that comes from the mouth of God."*(Matthew 4 : 4) He reaffirms this in John's gospel, *"The words I have spoken to you are spirit and they are life."* (John 6 : 63)

If we wish to grow in our faith, we must respond urgently to the prompting of the Holy Spirit to feed ourselves on the Word of God. It must become a priority. Are you recognising the need to prioritise feeding in order to grow? If we do not eat, we will be stunted in our growth and eventually starve. On the other hand, the more we feed, the greater our appetite will become and the stronger we will grow, just as we see in the life of the baby caterpillar.

Hunger, however, must not lead to careless eating. The caterpillar is a picky eater. It will eat only the fresh, tender leaves of the host plant where its eggs hatched. Most caterpillars will eat only from one plant or a small number of plants closely related to each other. It would rather starve to death than eat the wrong type of food. What a rich spiritual lesson! Be careful what you eat! Are you spending time digesting Scripture to help you in your spiritual growth, or are you getting indigestion, perhaps even, poisoning yourself, by chewing on the wrong things? The Apostle Paul, in his personal correspondence with young Timothy, exhorts him to devote himself to the public reading of Scripture and teaching. We, too, are instructed to watch our lives and our doctrine closely that we might not only save ourselves, but our hearers also. (1 Timothy 4 :16) We must be prepared to give an answer to all those who question us about our faith. We cannot do this, nor handle the word of God correctly, if we don't even know what the Word of God says.

# Eating to bring forth what lies within

*" ...... little groups of cells start developing very early in the caterpillar's life but then they stall, and so they're just in there waiting, and they don't start growing until the very end of the 5th instar (the last caterpillar stage). Then they start growing really rapidly....."* Prof. Lincoln Brower

Perhaps you feel like a hungry new-born baby, or like a ravenous baby caterpillar with no vision. Maybe your spiritual appetite is voracious and yet not accompanied by an awareness of where all your 'feeding' is leading. Do you yearn to serve God; to really show your true colours; to spread your wings and even to fly? Then I urge you - do not despise the day of small beginnings. Everyone has to begin somewhere. Although it is a hidden process, the caterpillar is already developing the cells it will need in the future to transform totally into a new creation. It may seem like a tiny, plain, even ugly worm to begin with but there is a glorious new creation within. The same is true of your life. Even if you feel small right now, take the initiative, like the baby caterpillar, to feed and grow where you currently are. Careful feeding will lead to the development of those 'cells in waiting' and will equip you for every good work the Lord has prepared

"Do not despise these small beginnings, for the Lord rejoices to see the work begin ...."
Zechariah 4 : 10a NLT

for you to do. It is easy to feel overlooked, or frustrated, when God does not seem to be immediately revealing a purpose for you. But he develops us according to his perfect plan. He has not forgotten you; quite the opposite. Your journey has begun if you feel those hunger pangs! He is rejoicing that the work is beginning.

Don't let resentment build up when you feel your talents are not immediately being used or recognised. A caterpillar would not be ready to become a butterfly at its first instar, even if it were prepared to surrender itself as such a tiny larva. It needs time to feed in order to develop defence mechanisms, to store up the energy for metamorphosis and adult life and to acquire the colours which will determine its identity in the future. Similarly, our Heavenly Father knows that his children need time to grow up spiritually; to gain strength and skills and to establish a character and an identity. To this end, he encourages us to use our 'spiritual childhood

A newborn baby has all the body parts it will ever need, yet it must grow up in order to use them as intended. The same principle applies spiritually in the life of faith.

Philip Yancey

and adolescence' to tuck as much knowledge and experience under our belts as possible. We must all go through experiences in our physical and emotional lives in order to develop the attributes God has placed within us and to be mature enough for the various ministries he has prepared for us. God knows us better than we know ourselves and he will not entrust ministry or responsibilities to us until he judges us to be ready.

Our Lord's early life served as an example. He came to earth as a baby and grew up in a normal family. He worked alongside his father developing life skills. He fed on the Word of God from an early age. He was so zealous to discuss Scripture, he was almost accused of disregarding the concerns of others. After his family's annual visit to Jerusalem to celebrate the Passover, Jesus went missing for three days. His parents eventually found their twelve year old son conversing with the teachers of the Law in the synagogue. His mother asked, *"Son, why have you treated us like this? Your father and I have been anxiously searching for you."* (Luke 2: 48) Jesus was surprised because he had thought his passion for his father's house would have been so evident, it would have been obvious where he was! Jesus went back to Nazareth and was respectfully obedient to his parents, accepting to grow up alongside them. Only a few verses later, we see the results of this period of his life: *"... Jesus grew in wisdom and stature, and in favour with God and men."* (Luke 2 : 52)

He did not bypass this time of maturing and growing. It was not until he was thirty years of age that he began his public ministry. We too must learn to wait and to grow as we abide in Christ. We must be patient. It is often said that the greater the task the Lord has for us to do, the longer the preparation time will be. Do not rush forward in your own strength or, like the tiny caterpillar, you will easily be picked off by 'the birds' - the enemies of your soul. In the meantime, seize every opportunity to build yourself up by feeding on the Word of God.

# My testimony

I am almost overwhelmed as I look back on the process of writing this story. Almost ten years have passed since I first received the butterfly vision in the summer of 1999. I was twenty-four years of age and had just finished my first year of teaching modern languages. After growing up in a Christian family, it was during my university years that my commitment to my faith was tested. I learnt the hard way that life outside of the Lord's will leads to painful emotional consequences. So, as I started into my professional life, I was searching for a deeper understanding of being a true disciple of the Lord Jesus Christ. I knew that I had a lot to learn. At the time of receiving the butterfly vision, I was reading "A passion for holiness" by J. I. Packer, knowing that I was far from passionate about holiness. I felt the desire to grow but I had to learn that the strength of one's desire is no substitute for the actual process of eating to grow. No-one can develop just by desiring to be mature. Like the caterpillar, we all have to pass through the stages of voracious eating to build ourselves up! Over the following five or six years, I spent many hours, especially on Saturday mornings, holed up in my bedroom, reading the Bible and many other devotional books. My journals are full of what I was learning. This gradual process of learning, preparation and growth felt painfully slow at times and was often frustrating. It is only now, as I read back over my journals, that I realize how much the Lord was using those hours of reading to give me strength, to help me to develop understanding of his Word and to teach me many lessons. Indeed, many of the things you will read in this book come straight from those diaries. Sometimes I marvel that I can quite clearly point back to certain points in my twenties where I learnt a specific lesson.

Alongside my spiritual development at that time, I also gained invaluable experience in my teaching post at the local high school. Not only did I become proficient at planning and teaching lessons but I also learnt leadership skills and how to handle a huge variety of situations in my role as Head of House. Step by step, the Lord gave me more and more responsibility and showed me that he could prepare me for any role he designed for me.

Most importantly, he used that time to build up relationships which have become foundation stones in my life. In addition to consolidating old friendships from school and university, I made new friends, both at my workplace and at church. These friends have helped me to become who I am today, and to overcome certain fears and discouragements.

Had God revealed to me at the age of twenty-four all that lay in my future, I would probably have been quite terrified. Whilst the Lord saw my desire to grow and to ultimately serve him wholeheartedly, he knew that the process required was going to stretch over many years. So, he gave me the words of the butterfly vision to encourage me. He revealed to me from the very start, that he was going to use my childhood, and everything I would subsequently live through and learn, to bring forth his butterfly. Sadly, I did not make the most of that initial revelation. I simply did not connect the vision to my life in any real sense. Like the caterpillar, I was blind. I did not understand my present because I had no real concept of my future even though my destiny had been pronounced and promised. I can remember being so frustrated that I had no sense of purpose. Probably despairing at my lack of understanding, the Lord gave me the butterfly vision a second time in 2004. It was only then, as I began to research the caterpillar and the butterfly, that I understood the significance of my butterfly promise and used it, as I am sure it was intended, to support me when I had a crisis of faith about the Lord's purposes for me.

I hope that through reading this book, you will be spared some of the frustrations and doubts I felt. I urge you to keep in mind the spiritual origins and promises the Lord has given you. Find encouragement there as you grow and mature. In particular, meditate on the metamorphosis of the caterpillar. That should act as a constant, powerful reminder that God has a plan for each one of us. Rather than waste energy fretting and doubting, prepare yourself for the God-given tasks that lie ahead through prayer, worship and feeding on the Word of God. Even doubts and fears can be turned into opportunities to fight back with revealed truth, to develop spiritual muscle and to become skilled in handling spiritual weapons. What do I mean by that? Let us move on to find out more.

# Eat to defend yourself

As babies feed, they are developing their immune systems in order to fight off diseases. Parents sometimes even deliberately expose their children to disease, whether through injections or "chicken-pox parties!" This may initially seem cruel but it is to encourage the growth of antibodies to ward off infections. God, as our heavenly Father, may allow some setbacks from time to time in our early lives, in order to develop a spiritual immune system. How do we survive such 'inoculations'? Feed well and submit to the care of the Father. He is always in control. He always knows what is best for us.

Likewise, the caterpillar uses the first stages of its life to prepare its self-defence mechanisms. Some species of caterpillar eat poisonous plants so that birds will not eat them, not even when they become butterflies. The Monarch butterfly is a perfect example of this. To most other creatures, milkweed is poisonous but the Monarch larvae can digest it and use its toxins to become poisonous itself to its predators.

We need to learn how to turn the Word we 'eat' into our defence mechanism. Ephesians 6 portrays the Word of God as a sword – a weapon against our enemies. The Lord himself showed us how to wield it when he was tempted by Satan in the wilderness. Each time Satan tempted him, Jesus responded with the word of God as his defence – *"It is written ..."* (Matthew 4, Luke 4) The acquisition of such a skill requires us to meditate on Scripture; memorise it and internalise it, so that we can apply it when necessary. Part of growing up is recognising that life will present many difficulties and not everyone will be for us. We will face enemies in all different guises, whether they come as physical, relational or spiritual problems. Are you learning who your enemies are and developing strategies to deal with them? One of the most crucial steps towards victory is recognising the enemy. Are you learning how to put on the armour of God so that you too can stand against the enemy's schemes? On this subject, the Apostle Paul's instructions in Ephesians chapter 6 are of paramount importance.

# Defence strategies

As well as gaining protection from their food sources, caterpillars have other defence strategies for their early days. Some species go for protection in numbers. The black, spiny caterpillars of the Peacock will feed in large groups hiding in silken tents atop nettles. As they get larger, they emerge from the tent together to feed. The wriggling heap of spiny bodies wards off would-be predators. The Small Tortoiseshell also spins a silk tent around nettle tips in order to feed in relative safety. They spin larger and larger tents as they grow until the caterpillars moult for the last time. Then, they become more or less solitary and protect themselves more through rolling leaves and hiding inside, like their relative, the Red Admiral.

These things serve to remind us of the 'spiritual protection' to be found within the church, the body of Christ. We gain strength and protection from 'feeding' at church, in home groups and conferences. These arenas can become our 'silken tents' where we can grow and learn through our mistakes in relative safety. Other Christians can help to protect us from our predators by praying with us and for us. Some churches seek to protect their members by introducing accountability partnerships in which Christians can share honestly about their spiritual growth. The church can also provide social occasions where temptation is minimized. As we will see through the later stages of the caterpillar, times of solitude and personal reflection are necessary for spiritual growth, especially when the Lord wants to take us through a period of change or transformation.

However, we must be careful not to become too isolated or introspective.

Caterpillars, in a bid to protect themselves, will even take advantage of what may seem very unfavourable surroundings. Nettles, for instance, far from being admired for their beauty, are usually regarded as undesirable weeds that sting. However, larvae of the Red Admiral will deliberately wrap themselves in a nettle leaf in order to munch away undisturbed, knowing predators will think twice before foraging around in a nettle patch!

Corrie Ten Boom, in her book "The Hiding Place", describes her initial horror at the lice-ridden dormitory she and her fellow prisoners were forced to endure in their wing at Ravensbruck Concentration Camp. However, her attitude to her surroundings soon changed when she realized that the German soldiers stayed away from the area because they feared becoming infested themselves. This left Corrie and her sister in relative peace to carry out Bible studies in the dormitory. Similarly, in the book "The Heavenly Man", Brother Yun describes how many Chinese believers used their years of imprisonment to spend much time with the Lord in prayer and meditating on the scriptures they had memorized. He also gives many examples of Christians turning unpleasant environments to their advantage. The fellowship between Christian prisoners was so strong that he actually claimed to miss prison after his release.

Be encouraged, therefore, to discover God's purpose in placing you in the particular church, neighbourhood, family or relationships, pertaining to your present situation. Recognise and affirm the advantages. Will you 'feed on a plant' that seems unpleasant but is the means the Lord has chosen for your nourishment and protection? Like certain caterpillars, you may have been given an ability to use a 'poisonous plant' to your advantage. As the old saying goes, "What doesn't kill you will only serve to make you stronger." Look to draw strength of character and wisdom from experiences and circumstances beyond your control. You will find that an acceptance of these learning curves will help you to become mature. The New Living Translation translates James 1 : 2-4: *"Whenever trouble comes your way, let it be an opportunity for joy. For when your faith is tested your endurance has a chance to grow. So let it grow, for when your endurance is fully developed, you will be strong in character and ready for anything."* (or as the New International Version reads – *"so that you may be mature and complete."*)

Are you prepared to accept the maturing process in the place of the Lord's appointment or are you impatiently pressing the Lord to move you on quickly?

## Accept camouflage

Camouflage is used by both caterpillars and butterflies to enhance the chances of survival. The larvae of the Comma mimics a bird-dropping by lying curled up and motionless on a nettle leaf, using its skin patterns of dark brown, tan and a white splash as a disguise! When we are disgruntled about being unnoticed or rudely handled, we sometimes equate it to being treated like 'dirt'. Surprisingly, however, the Lord may ask you to accept such experiences as a means of protective camouflage.

More often than not, caterpillars are simply deliberately drab and inconspicuous in their earlier stages. Do you find facing an inconspicuous start difficult to accept? Can you ever remember thinking, especially in your teenage years, "Why could I not have been prettier, or more sporty or gifted in a certain way?" I challenge you, however, to ask yourself where such 'blessings' might have led. Many who are 'blessed' with 'bright colours' have testified, usually later in life, concerning the problems arising therefrom because they received too much attention or were put under a lot of pressure. For girls, the problem is too many boyfriends of the wrong kind. For men, many talents often result in pride, leading them away from the Lord through a sense of self-sufficiency. To use the analogy of the first-instar caterpillar again – compare a small, drab caterpillar to a small, gaudy caterpillar with bright colours which have not been attained through a gradual process of retaining poisonous pigments from the plants. The colourful caterpillar would be very visible and yet totally unable to defend itself. As a result, it would be very vulnerable to its enemies. The same holds true for us spiritually. It is far better to develop 'colour' at the same time as learning how to handle it, than to be thrust into the limelight too hastily because of our potential. Very practical advice was given to the early church by the Apostle Paul when he cautioned against too hastily appointing men to positions of leadership. (1 Timothy 5 : 22) In the same letter, he warns of the risk in no uncertain terms. (1 Timothy 3 : 6,7)

There are some species of butterfly that have very similar markings and colours to a poisonous counterpart. It is hoped that this deceives would-be predators. As for ourselves, need I say, that flashy mimicry is hopelessly inadequate and inadvisable. To ensure our protection we must rely upon the adequate means specified in the Scriptures.

The spirit of dissatisfaction leads to deception. It causes us to doubt that the Lord has placed a beautiful and unique destiny in each one of us. Sadly, this often results in our prematurely searching for attention-grabbing 'colours', instead of waiting for our own to be unveiled from within, in the Lord's time.

The drab brown larva of the Morpho has no idea it is going to become such a beautiful, iridescent blue butterfly. Imagine if it wasted time and energy being unnecessarily angry against God for keeping the colour out of its life. Just as God purposefully designed the Morpho caterpillar, plain in appearance to reduce its likelihood of being attacked, so he designs defence-mechanisms for us to safeguard our future ministry. A very ordinary up-bringing is often a means of protection. A non-assuming start to our ministry gives us the time to develop our skills, even to make mistakes without affecting too many people.

> To find beauty we must carry it within.
>
> Ralph Waldo Emerson

Let us look at a biblical story of one young man who bypassed an inconspicuous start and prematurely gained his colourful coat, thereby attracting hostile attention! In Genesis 37, we read that Joseph, a young man of seventeen, was given a coat of many colours by his father, Jacob, who favoured Joseph over his brothers. His father's actions proved to be unwise. When we question God, asking why we still cannot have our 'coat of many colours', we would do well to consider what the consequences might be, and accept that, as a wise father, he has chosen to keep us anonymous for the time being. Joseph's coat and his father's favour led him to be proud and, in his immaturity, he shared a dream that provoked the hatred and jealousy of his brothers. They decided to silence the naïve "dreamer". They planned to kill him, but Reuben persuaded them to throw him down a well instead, hoping to rescue Joseph later. However, under pressure from Judah, the brothers sold Joseph as a slave to a group of passing Ishmaelites who took him to Egypt. Even in Egypt the Lord required Joseph to wait for years, many of which were in prison, before he elevated him to the place where his dreams would be fulfilled and he would save all Egypt from a famine that lasted years. Joseph had always known that he had a destiny. His dreams showed that he would one day occupy an exalted position. However, he needed time to develop the character and skills to carry out the work the Lord had prepared for him to do. So, as Psalm 105 tells us, the Lord tested Joseph's character until it was time to fulfil his word.

> 'Until the time came to fulfil his word, the Lord tested Joseph's character.'
> Psalm 105 : 19 (NLT)

There is another well-known biblical character, David, whose start in life was inconspicuous. As the youngest of the family, his father kept him feeding sheep whilst all the other boys were sent off to fight as soldiers. Imagine what that did to a young man's ego! In fact, he blended in so well into the background, that his father seemed to have forgotten him when he lined up his sons before Samuel, the prophet. Samuel even had to ask, *"Are these all the sons you have?"* Jesse replied, *"There is still the youngest but he is tending the sheep."* (1 Samuel 16 : 11). The Lord used that time alone in the hills to refine David's character. He became accustomed to solitude. He developed bravery in defending his sheep, to the extent of tackling a lion on one occasion and a bear on another. In due time, the Lord's time, his skill with the sling put an end to the Philistine giant, Goliath. The Lord used the talents David had developed in his everyday job. In early manhood, his courage and skill on the battlefield attracted the admiration of all Israel, but at the same time, aroused the jealousy of King Saul. Consequently, with his life threatened, David had to spend years in exile, hiding from the wrath of Saul. He learnt to wait. He learnt to feed on the word of God. He learnt to lead men in the wilderness. He dealt with attacks from his enemies. He grew to rely on the provision of the Lord. He learnt from his mistakes and progressed towards his true identity. Eventually, he became King of Israel! The one-time shepherd boy was now shepherding the people of God. It was years since he had been anointed by Samuel. All that time he had known that he had a destiny to become something so far beyond his current reality. But the Lord was not in a hurry. He is still not in a hurry. He is interested in the process as well as the end result. A study with his dealings with Joseph and David leads us to confidence in his handling of our lives.

Even the Lord Jesus had to wait for the time appointed by the Father. At the wedding feast of Cana, Mary tried to give Jesus 'a coat of many colours' – so to speak! She knew of his abilities and wanted him to put them to use, but Jesus told her, *"My time has not yet come."* (John 2 : 4) He knew that everything had to fall exactly into place as had been predicted by the prophets.

# Patience is a Virtue

Will you accept the Lord's timing in your life? Will you be patient with the Lord's plans? So often we can become very self-centred and forget that the things that happen in our lives do not just concern ourselves. The Lord, however, is aware of all the people and circumstances in your life. He is masterfully weaving a tapestry which intertwines all our lives in a way which develops us all in his perfect timing. When we become impatient and try to seize control, we affect more lives than just our own. Therefore, we must be careful not to stray from God's plans and his timing. When, in our impatience, we start to murmur and grumble, we create an atmosphere of unbelief and dissatisfaction which is dishonouring to God and detrimental to the lives of our associates.

Look at what happened in Abraham's family when Sarai persuaded him to take Hagar as his wife in order to produce the promised son. (Genesis 16) Why did she feel constrained to do such a thing? Because her natural circumstances (barrenness) outweighed her belief in the promise of Almighty God. As if God needed her assistance, Sarai devised a way to accelerate the fulfilment of the divine promise, never dreaming how far-reaching the disastrous consequences of her impatience would be. Abraham's immediate family suffered deeply. Ishmael and his mother were treated badly and sent away. The words God spoke over Ishmael concerning his continual strife with his brothers have remained true to this very day. Let us learn from this tragic incident that whatever we do in unbelief invariably has a very negative effect on the lives of others.

Rome was not built in a day.

Have you ever become tired of waiting and tried to 'sort things out' more quickly than God's timing? Did you consider the consequences? God's timing is as much for our benefit as for his. His perfect timing is a means of revealing something of himself. Sometimes he wants to show us a miracle. In Abraham's case, he wanted the child to be a child of promise, not of flesh (see Galatians 4 : 23); a child born supernaturally so that Abraham would always know his son was a gift from God. He went beyond the time limits of human possibility so that Abraham and Sarai would recognize and testify to God's supernatural hand upon their lives and the lives of their descendants.

Waiting on the Lord requires humble obedience and develops faith. In asking us to wait, the Lord is developing our characters. Character is not developed overnight. So often in our high-tech, instant world we become impatient and this impatience spills over into our spiritual life. We long for the glorious colours of integrity, perseverance, optimism, patience and fortitude to beautify our lives but we are not prepared for the long process such a transformation requires. Here again, the butterfly offers us great hope. Remember – no butterflies are born. Every butterfly begins life as a caterpillar; they grow, develop, suffer and emerge from this altogether different form. The butterfly is the glorious end-product of a marvellous maturing process. Similarly, no Christian is born in a state of maturity. Spiritual maturity is the end-product of years of feeding upon the Word of God; learning patience through various trials and learning to bear the fruit of the spirit by consistently abiding in Christ. Instead of bemoaning our current lack of colour or stature, let us continue to feed in faith, believing that the beautiful colours will be unveiled in our lives at a later date. As we feed on the word of God, the Lord will transform us from the inside out. Instead of wanting to put on a flashy show, we should be making every effort to develop inner beauty. Man may look at the outward appearance but God sees the heart. (1 Samuel 16 : 7) God is not just interested in what we will eventually do for him but in the process of our developing a relationship with him. Who we become is more important than what we do.

Spiritually, everyone starts at the same point, as a sinner redeemed by grace. The Lord has placed within each one of us, the capacity to grow to maturity and to live to the glory of God. The story of the butterfly teaches us to recognise this destiny as a process. The caterpillar in its early stages shows no promise of unveiling the glory of God as a beautiful butterfly. Yet, it is the same creature and everything it needs to that end already lies within its being. It is just in its immature phase. The time will come for it to radiate beauty and bless the environment in which it moves. For now, however, it must pass through the stages of growth and all its maturing trials. In all, the caterpillar has five instars to work through. May the following study of these instars cause you to reflect upon the various stages through which we pass in our progress towards spiritual maturity. Let us press on to maturity so God's glory can be more fully unveiled through our lives.

Remove my covering, Lord,
That I may see Thy light,
And be deceived no more,
But all things see aright.

Chorus
Oh, may Thy living light, Lord,
Scatter all my night, Lord
And everything make bright, Lord,
For this I pray to Thee.

I hardly know myself;
Deceived so much by pride,
I often think I'm right
And am self-satisfied.

I know Thee even less
In doctrine, shallowly;
True revelation lack
Of Thy reality;

As for Thy life within
In darkness I mistake-
If spirit or the flesh,
One for the other take.

As for Thy way, O Lord,
I often am not clear;
I toward seclusion tend
And from the pathway veer

As for Thy will for me,
I do not know it well;
I substitute my own
And often would rebel.

As for the church, I need
Thy revelation more,
The Body-life to know
Thy wisdom to explore

I long to be unveiled,
In everything made clear,
No more to be deceived
Or to my pride adhere.

Witness Lee
(1905 - 1997)

# Chapter 3

# Caterpillar Days
## Recognising Spiritual Immaturity

The early days of a caterpillar's life are, as we have seen in Chapter 2, an important time of growth and development. However, after a number of days, the greedy, little caterpillar reaches a point where it has grown to its maximum size for the small exo-skeleton it bears as a first-instar caterpillar. Due to various hormones within its body, it instinctively recognizes the limitations of this first immature stage and, in order to grow further, prepares for change.

In our spiritual walk with the Lord, we will also reach points where we must recognize that we have 'outgrown our skin.' Just as it is difficult for some teenagers to see their own immaturity so we, in our 'spiritual adolescence', need help to identify the characteristics and limitations of spiritual immaturity. Without such guidance, albeit potentially difficult to face and accept, we may remain as we are, deprived of the maturing process. At this stage, it may prove helpful if we consider the principal features of a caterpillar's life, representing as it does the immature stage of the adult butterfly. Our study of these features can then be used to assess the maturity of our own spiritual lives.

Briefly,

- A caterpillar has a self-gratifying hunger.
- A caterpillar has eyes but has little or no vision.
- A caterpillar, when compared with a delightful, pollinating and reproducing butterfly, is seen to live a self-centred lifestyle in the sense that it gives little, or nothing, back to its surroundings.

# Hunger

The caterpillar is almost exclusively characterised by hunger. Hunger defines the purpose of a caterpillar's life. Its body basically consists of one big gut! Its preoccupation with food is a self-centred and self-gratifying pursuit but there is a definite purpose behind the caterpillar's extraordinary hunger. It lives to eat and eats to grow. However, such an appetite cannot continue ad infinitum for its own sake. There will come a point where the caterpillar must shed its skin to reveal a larger, more flexible skin underneath.

During my twenties, I resembled the little caterpillar. I was hungry to grow spiritually.

However, I eventually came to an uncomfortable point where I recognized that my hunger was not matched with a readiness to accept change. I was feeding only to satisfy a rather selfish appetite. Ever feeding without accepting change, was leading to spiritual stagnation. Eventually, the Lord revealed to me that I was missing the real purpose behind my spiritual hunger. The divine purpose behind spiritual hunger, like the hunger of the caterpillar, is to produce the kind of growth which triggers all the changes needed on the route to maturity.

A small first-instar caterpillar can only eat the fresher leaves near the top of the host plant. It is also careful to eat only certain parts of the leaf where the toxins are not so strong. As the caterpillar changes, losing its skin to go into the next instar, it can cope, not just with more food, but also with older leaves and the part of the leaf that holds more toxins. This is a critical point to note. It is physical change, and subsequent growth, that enables the caterpillar to diversify its eating pattern. This leads to further growth spurts, the ability to build up its defence mechanisms and the ability to retain pigments for future colouration.

Babies and infants are normally fed directly by their mother, whether by means of breast or bottle. However, as the child gets older, the mother encourages a gradual self-help in the feeding process. The child becomes aware that it will now take some effort to abate hunger. He will have to become involved in feeding himself. Furthermore, his diet will no longer be restricted to milk. He will, in future, be required to chew solids, perhaps cut up into small parts. Gradually, the child's diet becomes more and more varied and the digestive system learns to cope with many different elements. Why do parents bring about all these changes? They do so, not only wishing to see their child grow, but also to see him enjoy the richness of discovering different flavours and textures. Any reluctance on the part of the child to engage actively in this process would automatically have a detrimental effect upon his growth and development.

As we look at these two examples from nature, they speak to us of the requirements for our spiritual maturing process. I believe the Lord, like a loving parent, wishes to see the same changes in our 'feeding patterns' – a difference not just in what we 'eat' but also how we are fed.

In Paul's first letter to the Corinthians, he acknowledges that there is initially a period of spiritual immaturity which limits 'our diet'. As "mere infants in Christ," we cannot 'digest' some of the deeper truths of scripture. *"Brothers, I could not address you as spiritual but as worldly, mere infants in Christ. I gave you milk, not solid food, for you were not yet ready for it."* (1 Corinthians 3 : 1)

However, as the writer to the Hebrews strongly conveys, the Lord does not want us to be content with milk and remain immature. He yearns for us to move on to "solid food" and to learn the deeper things of Scripture. He wants us to be able to chew over the full extent of his teaching and really take the goodness from it. He wants us to taste and see that he indeed is good. (Psalm 34 : 8) As we shall see further, tasting is linked to seeing and understanding God's nature more fully.

*"We have much to say about this, but it is hard to explain because you are slow to learn. In fact, though by this time you ought to be teachers, you need someone to teach you the elementary truths of God's word all over again. You need milk, not solid food! Anyone who lives on milk, being still an infant, is not acquainted with the teaching about righteousness. But solid food is for the mature, who by constant use have trained themselves to distinguish good from evil. Therefore, let us leave the elementary teachings about Christ and go on to maturity ..."* (Hebrews 5 : 11 – 6 : 1)

Such a change in diet calls for a change in our relationship with the Lord. There is a profound difference between childish faith and child-like faith. We expect a baby to be childish but, as it grows up, we hope it will develop a relationship with its mother beyond just crying out for food and attention. In the same way, the Lord longs for us to mature, not just to discover the delights of 'solids' but also to enjoy a new way of feeding. To this end, he prompts us to recognize the opportunity to commune with him over a meal. In the third chapter of the book of Revelation we are told that the Lord knocks at the door of his followers, wanting to come in and dine with us. He will still be providing the meal but how much richer the menu will be, and how much more meaningful our meal times will become, as we have fellowship with him. In order to enter into this level of communion with our Lord, we must willingly accept whatever changes he brings to our attention. Just as the caterpillar must shed a cramping skin in order to expand its capacity, it is commonly the case that the child of God needs to part with some personal restriction in order to expand his capacity for the things of God. Christlikeness must be our goal, though the route is costly. Our sanctification is the will of God. A readiness to accept changes in our personality, our attitude and our lifestyle is the sure test of professed spiritual hunger. Any professed hunger which does not produce positive changes in our lives needs to be identified as a deception. Otherwise, we will ignore, or even refute, the need to 'shed a skin' in order to grow. If we insist that merely our hunger is a sign of maturity, we are mistaken and we will not be able to grow into Christlikeness. Continual 'feeding' does not automatically produce spiritual growth. Continual 'feeding' is a form of self gratification, if it does not lead to the surrender of whichever "skin" we have outgrown, in active obedience to the Lord's desire for us to press on to maturity. In fact, gratifying such an appetite is more likely to lead to 'spiritual obesity', or even spiritual death. We can see this in the plight of the Pharisees in Jesus' day. There are still many who spend years studying theology, even dissecting the Scriptures in Hebrew and Greek. Sadly, instead of developing a clearer vision of the Lord, they remain blind, trapped by a refusal to allow the very Scriptures they study actually to change them. A greater knowledge of Scripture was not, and is still not, indicative of spiritual growth, maturity or vision.

"You will be ever hearing but never understanding; you will be ever seeing but never perceiving. For this people's heart has become calloused; they hardly hear with their ears, and they have closed their eyes. Otherwise they might see with their eyes, hear with their ears, understand with their hearts and turn, and I would heal them"

Matthew 13 : 14,15

Knowledge, in itself, cannot change us. Knowledge only becomes spiritually beneficial when it is accompanied by an aim and a willing spirit, to become more Christlike.

# Lack of vision

The caterpillar enhances its capacity to eat, and its range of food, by instinctively accepting the changes needed to progress through each instar to the maturity of the butterfly. In the event of a malfunction hindering ecdysis (the shedding of its skin), the caterpillar would be left incapable of growing beyond the stage of a near-blind, wormlike creature. A caterpillar's quality of vision is little more than an awareness of the difference between light and darkness.

In chapter five of Hebrews, quoted earlier, it is not difficult to see a link between the quality of our nourishment and the level of our understanding and discernment. A milk diet is associated with elementary teaching in contrast with solid food, associated with discernment and spiritual maturity. There are clear consequences if we will not mature and move on onto 'solids'. We too will remain spiritually 'blind' - unable to distinguish effectively between good and evil, not being acquainted with the teaching about righteousness. By contrast, those who discipline themselves to make the effort to 'chew on' deeper truths grow to be spiritually mature and acquire the corresponding discernment.

"You say, 'I am rich, I have acquired wealth and do not need a thing'. But you do not realise that you are wretched, pitiful, poor, blind, naked. I counsel you to buy from me gold refined in the fire, so that you can become rich; and white clothes to wear so that you can cover your shameful nakedness, and salve to put on your eyes, so that you can see."

Revelation 3 : 17,18

Before I received the butterfly vision, I was aware of my sinfulness, my old nature, but I still did not truly desire holiness. Rather, I suspected that spiritual maturity might make for a dry, dull, kill joy life. I was spiritually 'blind'. I did not recognize the treasure that was my spiritual birthright nor did I see the all-important significance of holiness. My lack of passion for holiness was the result of my failure to comprehend the true nature of holiness, and my failure to appreciate its intrinsic value. Worse still, I suspected that many around were having the same misgivings about the value of a life of holiness. Discouraged, I found myself questioning the purpose of maintaining a Christian testimony. I needed my eyes to be opened to a whole new dimension of life under the Lordship of Christ. The revelation needed to be a clear appreciation of the stark contrast between the restrictive, bland life of an earthbound caterpillar – crawling along with no vision, forever feeding yet never satisfied – to that of a winged butterfly, living a life of flight, beauty, vision and purpose.

Without this true perception of the rich quality of a life of holiness, I struggled to lead a life pleasing to the Lord, often despairing at my lukewarm attitude towards holiness. Does this sound familiar to you? Are you actually living a life of 'going through the motions' because you lack the motivation to press on to spiritual maturity? Such 'blindness' certainly hinders us from growing into Christlikeness. Why should we want to risk 'shedding an old skin' - throwing off the old nature - if we are not convinced that it will lead to something far better?

For me, a vicious circle ensued. I desperately wanted vision. I wanted a clearer revelation about the purposes of my life. You would only need to ask a few members of my church, who can remember that far back, and they will confirm how dissatisfied I felt. I would spend home-group Bible studies bemoaning my lack of passion! I knew that, as a Christian, I was supposed to live with zeal, enthusiasm and hope. However, I felt frustrated, and even burdened, by my short-sightedness. I felt as if I could barely see beyond the end of my own nose. I struggled with the absence of any desire to give up my free time and my hobbies, never mind to give up all I had and go to the ends of the earth to make disciples of all nations! Due to my failure to perceive the great promise of the beauty and superiority of a spiritually-mature life - portrayed to me through the butterfly vision in 1999 - I felt no motivation to 'shed a skin'. I wanted vision and the benefits of maturity without having to move on to the 'solids' which would require uncomfortable changes. There lay the obstacle to growth and vision. I wanted to stay in my room, meeting a self-gratifying hunger, reading excellent books and writing my journal. I loved to study my faith, but I felt no overwhelming passion or purpose, linked to putting it into practice. I feared that 'growing up' spiritually would mean surrendering my comfort zone and losing the freedom to do what I wanted, only to replace it with 'responsibility' and 'commitment'. With hindsight, I am now grateful to the Lord for allowing me to experience the discomfort of over-eating without shedding a skin. By that necessary, preliminary experience, he prepared me for the pursuit of heavenly things, encouraging me towards the changes necessary for my maturing process!

Can you relate to my plight? Have you settled for believing that 'feeding' your hunger is enough, whether that be through church attendance, quiet times, book reading or the conferences you attend? Are you trying to ignore the need for that 'food' to lead to change? Are you wrestling with the Lord, wanting to be committed to him on a deeper level, but afraid of what 'growing up' into spiritual maturity will actually mean for your life?

I praise God that, in his mercy, he intervened in my life and gave me the butterfly vision again in the summer of 2004. This time, I was explicitly told why I was feeling such wearisome sloth. I had not moved through the maturing process to become the butterfly of the 1999 vision. I was still a little worm. Like a ravenous caterpillar, I was trying to squeeze more and more 'leaves' into my old skin, rather than making room for more by shedding a skin. So, instead of my 'food' providing the energy and motivation for change, it was progressively making me feel more and more heavy and tired.

In my attempts to unlock the significance of the vision, I remember looking up the word "caterpillar" and found it certainly matched my feelings, even in its secondary meaning. I indeed felt as if I was going endlessly round in circles, carrying a heavy load. Through those five years I had been 'blind', acutely aware of my hunger, but having little view of where all this 'feeding' was leading! How sad! I had been given my purpose from the Lord in August, 1999, right at the start of my quest for "a passion for holiness". He had already given me the full answer but I had failed to see it. If I had sought to understand the analogy then, I would have foreseen the reason for the stages of hunger and blind immaturity. I would also have perceived not only the way through them but also a great motivating reason to do so.

Caterpillar ©
Endless track driven by cogged wheels used to propel a heavy vehicle.
Collins Pocket English Dictionary

## Selfish lifestyles

The caterpillar leads a very self-centred life. It eats its host plant for its own gain and, unlike the pollinating butterfly, gives very little back to the surroundings in which it grows. There are some caterpillars that have symbiotic relationships with ants but, generally, it is fair to say that caterpillars live unto themselves and their own survival. As I studied the caterpillar, I came to recognize my own self-centredness as spiritual immaturity. Above all, I began to see that it was this stubborn immaturity which was hindering any further growth or vision and so causing all the frustration and unease I was experiencing!

Immature relationships are often characterized by selfishness. According to many psychology studies, even the most balanced of children, up to a certain age, are ego-centric. They are physically incapable of true empathy. Like the caterpillar, they live for their own interests and seek to secure their own growth. Commitment, to something or someone else outside of these purposes, is seen as an infringement on their time and a waste of energy!

As adults we do not have the excuse of physical immaturity and yet many remain relationally immature. Many want the benefits of a relationship without commitment. Some enthusiastically take all the help that is available but are not so enthusiastic about helping others. Others revel in helping others but find it difficult to accept help themselves. Most of us like to have someone to listen to all we have to share but not many of us show the same attention when it comes to listening to what others have to say. A relationship which is intentionally superficial, and perhaps unequally balanced, can be of no lasting value to either party. The cry of a hungry baby will invariably prompt the mother to put on hold whatever she is doing in order to satisfy the baby's need as a priority. We accept that one-sided, sacrificial relationship as normal but only for the duration of the baby's weaning. As the child matures, a more balanced relationship, beneficial to both child and mother, is to be expected. Our choice of relationship is often an indicator of our level of maturity. Whilst a superficial relationship may, for a time, have some appeal as convenient, or even advantageous, its superficial nature will prevent the development of a real soul-bond.

Immaturity creates tension in our lives. You may well remember the desire as an adolescent to be treated as an adult and enjoy the benefits of mature relationships. On the other hand, you can probably also recall fearing growing up, believing, ironically, that the adulthood you so desired in other ways, would somehow take away your identity, or burden you with too many commitments. A similar conflict of interests may confront us in our spiritual lives. We often call on the Lord when we need him, pray when we want to off-load and only give our time when we want fellowship or teaching. But, when it comes to waiting upon the Lord and listening to perceive what is on his heart, going out of our way to serve him with the work of his Kingdom or lending a hand to one of his family, we suddenly feel inconvenienced. In our immaturity, we tend to resent calls for help which involve being actively present. Commitment is seen as a burden, not as the pathway to a closer and more mature relationship which will bring a joy all of its own.

Such self-centredness also causes 'blindness'. It's not uncommon these days for men or women to terminate a marriage, or a friendship, or membership of a church, on the grounds that they see no future in the relationship. There is nowhere to go. Further growth in the relationship requires a compromise, a sacrifice. Is your relationship with the Lord under a similar threat? Satan will do all he can to persuade you, both in your human and spiritual relationships, that you are happier in a non-committal relationship. He knows that relationships and community encourage maturity. So, in order to minimize growth and vision, Satan will persistently interfere with our relationships with one another and with the Lord. Strong relationships guarantee a greater chance of survival when hard times or temptations come, a greater kingdom-growth as people work together as a team, more fun in fellowship and the development of character as iron sharpens iron. Yes, there is a price to be paid, but it's worth it! To know each other well, you have to know each others' weaknesses and share what

> Spiritual maturity is not a solitary, individual pursuit. You cannot grow to Christlikeness in isolation.
>
> Rick Warren

causes you to stumble, or to get angry. You have to deal with the times when being close gets too close, and you rub each other up the wrong way. You may have to listen to criticism you would rather not hear. But, through all of this, you develop maturity and a rich depth to life that cannot be gained through superficial relationships.

Let me give an example from my own church. Each year, many people in the congregation will give up their summer holidays to help run a children's summer camp. They even pay to go and work in the kitchen, clean the toilets or be tent-leaders supervising the children etc. When first asked to go to camp, my initial reaction was to ask myself, (particularly as a teacher) "Why would I want to give up my summer holiday to do that? The last thing I need is further involvement with teenagers! I should take the time for myself after the hard work of term-time to relax and be self-indulgent." However, after praying about the need, I chose to give those ten days to the Lord each summer for five years.

Were there days when I wished I'd gone to a beach resort in France instead? Did leaders get tired? Were there arguments and frustrations at camp? Of course! That is the messy part of being a 'caterpillar'. Caterpillars are eating to grow. Because of this, they produce copious amounts of dirt, known as frass. Waste production comes with growth.

We know that from our own bodies. As we are growing spiritually, we may leave a 'trail of waste' behind us too! This is all part of the caterpillar stage. Experiences that deepen relationships, and sharpen our characters, may leave some 'frass'. But caterpillars do not, and must not, sit around in their waste. Those who watch caterpillars grow in captivity know that frass must be cleaned out of the container every day in order to prevent the growth of mould and to create a healthy environment for the caterpillar. Don't be surprised if your growth creates some mess. Clear it up and move on. Don't hang around in your mess! It can endanger your spiritual health.

By going to camp, I not only had a lot of fun and developed closer friendships with people from my church but I also had a glimpse of the Lord's work. I saw young people give their lives to Christ and then, in years to come, their parents follow suit! I saw many people within my own church grow spiritually through their involvement in camp. Above all, in the midst of that new level of commitment, I received my butterfly vision.

# Healthy Pain

Think of your personal relationships and, most especially, your walk with the Lord. Are you feeling the discomfort of 'stalemate' (if you will pardon the twist on words) as you refuse to change? What is it costing you?

Growth can be uncomfortable. As we have seen in the life of the caterpillar, growth necessitates and produces change. We shall be changed permanently by what we eat. Change is never easy. Change involves loss as well as gain. The caterpillar's appetite brings it to a very uncomfortable position of becoming too big for its own skin! The only way to grow further is to shed a skin. In our lives, we shall also be brought to a point where God will cause us to admit our immaturity for, indeed, immaturity has to be recognized and challenged in order for us to grow up. Immaturity betrays itself in the refusal to admit one needs to grow up. In contrast, accepting that life is a learning curve and acknowledging that we have not yet figured it all out is a sign of maturity. But, often, that is not easy, for if there is one thing that grates on us, it is being called immature. Nevertheless, God will ask us to acknowledge our current state before him. If you are anything like me, you will probably cringe as you read these words and may even feel some resentment. Why does it always seem so undesirable to grow up and surrender our 'immature skins' in order to mature? It is undoubtedly our old nature which holds us back. Strong measures are needed whenever spiritual immaturity manifests itself in the form of resistance to change. Teenage angst is a phenomenon not uncommon. Why? Because so many teenagers feel the world, especially parents and teachers, to be against them, compelling them to grow up by enforcing discipline or requiring them to think beyond their immediate circumstances and set goals for the future. Our Heavenly Father, our greatest teacher, wants us to grow up, not because he wants to rob us of the carefree spirit of childhood, but because we were designed to find fulfilment in a mature relationship with him. This may bring discomfort at first but, as Philip Yancey says in "Reaching for the Invisible God", it is a healthy pain which pushes us on to maturity.

Let us look back at the biblical character, Jacob, who had to learn some painful lessons from his mistakes. He had to come to the point of acknowledging his immature self before he could go on to grow into his new nature. Jacob struggled with selfishness. His name, figuratively, means "supplanter" or "he deceives" because, at birth, he grabbed his twin brother's heel, in an attempt, it would seem, to stop him being the first-born! Jacob had a clear destiny. His mother, Rebecca, had been told by God while she was still pregnant, *"The older will serve the younger"*. (Genesis 25 : 23b). Yet Jacob and his mother did not wait for the Lord to bring this about in his time. They took matters into their own hands! They sought to secure his future independently of the Lord. As we saw in the first chapter, Jacob, in order to acquire the first-born's birthright, took advantage of his brother's hunger. In his greed, he even stooped as low as to deceive his elderly, infirm father into giving him his brother's blessing. Selfishness led to separation. He was at odds with his brother and had to leave home for fear of his life. For twenty years, he did not return home; he never saw his mother again! But God still had his hand on Jacob and blessed him although he also allowed Jacob to suffer at the hands of other tricksters and selfish family members, probably to teach him a lesson. The wonder of this story still continues for, despite Jacob's nature, God met with him. God saw that Jacob passionately understood the value of God's blessing and birthright. It may, initially, have been a misguided zeal but God saw what Jacob could become; he saw his destiny. At heart, Jacob wanted to be at peace with God and have his blessing. Eventually, he came to the place where he wrestled with the Lord and, recognising his desperate need of the Lord, held on determinedly, begging God to bless him. However, there was an important interaction between Jacob and God before he gave him a new title. God asked Jacob his name. A person's name held such significance in those days. In Jacob's case, it was his identity, his nature. I wonder how Jacob gave his name. Did he shamefully whisper "Jacob" knowing his name stood for his selfish nature– "the deceiver and the supplanter"? The Lord wanted him to state openly his nature. Only after stating his name, did the Lord endow him with a new name and a new heart. He was given the name Israel – "a prince with God" or "he wrestles with God."

The second time I received the butterfly vision, I prayed the Lord would help me to understand its meaning. I opened my Bible and the Lord led me straight to Isaiah 41 : 14:- *"Do not be afraid, O worm Jacob, O little Israel, for I myself will help you,"declares the Lord, your Redeemer, the Holy one of Israel.*

At that time, I saw only the worm. I had just been told I was still at the caterpillar stage. However, the promise that God was still prepared to walk with me, and help me, really encouraged me. It was not until two years later, after reading a book called "Struggling with Selfishness" by Woodrow Kroll that I understood that the butterfly had been in the verse too! Israel is not just the name of the country, as I had originally read it; Israel was Jacob's new name! At one and the same time, in God's eyes, Jacob was both a caterpillar - "O worm Jacob"- and a butterfly - "O little Israel" - as though the transformation was already underway. Jacob became a new creation with a new name and a totally new nature, just like the caterpillar. From the very point of giving me the vision for the second time, God showed me through this verse that he did not just see my 'wormlike' state, but he also saw what I would become. Furthermore, despite all my failings and selfishness, he was prepared to work through the maturing process with me, just as he was with Jacob.

Perhaps seeing yourself as a "Jacob", you may well be asking yourself, "Who am I that the Lord should choose to display his glory in and through my life?" Therein lies the mystery of his grace. The wonder of God's glory is made even more awesome when he deigns to display it through weak and imperfect human beings. Our unexpected ability to reflect God's grace brings more glory to God because of our original wormlike nature. I have often marvelled at how the ugliest looking caterpillars often become the most beautiful butterflies. Doesn't this bring even more glory and honour to the Creator? If the caterpillar had any beauty of its own to begin with, the transformation would seem less miraculous.

> No-one reaches adulthood without undergoing such a period of immaturity. Equally, no healthy person wants to remain there. I know nothing sadder in life than a rupture in the maturing process: a caterpillar that never becomes a butterfly.
>
> Philip Yancey

We receive the grace of the Lord for the praise of his glory. (See Ephesians 1 : 12) What's more, he delights to show his love and his glory to us and through us. However, our starting point has to be the acknowledgment that we are, indeed, 'immature caterpillars' and things need to change. None of us can escape the questioning of the Lord, any more than Jacob could.

# A concluding challenge

So, to conclude, we have seen in the last three chapters that, as in the case of the caterpillar, the Lord will use our start in life, and our childhood days, to create our identity and to build us up with much feeding on 'young and tender shoots'. But, once strong enough to pass on to the next stage, he will begin to reveal to us the fact that we are immature and need to change, grow up and move on. How we choose to respond is critical to our spiritual growth. If we take offence at the charge of immaturity, we miss the intention. Are you prepared to miss out on future growth because you don't want to face the reality of your immaturity? Immaturity at an early age is normal and no cause for concern. God created it that way and, in previous chapters, we have already considered its importance as a time of development. But we are not meant to remain immature.

Are you tired of having no vision? Are you aware of the limitations imposed on you by your old nature? Do you sense that "there must be more than this", but feel unable to give up what you have, to gain something new? Perhaps it is time for you to ask the Lord to begin the work of apolysis and ecdysis in your spiritual life.

All the days ordained
for me were written in
your book before one
of them came to be ...

Psalm 139 : 16

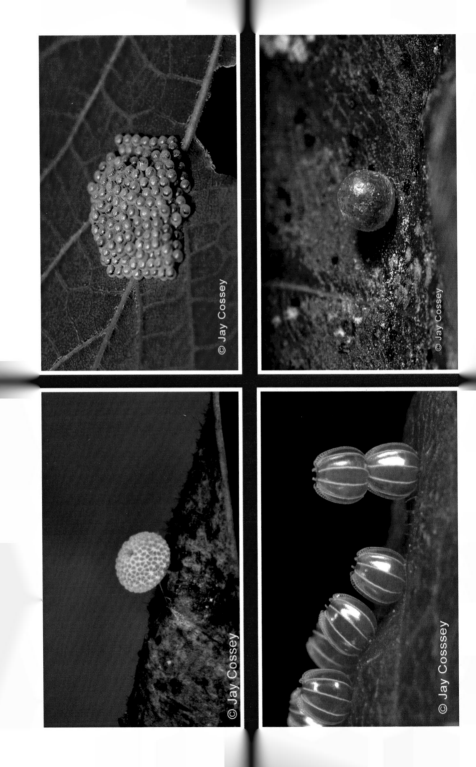

# Out it Pops

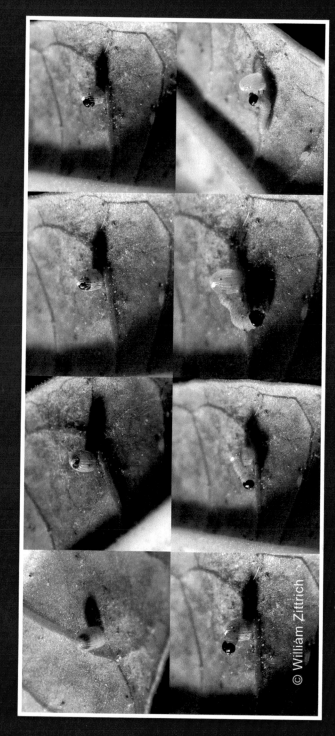

A tiny Monarch (Danaus plexippus) larva eating its way out of its shell

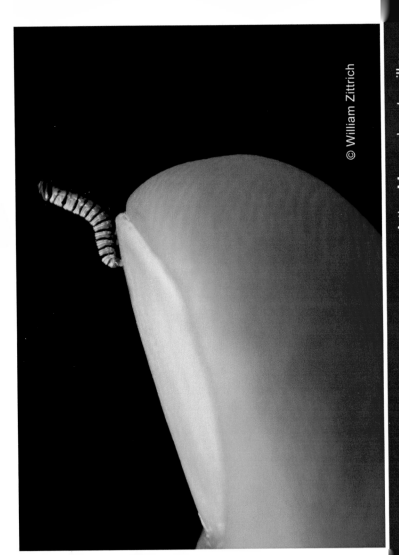

© William Zittrich

A tiny Monarch caterpillar

I asked the Lord that I might grow
In faith, and love, and every grace;
Might more of His salvation know,
And seek, more earnestly, His face.

Twas He who taught me thus to pray,
And He, I trust, has answered prayer!
But it has been in such a way,
As almost drove me to despair.

I hoped that in some favoured hour,
At once He'd answer my request;
And by His love's constraining pow'r,
Subdue my sins, and give me rest.

Instead of this, He made me feel
The hidden evils of my heart;
And let the angry pow'rs of hell
Assault my soul in every part.

Yea more, with His own hand He seemed
Intent to aggravate my woe;
Crossed all the fair designs I schemed,
Blasted my gourds, and laid me low.

"Lord, why is this?", I trembling cried,
"Wilt Thou pursue Thy worm to death?"
"'Tis in this way," the Lord replied,
"I answer prayer for grace and faith."

"These inward trials I employ,
From self, and pride, to set thee free;
And break thy schemes of earthly joy,
That thou may'st find thy all in Me."

John Newton
(1725-1807)

# Chapter 4

# Apolysis and Ecdysis
## Dealing with Self-life

*"When I was a child, I talked like a child, I thought like a child, I reasoned like a child. When I became a man, I put childish ways behind me."*    *1 Corinthians 13 : 11*

The caterpillar will usually have to undergo the process of moulting four times before shedding its final skin to reveal the pupal skin, otherwise known as the chrysalis. The shedding of a skin in order to grow may seem natural and painless when we consider the caterpillar. However, moulting is an incredibly complex internal upheaval where many factors must come together perfectly if the insect is not to die during the process! Moulting requires the combination of two breathtaking processes within the caterpillar's body – apolysis and ecdysis.

Apolysis is a process of preparation. It requires the caterpillar to become inactive, or dormant, for a short time. A hormone, ecdysone, is released into the body, telling the cells of the old skin to move ever so slightly away from the insides of the caterpillar. The old skin gradually lets go, leaving a narrow space. A digesting fluid is then released into this space. These digestive enzymes remain inactive until a new skin has formed underneath. When the new skin is ready, and only then, the enzymes get to work and the old skin peels off completely. This moulting is called ecdysis and only occurs after apolysis.

Our spiritual growth requires a similar combination of processes. First, there must be recognition of the restrictive 'old skin' and a preparation to let it go. Then, there must be an active process of shedding it. Change and progress in any area of our lives is often accompanied by a familiar pattern –

- an uncomfortable period of accepting that things must change
- fear of those changes
- being out of our comfort zone during times of change
- new growth as we then adapt to our new circumstances.

Let us consider how we move through these stages spiritually.

# Apolysis – Accepting things must change

*The truth will set you free, but first it may make you miserable! God's word exposes our motives, points out our faults, rebukes our sin, and expects us to change. It's human nature to resist change, so applying God's word is hard work. Rick Warren*

The Lord longs for an ever-increasing commitment and maturity in our walk with him. Going deeper into any relationship entails decision-making, changes, compromise and, ultimately, sacrifice. This process usually requires changes in both our circumstances and our character. It is often close relationships which cause us to see the worst in ourselves. We simultaneously see the undesirable, immature characteristics we want to leave behind and the desirable person we actually aspire to be. (This is especially true of our relationship with the Lord.) The survival of a relationship hangs on achieving the often complex internal changes needed to move progressively from one nature to the other, without disheartening each other. In our relationships with fellow men and women we may be tempted to question the love and the motive of a person who points out our faults. In our relationship with Christ that kind of doubt need not arise because of his unique sinless perfection. Even when spending time with him serves to make us painfully aware of our need to be more like him, we can be assured it is time well spent. Christ loves us too much to leave us content with our immaturity. So, he begins to work through this merciful combination of 'apolysis and ecdysis' - encouraging us to let go of our old nature whilst building in us a 'new skin'- our Christlikeness - to ensure our survival, before the 'old skin' falls away. In the words of the Apostle Paul: *"You were taught, with regard to your former way of life, to put off your old self, which is being corrupted by its deceitful desires; to be made new in the attitude of your minds; and to put on the new self, created to be like God in true righteousness and holiness."* (Ephesians 4 : 22-24)

In Chapter 3, we looked at becoming aware of spiritual immaturity through understanding its characteristics. Having once established the need to press on to maturity, the next step is to identify our old nature in order to shed its various 'skins'.

Our old nature is not a pretty sight. Colossians, chapter 3, and Galatians, chapter 5 list the following as indicative of our self-life: sexual immorality, impurity, lust, evil desires, greed, anger, malice, slander, filthy language and lies. These sins are not ones to which we readily like

"The acts of the sinful nature are obvious: sexual immorality, impurity and debauchery; idolatry and witchcraft; hatred, discord, jealousy, fits of rage, selfish ambition, dissensions, factions and envy; drunkenness, orgies, and the like. I warn you, as I did before, that those who live like this will not inherit the Kingdom of God." Galatians 5 : 19-21

to admit. Many of us are in denial of our self-life and, as such, very defensive when our faults are exposed. All too frequently, we silence our conscience with contradictory excuses like "No-body is perfect" but "I'm a good person." Only the Holy Spirit, therefore, can open our eyes to the true nature of our self-life, and convict us. We can anticipate a spiritual battle over this preparatory process of spiritual 'apolysis' because the human heart does not like to face the need to allow God to work in us and change us. Conviction from the Lord can therefore be disturbing. Rick Warren, in his book, 'The Purpose Driven Life', teaches that the truth will set you free, eventually, but it may make you miserable first.

The process of change has to start with an admission of our own faults and a genuine desire to be transformed from the inside out. We may have to acknowledge that we have known for some time what is hindering our spiritual growth but have chosen not to make the necessary changes to move on. The pursuit of happiness through materialism, relationships or career aspirations can be a very good disguise for a restrictive 'immature skin'. The desire to be "happy" is not a bad thing in itself but it is often the cause of spiritual stagnation.

It is indeed a challenge to allow the Lord to work out the process of spiritual 'apolysis and ecdysis' in our lives, unhindered. However, if our Creator-God watches over a caterpillar's struggle, with the beauty of a butterfly in mind, how much more will he watch over our struggles, until the beauty of Christ is seen in us!

# A sympathetic high priest

*"For we do not have a high priest who is unable to sympathise with our weaknesses, but we have one who has been tempted in every way, just as we are – yet was without sin. Let us then approach the throne of grace with confidence, so that we may receive mercy and find grace to help us in our time of need."*      Hebrews 4 : 15-16

During my first year of service on board OM mission ship, MV Logos 2, I experienced the discomfort of confronting issues arising from my old nature. During a particularly challenging time, I was asked to speak at an Easter service. I wanted to speak about the butterfly vision so I specifically prayed to the Lord for new insight from within the butterfly vision that related to Easter, apart from the obvious symbolism of death and resurrection. In response, the Lord gave me much encouragement for my own spiritual walk through the prophetic Psalm 22 : 6: *"But I am a worm and not a man, scorned by men and despised by the people."*

I marvelled as I realised that the Lord empathised with us in our internal struggles. He understood the shame I was feeling. Not only did our Lord lay aside his heavenly glory in order to be made man, but he also laid aside the earthly glory of man in order to be made a "worm", scorned and despised by the religious and the irreligious. *"God made him who had no sin to be sin for us, so that in him we might become the righteousness of God."* (2 Corinthians 5 : 21) All manner of guilt and condemnation pertaining to our fallen, sinful nature was heaped upon him – not metaphorically, but in such actuality that the bond with his Holy Father was temporarily broken.

As the Holy Spirit begins to convict us of the true horror of our old nature and self-centredness, or we perhaps feel the shame of our battle for self-control, let us remember that our Lord sympathises with our every weakness. He bore our wormlike nature on the cross, scorning the shame of it because of the joy set before him. (Hebrews 12 : 2) Surely, this is the Lord's ultimate encouragement to change us without disheartening us to the point of despair. Yes, he calls us to face up to our old nature but only as a necessary first step to discarding it and moving on to the joy of spiritual maturity set before us. We are neither to continue living in the mentality of the old nature, nor in a permanent state of self-defeat, condemnation or guilt.

The conviction we feel may sometimes seem harsh, but Christ is calling us to a better way of living not trying to spoil our experience of life. Christian discipleship is not about setting our own standards or adopting the local cultural norm. It's about engaging with the standards set by our Lord and Teacher. Jesus was well aware that his first disciples were ordinary men, like ourselves, and yet he set standards for them, in his 'Sermon-on-the-Mount', which must have sounded unattainable. For instance, in the section dealing with our attitude towards our enemies,

"If anyone would come after me, he must deny himself and take up his cross daily and follow me. For whoever wants to save his life will lose it, but whoever loses his life for me will save it. What good is it for a man to gain the whole world, and yet lose or forfeit his very self?"

Luke 9 : 23-25

and towards people of whom we disapprove, Jesus said, *"Be perfect, therefore, as your heavenly Father is perfect."* (Matthew 5 : 48) Let us take note, however, of the objectives Jesus had in mind – *"that you may be sons of your Father in heaven."* (v 45) He was seeking to lift his disciples out of the old 'religious life' *("You have heard that it was said"* v 43) and into a new 'relationship life' *("but I tell you"* v 44). In other words, Jesus was telling his disciples to leave behind their former way of life, in order to enter into a dimension altogether more glorious.

Scripture tells us that we, too, will find a new life – everlasting life - if we are prepared to lay down our sinful lives. God does not want us to live our lives trapped in our old natures. He has a destiny and purpose for each one of us. The caterpillar does not consciously control its own process of metamorphosis. It is a gift already within its genes. In the same way, God has put the Holy Spirit within us as a guarantee of our inheritance. (Ephesians 1 : 13,14) We are not expected to bring about our own transformation. The transforming power is the work of the Holy Spirit. However, we must co-operate and respond to the workings of the Holy Spirit. Like the hormones which prompt change within the caterpillar's body, the Holy Spirit will stir our spirits to evoke change by convicting us of the particular elements of our lives which are hindering our spiritual growth.

## Apolysis: Facing the Fear of Change

Once we have accepted that we do need to ask God to work in our lives, we can still be paralysed by the fear of the process of change. I can remember wondering what would happen if I asked God to mature me by stripping away the sinful nature. What did 'shedding a skin' entail in my life? If I fully surrendered my life to God, would he ask me to give up everything and send me to Africa? How would he deal with my sins? Would he convict me in front of everyone at a church meeting? Would he force me to stand and confess all my sins publicly? Would I start to feel terrible about every 'little' thing? These fears held me back.

Are you afraid of what the Lord would do if you were to surrender yourself to him and ask him to peel away the old nature? Satan loves to deceive us. He would have us believe that the Lord's work in our lives will mean losing our personality; giving up what we love; being publicly shamed or living in a permanent state of guilt. He will cause us to doubt the Lord's motives for changing us. He may try to persuade us that we will be just be exploited by the Lord. Why? Elisabeth Elliot gives us a clear answer in her book, 'The Glad Surrender': *"If, deep in our hearts, we suspect that God does not love us and cannot manage our affairs as well as we can, we certainly will not submit to his discipline.... It is on the basis of a solid conviction that He is both sovereign and loving that we commit ourselves to him unconditionally,* **believing that what we leave behind is less than nothing compared to what we hope for.***"*

Satan knows that if we, in our love for the Lord, are prepared to submit to divine discipline, including the 'shedding of immature skins', the level of maturity reached thereby will make us capable of carrying out the will of God with vision and purpose. Of course, Satan does not want this. Consequently, he plagues us with doubts and denial! We should always answer Satan with the sure word of God. In addition, let us take heart from the story of the caterpillar in which it is so evident that the changes a caterpillar must undergo are only to bring about something of breathtaking beauty. Be encouraged to entrust yourself to the transforming power of your Creator-God. Only by persevering faith will we prove that what we purposefully leave behind is less than nothing compared to what we will gain.

If you feel fear about asking the Lord to begin the process of ecdysis (shedding skins) in your life, remember that God has determined that apolysis will always come before ecdysis. Although moulting time does leave the caterpillar more vulnerable than usual for a short period of time, the creator of the caterpillar does not let it become totally exposed. It is not stripped of its skin and left with all its 'guts hanging out', ready to be gobbled up by its nearest enemy. No, as we have seen, the new skin is prepared beforehand in secrecy, ready to replace the obsolete one. Furthermore, when the old skin falls away, some new skins incorporate extra features which make the caterpillar more able to defend itself. These features might include brighter colours, more defined markings, long spiny hairs, or even the ability to ward off predators with a noise, or a smell. The Swallowtails acquire a bright orange protrusion called an osmeterium. Resembling a snake tongue, the osmeterium pops out from the caterpillar's head, releasing a foul smell whenever the caterpillar is in danger.

It is encouraging to keep this in mind when the Lord calls us to surrender a part of our old nature. Rather than yield to the fear of change, we can rest assured that the Lord will not leave us unprotected. If he carefully provides protection for the caterpillar at each stage of development, how much greater will be his care for us. When we recognize our desire to grow spiritually as a preparatory work of the Holy Spirit, it can be likened to the formation of a new 'inner skin', ready for our next stage of development. By the time the change actually occurs, the necessary protection is already in place. This has been my experience when, more than once, I have faced 'spiritual ecdysis.' Let me share with you one of the biggest changes in my life.

# Letting go of an old life

The start of 2005 did not seem promising. I lay in bed for weeks with a severe chest infection, tired out from over six years of teaching in a secondary school. During this time of enforced 'dormancy' (just like a caterpillar who is about to moult) the Lord began to challenge me to 'shed an old skin' in order to grow. Over the course of one week, the Lord asked me to lay down all the basic elements of the framework of my life at that time. I began to feel the secretion of the 'moulting hormone' into my life!

The first two days I wrestled against letting go of my material possessions. A friend came to visit to cheer me up and gave me a very helpful picture, which, I believe, is traditionally attributed to Corrie ten Boom. She said, *"If you hold on to what you have now with a clenched hand, the Lord will have to painfully bend your fingers back to open up your hand. Above all, you cannot receive anything new with a closed hand. However, if your hand is open, you may not even notice anything being lifted off and who knows, the Lord may be waiting to put a new blessing into your hand!"*

However, despite this excellent advice, it took an accident, that very same day, which ruined my favourite handbag to realize that possessions can be lost in the blink of an eye. I suppose you could say my fingers were forced a little there!

During the following days, I consciously laid down my job; the status associated with a good job; my friends and family; and my home. I did not know whether the Lord was asking me to lay those things down figuratively or literally, but I knew that I had to be able to lay them before him as if it were literally. By the end of the week I understood it to be literally. A couple of weeks earlier I had seen an article about the MV Logos Hope, the new ship owned by OM Ships. OM desperately needed volunteers to help prepare the ship for ministry. In response, I seriously considered spending my summer holidays there. However, all my close friends and family judged this to be inadvisable, as I had just been signed off ill for two months. How would I face a new academic year in September if I had not rested and prepared properly in the summer? When sharing with a friend the details of that week of surrender, she asked me what came of my notion to spend my summer holiday working on MV Logos Hope. I explained that cold water had been thrown over that idea. Her response made everything fall into place - *"Such reasons for not working on OM Ships would no longer be valid if you joined long-term!"*

If the Lord had told me, at the time of reading the article, "I want you to leave your job, and all you know and love, to join OM Ships for two years", there is no way that I would have been able to handle such a challenge. Instead, over the course of a week, without alarming me with the reasons, the Lord had been gradually breaking away 'the old skin,' bit by bit, and asking me to let go. With hindsight, I now perceive that he had been preparing me for that move for a number of years, giving me a hunger for a purpose, which I could not ignore, and a desire to know God more. Over the following six months he prepared the new inner skin. I cannot deny that the internal upheaval was very stressful but, by August, I was ready to go to sea. The 'old skin' fell off completely.

It took many months to adapt to life onboard but, gradually, I began to grow as I 'fed' on all the different opportunities within my new environment. After two amazing years of adventure with the Lord; visiting nearly forty different countries; making friends from all over the world and being involved in ministry, I can truly testify that what we leave behind is nothing compared to what we gain.

You, too, will find that as you surrender 'an old skin', the Lord will already have everything covered. He has gone ahead of you to prepare a way for you. Your 'new skin' might seem uncomfortably big, at first, but if you feed on God's word and learn from the new experiences, you will soon grow into it! As with the caterpillar, a greater capacity for food will produce not only growth and strength but an increased level of protection. Without stretching the analogy too far, I dare to say that by putting on the whole armour of God and 'feeding' on the Word of God, we make ourselves 'poisonous' in the eyes of our predators.

# Ecdysis – Moving Out of the Comfort Zone

I believe there are two principal ways in which the Lord asks us to 'shed skins' – the laying down of our lifestyle, as described above, and the laying down of our self. Of the two, I think the second is often the more difficult to accept.

Many people have remarked on the enormous step I took in leaving my job, home, church, family and friends to join OM Ships. However, whilst serving onboard the MV Logos 2, I was often challenged by the Lord in a much deeper way to deal with my selfish and immature 'old skins'! Facing up to the truth about oneself is not a pleasant experience, to put it mildly. Personal pride is probably the most restricting 'old-nature skin' and the most difficult to shed because the shedding becomes all too public for comfort. Accepting the peeling away of our personal reputation is far more painful than laying down our material possessions. It was a real struggle, at times, to go and ask for a friend's forgiveness, especially if they had not even been aware I had sinned against them in thought, word or deed. It is a humbling process to reveal one's old nature to those concerned.

Sometimes I was so ashamed of what I saw in myself, I felt really disheartened. There were so many things to which the Lord drew my attention that I felt as if I was never going to be done with 'shedding skins.' Like John Newton (see the hymn at the start of the chapter), in wanting to be close to the Lord, I soon found myself echoing his confused and frustrated words *"Lord, why is this? ..... Wilt Thou pursue Thy worm to death?"* Sometimes I wondered why I ever "asked the Lord that I might grow in faith and love and every grace" and "more of his salvation know". However, by means of this experience, I came to realise that the Lord's purpose in exposing 'the worm' is to intensify our desire for 'the butterfly'. Newton's hymn records a similar recognition. Having bemoaned the strains of being refined, he notes the Lord's gracious answer, revealing his purpose for employing the trials.

> These inward trials I employ
> From self and pride to set thee free
> And break thy schemes of earthly joy
> That thou mayst find thy all in Me

The biological process of apolysis and ecdysis provides an encouraging analogy of the sanctifying process of dying to self. To me, they are like the spiritual trials which break our "schemes of earthly joy" – peeling away the old nature - our attachment to the world - yet simultaneously developing 'a new skin' to continue the journey towards spiritual maturity. The spiritual process of 'apolysis and ecdysis' is necessary and indeed life-saving but not without risk and struggle. Satan persistently tries to convince us that our old nature is not so bad and that it is safer to remain as we are. "Keep the old covering firmly in place!" he cries. He persuasively reminds us that the surrender of our 'old skins' will be costly and hurtful to our pride, involving repentance and confession. As with me, spiritual growth may require you to confess your wrongdoings to others and to ask for their forgiveness. It may be advisable to make yourself accountable to a friend or partner in order to protect yourself from tenacious old habits which you now wish to lay down. Nobody enjoys this kind of transition in life; invariably it is painful and embarrassing.

To aid me in my commitment to press on towards spiritual maturity, I sought the help of a ship leader. She became my accountability partner and would meet with me from time to time. In our first meeting, she impressed upon me the necessity for openness and honesty in order to tackle effectively any sin that was hindering spiritual growth. Perhaps sensing my hesitation, she gave me a very powerful analogy to help me understand my choices and their consequences. Imagine a tranquil lake set up in the mountains, surrounded by beautiful scenery. But, as you sit by the lake, you cannot appreciate its beauty because you know a secret. You have carelessly allowed some toxic waste to fall from your boat into this lake and sink to the bottom. Beneath the still waters, the poison is gradually leaking out, threatening the beauty of the lake and all its wildlife. The surroundings still look beautiful but you know what lies beneath. You have a choice; to leave the waste and face the devastating pollution that will eventually come for all to see and suffer, or to face the exposure and removal of that waste now and restore the former glory of the lake. The removal may be ugly. Heavy machinery will have to move in and drain the lake and lift out the waste. They will reduce the grassy banks of the lake to mud and leave scars across the landscape. The waste will no longer be a secret as it is lifted out. You will doubtless be ashamed. But, in time, the machines will all drive away, the grass will grow over the mud again and the lake will be refilled. As you sit by the lake, you will, once more, be able to appreciate its beauty with peace and joy.

In the context of spiritual development, fear is usually the greatest obstacle to unconditional surrender. Do we not fear that by submitting to the humbling exposure of our sins we will lose our standing in the eyes of our fellow Christians? But what justification is there for such fear? In truth, the opposite is invariably the case. One person's brokenness can be beneficially 'infectious'. In fact, it is often the catalyst to revival or, at least, to a heart-warming visitation of the Holy Spirit. I cannot deny that my surrender to the Lord, which involved the naming of my weaknesses and secret sins, initially left me feeling exposed and vulnerable.

"But God chose the foolish things of the world to shame the wise; God chose the weak things of the world to shame the strong. He chose the lowly things of this world and the despised things - and the things that are not - to nullify the things that are, so that no-one may boast before him. It is because of him that you are in Christ Jesus, who has become for us wisdom from God - that is, our righteousness, holiness and redemption."
1 Corinthians 1 : 27 - 30

However, I must tell you that, like the caterpillar as it sheds its final skin to reveal the pupal skin, that exposure was over in minutes, and I was free of one of Satan's toughest skins - the secrecy of shame - which keeps so many of us bound up. Not all times of exposure will be so short or so contained to one person. However, no matter which area of your life you need to deal with, the cleansing time will be relatively brief when compared to living with 'the waste' for the rest of your lives. The Lord, in his faithfulness, will cleanse you as you confess your sins. As we have learnt, the Lord will also not bring you to such a point without preparing you through the wonder of 'spiritual apolysis'. This often takes the form of feeling "godly sorrow" and regret for the secret shame you are hiding. This may last weeks, months or even years, before you decide to allow the Lord to change your total inner-self and peel off that final 'old skin' to reveal the 'pupal skin'. The Bible promises: *"Godly sorrow brings repentance that leads to salvation and leaves no regret, but worldly sorrow brings death."* (2 Corinthians 7 : 10)

What is worldly sorrow? It is a paralysing remorse – a sitting at the edge of that lake all your life, fearing the day the pollution finally spills out. It is a constant insecurity about being exposed for who you really are. It is a deception to think that continuing in your 'old skin' will be less costly. You must be clear-minded about that. Epictetus, a Stoic Philosopher (50-130), once said *"What punishment is there for those who will not accept things in this spirit? Their punishment is that they remain as they are."* This is even more poignant when we remind ourselves that we are everlasting beings. We were designed to become new creations, son-worshippers. If we refuse to give up our 'wormlike nature' in this life, it will remain with us forever. In this light, I now see one of the Bible's definitions of hell with a deeper understanding: *"Hell ... where their worm does not die."* (Mark 9 : 48)

Imagine remaining in the old nature with all "hope of glory" gone for ever. Imagine knowing you will never be rid of the things you despise about yourself. Imagine your persistent failure to overcome besetting sins culminating finally in a self-condemnation which is irreversible. Over and above the biblical description of Hell, one can imagine the bitter mixture of sorrow and remorse over the tragic neglect of *"such a great salvation"* (Hebrews 2 : 3) – man's opportunity to reflect God's glory.

# Ecdysis: A swift shedding of the skin

The moment of ecdysis is still one of extreme vulnerability for the caterpillar despite all the preparation of apolysis. As it sheds its skin, the caterpillar is momentarily incapacitated. It therefore cannot afford to act slowly; rather, the skin comes off in a flash and the caterpillar quickly wriggles out. If not, the birds and other predators would seize their opportunity and swoop in!

This picture in nature provides an important lesson for us. Satan has several techniques to deceive us to stay within our 'old skin.' He will try to convince us that we will never be able to change or there is no point dealing decisively with sin and that a gradual approach will be sufficient. He will try to delay our action through reasoning. If we once begin to reason, we are half way towards defeat. Be determined to act swiftly for if you linger too long, the enemy will pounce on you, just like a bird snatching a vulnerable caterpillar.

'The Great Divorce' by C. S. Lewis contains a story which illustrates the battle we may face in dealing with sin but also the amazing strength we gain in taking decisive action to rid ourselves of the old nature. A "ghostly man" approaches heaven's borders carrying a little, red lizard on his shoulder. It represents lust. The ghostly man turns away from the high places because he cannot silence the lizard and fears embarrassment and shame. An angel immediately steps in and offers to kill the lizard and stop him from tormenting the man anymore. The man draws back at such drastic action and suggests that silencing him would suffice and that there was plenty of time to deal with the lizard more decisively at a later date. The angel corrects him, pointing out that time is short and the gradual process is of no use. The man tries to make all sorts of excuses. Meanwhile, the lizard desperately whispers into the man's ear to try to persuade him that living in this 'old skin' is not so bad and that it would be a big mistake to give it up! Let us look at the 'reasoning' that ensues.

*"Why are you torturing me? You are jeering at me. How can I let you tear me in pieces? If you wanted to help me, why didn't you kill the damned thing without asking me-- before I knew? It would be all over by now if you had."*

*"I cannot kill it against your will. It is impossible. Have I your permission?"*

*The Angel's hands were almost closed on the Lizard, but not quite. Then the Lizard began chattering to the Ghost so loud that even I could hear what it was saying.*

*"Be careful," it said. "He can do what he says. He can kill me. One fatal word from*

*you and he will! Then you'll be without me for ever and ever. It's not natural. How could you live? You'd be only a sort of ghost, not a real man as you are now. He doesn't understand. He's only a cold, bloodless abstract thing. It may be natural for him, but it isn't for us. Yes, yes. I know there are no real pleasures now, only dreams. But aren't they better than nothing? And I'll be so good. I admit I've sometimes gone too far in the past, but I promise I won't do it again. I'll give you nothing but really nice dreams--all sweet and fresh and almost innocent. You might say, quite innocent .... "*

*"Have I your permission?" said the Angel to the Ghost.*

*"I know it will kill me."*

*"It won't. But supposing it did?"*

*"You're right. It would be better to be dead than to live with this creature."*

The angel immediately strikes the lizard dead. The "ghost" becomes his true self, a strong man, and the lizard changes into a magnificent horse which the man then uses to ride towards the high places. He has a changed nature with authority and control over the former lizard. In a similar way, the caterpillar may even sometimes eat the skin it has just shed. The skin which formerly trapped the caterpillar, now becomes a source of food and energy.

Herein lies the reason for Satan's desperate attempts to keep us in our old skin, unchanged. He does not want you to change for he knows that each time you 'shed a restricting skin' you become stronger and stronger, moving ever closer to your destiny! Maybe you struggle with jealously, pride, a quick temper, lust or an addiction. Perhaps you feel powerless to shake them off? Do you doubt the Lord's power to transform your life as dramatically as a drab caterpillar is transformed into a beautiful butterfly? Perhaps you only believe it possible for others, who don't seem to have as many weaknesses or as many regretful experiences in their past, and just appear to be naturally 'nicer'. I encourage you not to lose heart but to turn over your old nature to the Lord. He will transform you. Read Hebrews 11, especially verse 34, to learn how, by faith, the weaknesses of the heroes of old were turned to strength, making them powerful in battle, able to rout the enemies of the Lord.

## Adaptation : Growing into the new skin

Growth is an inevitable part of adaptation. Once free of its old skin, the caterpillar wastes no time taking full advantage of its new, bigger and more flexible skin! Do you think that, even if it were possible, you would ever see a caterpillar looking back wistfully at its old skin? I think not! Nor would you see it deliberating whether to carry on eating, worrying that it will only lead to another moult! Rather, the caterpillar greedily devours more food, instinctively focused on the growth process towards maturity. The beautiful end result determines the worth of this cyclic process of eating, growing and subsequently, facing apolysis and ecdysis again and again.

We must adopt the same attitude. In Philippians, chapter 3 : 13-15, the Apostle Paul urges all those who are mature, to be as determined as himself to *"forget what is behind"* and to *"strain towards what is ahead, pressing on to win the prize for which God has called us heavenwards in Christ Jesus"*. Rather than dwell on the 'old skins' we have left behind, we should, like the caterpillar, actively set about ensuring new growth, making the most of our

"Therefore we do not lose heart. Though outwardly we are wasting away, yet inwardly we are being renewed day by day. For our light and momentary troubles are achieving for us an eternal glory that far outweighs them all. So we fix our eyes not on what is seen, but on what is unseen. For what is seen is temporary, but what is unseen is eternal."

2 Corinthians 4 : 16-18

'new skin'. It is true that we, too, will inevitably face another period of 'apolysis and ecdysis', but let us rejoice that we have an even greater motivation to endure it than any caterpillar. Chapters three and four of the Apostle Paul's second letter to the Corinthians tell us that we have the opportunity to be Christlike, to reflect his glory (with even greater splendour than a beautiful butterfly!) With this perception of who we are and the glorious destiny to which God is calling us, let us press on to maturity (Hebrews 6 : 1), not despising his discipline, but prepared in heart and mind to engage with the challenges of change and to throw off anything that hinders us. Praise God, he will complete the good work he has begun in us (Philippians 1 : 6) for the sake of his honour and glory.

*"To him who is able to keep you from falling and to present you before his glorious presence without fault and with great joy, to the only God our Saviour be glory, majesty, power and authority, through Jesus Christ our Lord, before all ages, now and for evermore! Amen." Jude : 24,25*

.

Lord, we've seen Your purpose to bring the many sons
To share in Your full glory and see Your kingdom come.
We praise You, Lord, this glory is You, Yourself within,
Spread out in all Your people to shine in all of them.

Since we received Your life, Lord, a seed's been growing there:
The seed of inward glory, the glory we will share!
By growing 'til the blossom of glory blooms in full,
We'll thus enjoy Your increase and glory bountiful.

Hail! Captain of Salvation! Our heav'nly Pioneer!
Our praises, midst the battle and tumult, You will hear.
We're following our Captain all through the mighty fray.
Our glorious, faithful Captain sustains us all the way.

Lord, fighting on to glory, You now have gone before:
Now fighting in Your footsteps we'll conquer o'er and o'er.
From glory unto glory, we'll fight until we see
The glory from within us shall manifested be.

Then, Lord, at last the fighting and battle cry will cease,
And we'll appear in glory, Your kingdom and increase.
That day we'll be completed, that day Your face we'll see,
For in that blessed day, Lord, we'll in the glory be!

Henry Thomas Smart
(1813 -1839)

# Chapter 5

# Predators, Parasites and Pathogens
## Enemies without and within

*"Then the dragon (Satan) was enraged at the woman and went off to wage war against the rest of her offspring - those who obey God's commandments and hold to the testimony of Jesus." Revelation 12 : 17*

Caterpillars and butterflies live under constant threat of attack, from their earliest days as larvae in the egg, to adult-life as a butterfly. As if aware of danger, albeit instinctively, both caterpillars and butterflies live their lives in such a way as to avoid predators wherever possible. Nevertheless, despite being endowed with certain defence mechanisms, the majority of caterpillars are destroyed before they ever reach metamorphosis.

They are at risk from three main enemies:
- predators (outside enemies that attack their prey to eat them, such as spiders, birds, etc)
- parasites/parasitoids (enemies that live in/on their prey to their own advantage, often resulting in the death of the host such as wasps/flies/mites)
- pathogens (disease)

Some of the unpleasant facts of life and death we discover, as we study these enemies of the caterpillar and the butterfly, serve to remind us forcefully that we too face many dangers in this world which threaten our spiritual lives. They also give us new insight into the means used by Satan to attack and devastate the lives of men and women – lives full of potential. He knows our personal individual weaknesses; he knows the areas in our lives where we are most vulnerable and he will not hesitate to exploit any unbelief, or carelessness, which we fail to deal with in our own lives. Satan does not want us to reach spiritual maturity. His ancient rebellion against his Creator is now played out on planet earth, with his hatred directed towards any man or woman who aspires to walk with God. His main strategy is to attack our self-worth and, consequently, our ministry. In personal spiritual warfare, our enemies, driven by the unseen spiritual principalities of darkness, will come in various disguises. The Apostle Paul warns us that Satan himself masquerades as an angel of light. (2 Corinthians 11 : 14) To say that there is a war raging over the eternal destiny of your soul, as well as over your life here on earth, is no new mention of mine. In Ephesians, chapter 6, we read, *"For our struggle is not against flesh and blood, but against the rulers, against the authorities, against the powers of this dark world and against the spiritual forces of evil in the heavenly realms."* (Ephesians 6 : 12)

Does this seem far-fetched to you? Beware! One of the greatest tactics the enemy will use is the persuasion that there is no enemy and, therefore, no war. This lie has to be exposed for it is perhaps the most lethal. It results in apathy and indifference, leaving the victim vulnerable to the full extent of Satan's subtleties against us. Beware of consciously, or unconsciously, living in denial. Involvement in spiritual warfare is not optional. The Word of God instructs us to equip ourselves actively with our God-given spiritual armour and spiritual weapons.

The caterpillar in its early instars is unconsciously protected by its God-given camouflage and tiny size. Early in our spiritual development there will be times when the Lord protects us without our conscious awareness. The larvae in their later instars, however, are endowed with a greater ability to defend themselves actively, rather than just avoid attack through camouflage. Similarly, as we mature we are required to *"watch our lives and doctrine carefully."* (1 Timothy 4 : 16) We have a personal responsibility to protect our own souls. If we leave our lives unguarded, we shall have only ourselves to blame if the enemy makes devastating inroads into our lives.

Having once acknowledged there is a war, no time must be lost in establishing the true identity of our enemies. In order to win the battle, we must learn as much as possible about the enemy, his techniques and his weapons. "The Parable of the Sower" in the fourth chapter of Mark's gospel identifies common 'enemies' that prevent the Word of God from taking root in our lives, thus hindering healthy growth and fruitfulness in our walk with the Lord. Let us then consider this passage in conjunction with the study of predators, parasites and pathogens.

# Predators

*"Listen! A farmer went out to sow his seed. As he was scattering the seed, some fell along the path, and the birds came and ate it up. Some fell on rocky places, where it did not have much soil. It sprang up quickly, because the soil was shallow. But when the sun came up, the plants were scorched, and they withered because they had no root."* Mark 4 : 3-6

*"The Farmer sows the word. Some people are like seed along the path, where the word is sown. As soon as they hear it, Satan comes and takes away the word that was sown in them. Others, like seed sown on rocky places, hear the Word and at once receive it with joy. But since they have no root, they last only a short time. When trouble or persecution comes because of the Word, they quickly fall away."* Mark 4 : 14-17

Predators are commonly known as animals which habitually hunt other animals for food. The caterpillar and the butterfly have many predators. They are pursued principally by spiders and birds. Occasionally, they are also attacked by a large dragonfly or by small mammals such as mice and voles. These creatures attack caterpillar eggs, larvae and butterflies. Take a closer look at the next butterfly you see, and you may well find a clear, bird-beak shaped hole, in one, or both, of the wings. Spiders spin webs in mid-air to trap butterflies, lie in wait in flower-heads or pounce on their prey on the ground. They may even attack sleeping butterflies at night.

However, the words 'predator' and 'predatory', can also have a much wider meaning. Being a predator means living at the expense of the well-being of others – a means of survival characterized by plundering. Indeed, the word "predator" comes from the Latin term – 'praeda' - which means 'booty'. From this perspective, man can also be seen as a predator. We may not catch larvae and butterflies for food, but we do intentionally catch them for display, for breeding, for commercial sale or for research. Furthermore, whilst we have no intention of deliberately killing butterflies, our modern lifestyle is plundering their environments for the sake of our well-being and profit margins, leaving many species close to extinction! Garden plants and crops are sprayed with insecticides to ensure a prosperous harvest. These chemicals can either harm the larvae of some butterflies, or kill their host plants and thus, indirectly, threaten their survival. Both the caterpillar and the butterfly are also suffering from another increasing environmental concern – the uprooting of wildlife areas in the name of development and civilization. This is not just the mass destruction of rainforests but, also, the smaller decisions we make, for example, to tarmac over our front gardens to make a driveway! Although such actions are not seen as a direct attack on caterpillars and butterflies, they are, nevertheless, detrimental to their chance of survival.

Man's spiritual predators can be divided into two similar categories:

- those that are openly attacking Christians as individuals
- those that are plundering our Christian heritage so that there seems to be little hope for our continued existence.

The Parable of the Sower makes it clear that there are spiritual predators - Satan and his evil spirits - represented in this parable by "the birds". Evil powers use other human beings and circumstances, political ideas and other religions to wage war against Christians as open enemies of the gospel. One only has to read the accounts of organisations like "Open Doors" or the "Barnabus Fund" to realize that there are very real, determined enemies of the Christian faith. They will stop at nothing to silence, if not destroy, all those who follow Christ, especially, those who seek to 'lay eggs' and 'pollinate'. In many areas of the world, where the church is trying "to sow seed on hard or rocky ground", pastors and professing Christians are suffering terribly for their faith. They are openly attacked and thrown into prison, brutally tortured and murdered. Their families are often assaulted as well and it has been known for whole Christian communities and villages to be burnt down and the residents driven away. Such atrocities have recently taken place in countries such as Indonesia, India and parts of Africa, though rarely reported by the secular media. Some converts, who perhaps formally accepted the word of God with joy, are becoming discouraged and afraid. They are at risk of returning to their former religions, their faith withering under the "scorching sun" of persecution and trouble.

In the West, we may not yet be seeing physical persecution and martyrdom of Christians but there is no room for complacency. For decades, human 'predators' have been actively seeking to prevent the preaching of the gospel, whether that be in our schools and universities, on our streets, in prisons, in hospital chapels or even from our church pulpits! Unseen spiritual forces are an even greater threat. Unexplained incidents can occur when you are heavily involved in evangelism, or simply seeking to discipline yourself to spend more intimate time with the Lord. These events invariably cause distraction, if not distress. Occasionally, they succeed in disabling you from your involvement or commitment. Be alert and ready to defend yourself. Just as the predators of the caterpillar and butterfly are varied, so, too, are our spiritual enemies. Watch out for things that seem to be deliberately placed in your way to trip you up or temptations designed as entrapment – like the spider's web spun across the plants to entangle the butterfly. Be especially alert if you are directly involved in church leadership, discipleship work amongst any age-group, restoration ministries, worship leading, intercessory prayer and any form of mission. That is not to say that we are out of danger when at rest, so to speak. Even in our leisure time, we can be at great risk of temptation. Consider at all times Jesus' warning to his disciples: *"Watch and pray so that you will not fall into temptation. The spirit is willing, but the body is weak."* (Matthew 26 : 41)

Our enemies are closer to hand then we care to imagine! Spiritual forces of darkness are clearly manifesting predatory behaviour as they deliberately plunder our Christian heritage. In the last few years, our society has witnessed a decisive move away from the teaching of the Bible. Where once our laws and legal systems were built upon Christian foundations, now we see laws, hostile to Christianity, rushed through Parliament, often without adequate debate. It is now illegal to preach certain teachings from the Bible, especially with regards to homosexuality. With "freedom of speech" now in the history books, one can be accused of "incitement to religious hatred" if you declare that "Jesus Christ is the only way, the truth and the life, and that there is no other way to God except through him." (John 14 : 6). Our 'host plant' – our food source, the Word of God - is being 'sprayed' with deadly poisonous lies and mockery as both secular enemies, and to their shame, clerical enemies, cast aspersions on the validity and truthfulness of certain portions of scripture. Whilst in the process of doing research on scientific websites for this book, I have been moved to tears by reading some of the vitriolic propaganda against those who believe in creation. These people are real enemies of the gospel. It is not rational, intellectual disagreement, or even mere ridicule, but active persecution to the extent of 'naming and shaming' Christian scientists who testify to a young earth and intelligent design by the awesome power of our Creator-God. Even though there are Christians who differ on their views regarding creation, it cannot be denied that fellow brothers and sisters are now being unjustly discredited and singled out for verbal abuse. Indeed, it may not be long before we find our 'host plant' being uprooted all together. It has happened in many countries already. Wherever communism or Islam gains ascendancy, the Bible is confiscated and outlawed.

Brother Andrew, in his book, 'And God changed his mind because his people prayed', tells how he was once deeply challenged by an Eastern European pastor. Having just been released from prison, the pastor enquired why West Europeans did not suffer persecution, when it clearly states in Paul's second letter to Timothy, chapter 3 and verse 12: *"...Everyone who wants to live a godly life in Christ Jesus will be persecuted..."* Brother Andrew went on to comment on what he learnt from this experience: *"It was a powerful reminder of a fact Satan wants us to forget: We are living in enemy territory, all of us - not just those in the restricted nations of the world."*

In every section of society, we now see evidence of this. Mass media and the entertainment/leisure industries are manipulated to serve the purposes of evil powers. They plunder our society of its stability and integrity by deliberately promoting godless, self-centred and self-gratifying behaviour. The media consistently promotes a culture which mocks God, those who believe in the Lord and even those who simply uphold Christian values. With less and less subtlety, our minds are bombarded with worldly values and selfish priorities which militate against spiritual growth. Unless we determine to exercise rigorous personal discipline, in the area of entertainment and recreation, television in particular, the seeds of the Word of God will be snatched from our hearts before they have chance to germinate and bear fruit. Our spiritual lives will be plundered.

> "The thief comes only to steal and kill and destroy: I have come that they may have life and have it to the full."
>
> John 10 : 10

You may now be asking yourselves, "Why do the majority of Western Christians live as though unaware of being targeted?" or "Why is it that even when forced to acknowledge spiritual warfare, we still do not identify and engage our enemies?" Some clues will be discovered as we continue our study of the caterpillar's enemies, parasites in particular.

# Parasites

One of the greatest threats to a caterpillar's survival is the parasite. Parasites and parasitoids are creatures which live either on, or within, the body of another animal - the host. (To make a distinction - a parasitoid will kill the insect outright.) Several types of parasites attack caterpillars in many different subtle ways. Tachinid flies, for example, may stick their eggs directly on the host, or deposit eggs on the plants which the caterpillar will subsequently eat. Ichneumon wasps inject their eggs into the body of the caterpillar, or even into the pupa of a developing butterfly. Whichever way, if a butterfly is attacked by parasites in the immature stages of its development - egg, larva or pupa, the results will be fatal. In the early stages, the parasites will not kill the caterpillar. The caterpillar continues to eat, accommodating its parasitic guest, which, feeding on non-essential tissues of the caterpillar, grows with the unsuspecting host. The caterpillar appears normal. Later, however, the parasites paralyse the caterpillar so that it becomes lethargic and stops feeding. They then begin to feed on essential tissues and will determine the caterpillar's fate in various ways. Some kill the caterpillar before it enters the pupa; others kill the caterpillar within the pupa and hijack the pupal skin for themselves. Flies and wasps can pupate inside the dead hosts. One to two weeks later, instead of a beautiful butterfly breaking out gloriously from its chrysalis, an adult fly or wasp emerges, mates and looks for the next host. The cycle starts all over again.

# Identifying parasites affecting the 21st century Christian

The journey of 'spiritual metamorphosis' is not just an individual pursuit, but one that the whole body of Christ should also be undertaking together. Our churches should collectively desire to go deeper – to move from spiritual immaturity to spiritual maturity. However, in doing so, churches will face as many enemies as their individual members. What lessons, therefore, can the churches learn from these chilling examples in nature of being unwittingly overtaken by an enemy? Have our enemies crept up on us from behind and injected their own agenda to grow even within our churches? Have we become inert, paralyzed by 'parasites'? Are we being 'eaten up' by something from the inside out? Are we aware of anything in our lives that is seeking to abort our spiritual growth and the fruit of 'spiritual metamorphosis' in our lives? The parasite is designed to ensure it is not detected thus avoiding eradication. Similarly, the devil has found many well-disguised and subtle 'parasites' to devour surreptitiously all our 'vital organs' before we ever make it to the choice point of surrendering our lives to Christ to become effective workers in his kingdom. Let us identify some of the 'parasites' which have found their way into the body of the church or into the lives of individual members.

## Compromise

In his book, "The Heavenly Man", Brother Yun describes how the Chinese church was faced with the challenge of recognising and confronting the stealth attack of the 'parasite' called compromise. He writes: *"...the devil used a new way to try to tempt and deceive us. Instead of torture and force, he started to use subtle suggestions and sly trickery. The government called a gathering of 120 religious representatives from all over our country. Muslim, Buddhist, Daoist and Christian leaders were all invited to attend. At that time we didn't know anything about the Three-Self Patriotic Church that the government was forming. "Three-Self" stood for the movement's three guiding principles: Self-Propagating, Self-Supporting, and Self-Governing. Most Christians considered it a good thing and rejoiced that a new day appeared to be dawning when believers could worship freely without interference or persecution."*

*"Over the ensuing weeks and months the Lord started to teach me to know the difference between his church and the Three-Self Church in China. We knew the government had only created the Three-Self Patriotic Movement and allowed "open, legal" churches in a bid to control Christians and to promote their own political agenda inside the churches."*

During the repressive Communistic regime, this "Three-Self" church was allowed to continue as a means of propaganda. By this means, the Chinese government was able to justify its claim of religious freedom in China. Like the larva attacked by a parasite, The Three-Self Church's outward appearance was normal enough. However, the church was actually controlled by the government, and infiltrated with government spies, to ensure it stayed within its designated boundaries. The church was not permitted to preach about the Second Coming of Christ, nor on divine healing, nor on the deliverance from evil spirits. The whole of the book of Revelation was also banned. Evangelism was discouraged and it was strictly forbidden to teach children about the Lord. There were true believers in the 'Three-Self' church but they were so restricted they could not effectively preach the gospel in its entirety. Brother Yun equated these restrictions to clipping the wings of a bird and caging it. Whilst not dead, birds in cages will have difficulty reproducing. By contrast, the Christians who refused to be so controlled and remained within the secret house-church movement were "free as birds", "flying" all around the country, spreading the gospel.

One could say that the Christians within the Three-Self Church settled for the compromise of being allowed to continue as 'caterpillars'. Their existence, as such, made them useful 'hosts' for the political agenda of their 'parasites' but any signs of 'metamorphosis' would have put a swift end to their existence. Within the imagery I am adopting, being a 'caterpillar' rather than being a 'butterfly' does not equate to being lost but to being spiritually immature. The 'metamorphosis' which would bring spiritual maturity and with it, the ability to 'pollinate' and 'reproduce' will always be restricted by compromise or various aspects of the old nature.

Could it be that we also may one day be promised the freedom to remain 'caterpillars' on condition that we do not aspire to become 'butterflies', with freedom, vision, and the desire to 'pollinate' and 'reproduce'? Has that time, in fact, already come upon us as stealthily as a parasitoid wasp? Already our freedom to 'pollinate' and 'reproduce' has been deliberately curtailed by anti-Christian legislation which reached the statute book without encountering any resolute opposition from the Christian minority. Political

"For certain men, whose condemnation was written about long ago, have secretly slipped in among you. They are godless men, who change the grace of God into a licence for immorality and deny Jesus Christ, our only Sovereign and Lord." Jude : 4

correctness already asserts that the holding of 'religious' views is acceptable as long as those views are not imposed on others. This kind of intimidation is not much different from the restrictions imposed on Christians in China. Has political correctness so disabled the church that we no longer actually attempt to 'pollinate' and 'reproduce' but remain as lethargic, paralysed 'caterpillars' in our churches? Here is a startling statistic: it is estimated that ninety-five percent of Peacock larvae in the United Kingdom never make it to adulthood, due to parasites. Could the statistic be the same in the church, with ninety-five percent of us still 'in the dark', trapped within 'immature skins' inside our church walls, never actually surrendering everything to the Lord? How many of us make it through to complete 'metamorphosis', enabling us to 'reproduce' by going forth in obedience to the great commission to make disciples of all peoples?

As in former generations, today's Christian church has been penetrated and corrupted by many false teachers. The result is confusion and lowering of standards. Many of them actively promote collusion with the world's secular political structures. Jude's description of them as *"shepherds who feed only themselves"* (v12b) cannot fail to point again to the analogy of the parasite. Jude's whole letter condemns them in no uncertain terms.

Sadly, the majority of 'infected' churches or individuals are unaware of their predicament. Just as the infected caterpillar continues to eat, oblivious to the lethal corruption taking place within, these Christians are unwittingly accommodating 'parasites'. What a picture from the natural world to illustrate the danger of failing to recognise the source of subtle, corrupting influences! The parasites feed initially on non-essential tissues but before long the true agenda of these parasites manifests itself – the complete destruction of the host. Would it be stretching the imagination too far to liken non-essential tissues to those elements of the Christian life which are currently being attacked and eaten away by the enemies of the gospel? If not, then how long will it be before the 'host' is ultimately destroyed?

Perhaps it is all too easy to look at the church as an establishment and find fault. It is harder to identify the 'parasite' called 'compromise' within our own lives. We may think that we are growing strong, 'feeding' by means of our religious disciplines. The warning of the caterpillar's fate is that the parasite feeds off the very eagerness of the caterpillar to eat and grow. It takes full advantage of the caterpillar's efforts in order to grow itself, only destroying the caterpillar in its fifth instar to prevent metamorphosis. Satan employs the same strategy. He is not overly concerned if we are just constantly 'feeding' ourselves. He would prefer to 'kill' all immature Christians outright, but he realizes that such action would lead to a higher risk of detection and counter-attack. Instead, he slyly works to prevent 'spiritual metamorphosis'. He knows that if he can keep us preoccupied with the things of this world and content with a half-hearted devotion to the Lord, we shall never reach 'the butterfly stage'. Without fully surrendering our lives to 'spiritual metamorphosis', we remain immature and ineffective. No caterpillar can reproduce. Consequently, without metamorphosis, the species would die out soon enough! Sadly, many Christians, in their spiritual immaturity, have already succumbed to 'parasites' that have left them inert and paralysed. In one website about parasites in the human body, the writer identified ignorance of the problem as one of the main reasons for large-scale infection. Is it not equally true in the spiritual realm? Despite easy and unlimited access to the Word of God, ignorance of Satan's devices is still a common problem. Having already dealt with compromise, let us address this problem by identifying further parasites. If you become conscious that you are having the life squeezed out of you by one of these 'parasites', I urge you to seek further advice as to how, with the Lord's help, to rid yourself of that debilitation.

# Other priorities

The Parable of the Sower once again helps us to uncover issues that can choke our spiritual life and prevent us from bearing fruit: *"Other seed fell among thorns, which grew up and choked the plants, so that they did not bear grain."* (Mark 4 : 7)

*"Still others, like seed sown among thorns, hear the word; but the worries of this life, the deceitfulness of wealth and the desires for other things come in and choke the word, making it unfruitful."* (Mark 4 : 18-19)

The good seed of the Word of God can be choked and rendered unproductive by …. *"the worries of this life, the deceitfulness of wealth and the desires for other things"*. Luke's version of the parable further confirms that *"the desire for other things"* aborts the process of spiritual growth, leaving us immature. *"...they are choked by life's worries, riches and pleasures, and **they do not mature.**"* (Luke 8 : 14)

In the lives of some men and women, the deceitfulness of wealth becomes a 'parasite'. If we wish to prioritise spiritual growth and, ultimately, 'spiritual metamorphosis', we must ask ourselves some searching questions. Has materialism taken a hold of our lives? How would we feel if the Lord called us to surrender everything to him? Would we rather choose the slow death of 'parasitic' comfort and self-centred fulfilment?

Many in the church suffer from spiritual inertia. Spiritual inertia can usually be traced to either physical or mental exhaustion caused by an unhealthy work-load or burden of responsibility. Christians who exhaust all their physical and mental capacity in pursuit of a certain lifestyle need to examine their priorities. Of course, our workplace can be our place of ministry but we must beware if our work is draining us of all our energy, so that we have nothing left to help in outreach, or to attend meetings designed to disciple us.

We can legitimately desire a variety of good things in life but, if any is given priority over our relationship with the Lord, it will inevitably hinder our spiritual growth and prevent fruitfulness. These desires will understandably vary from person to person depending on age, sex and circumstances. The desire for marriage and raising a family is both natural and legitimate but when wilfully pursued outside of the will of God, it is unlikely to provide the fulfilment hoped for and is more likely to lead to spiritual back-sliding. The sadness, sometimes even bitterness, a single person can feel because they are not yet married can choke their faith as they question God's plan for their lives. Disappointment, and often compromise, can tarnish the radiant joy of salvation. The desire for a career also falls into the legitimate category but, if it overrides the call of God upon our lives, it will eat away at our spiritual growth. Real opportunities for spiritual growth during retirement years are often squeezed out by plans to cruise and live "the good life". Even hobbies, which may be totally harmless to others, may hinder spiritual growth. Isobel Kuhn, in her book, "By searching", testifies that the Lord asked her to stop reading novels. When she queried this, the Lord revealed to her that a child who fills its stomach with ice cream and soda water would subsequently, lose its appetite for meat and potatoes. She realized that she was indeed often choosing a novel over the Bible. We must all personally search our hearts and ask the Lord to show us where we have set our affections on things of this world, instead of on the Lord.

# Disunity

When Jesus prayed for his disciples one of his greatest concerns was for unity. Our love for each other identifies us as his disciples and draws others to the Lord. 1 John chapter 4 : 12 tells us that *"no one has ever seen God, but when we love one another, God lives in us and his love is made complete in us."* Satan, not wanting others to see the love of God, causes people to focus selfishly on their own needs and desires, knowing this will lead to bitterness and strife. James 4 : 1-3 reads, *"What causes fights and quarrels amongst you? Don't they come from your desires that battle within you? You want something but don't get it. You kill and covet, but you cannot have what you want. You quarrel and fight. You do not have, because you do not ask God. When you ask, you do not receive, because you ask with wrong motives that you may spend what you get on your pleasures."* Once distracted, arguing amongst themselves, the Lord's people will no longer be fighting together for the souls and hearts of the lost. Indeed, disunity, at its worst, has been known to close ministries down altogether.

# Unforgiveness

Confronting disunity may prompt you to think of issues in your life that remain unresolved. Maybe you have fallen out with an old friend, or a family member, or a member of your church. Unforgiveness gives Satan a foothold and, therefore, has serious spiritual consequences. Matthew 6 : 14 gives the grave warning, *"For if you forgive men when they sin against you, your heavenly Father will also forgive you. But if you do not forgive men their sins, your Father will not forgive your sins."* Unforgiveness very often leads to bitterness, and bitterness eats its way into our soul.

# Habitual Sins

Whilst writing this book, I saw the most disturbing, yet fascinating, piece of film in a National Geographic / Channel 4 production called "Extraordinary Animals in the Womb". The clip showed a wasp injecting its eggs into the caterpillar. By the amazing wonder of the latest high-definition cameras and 4D scanning technology, the film-makers then showed the development of these parasitical, maggot-like creatures within the caterpillar's gut. Having grown to their optimum size, the parasites drugged the caterpillar whilst they ate their way out of the caterpillar's body. The caterpillar became lethargic and stopped feeding. At first, just a few parasites seemed to crawl out of the skin of the caterpillar but then, I watched in horror as the caterpillar's body literally broke out in a teeming mass of maggots. These maggots quickly spun silk cocoons within which to metamorphose. Incredibly, the caterpillar having been further poisoned by the parasites as they left their host, was left to spend its dying moments frantically producing its own silk to cover the mass of newly-formed cocoons. It went on to actively protect the killer maggots from their would-be predators. Finally, the exhausted caterpillar collapsed on top of them, dead.

This dramatic picture from nature provides a startling warning of the fatal consequences of accommodating parasitical, sinful habits in our lives, with no attempt to expel them. These 'parasites' often seem harmless at first, and may not appear to stop you from growing spiritually. But, over time, they will start to eat away at your soul. Compromises in the use of your leisure time, your relationships and your thought-life must be addressed. If not, other desires will start to take priority over your walk with Christ. Eventually, you may find yourself being literally consumed from within by an addiction that demands constant feeding. Your desire to become a new creation will gradually be destroyed, and the process of 'metamorphosis' in your life will be aborted.

"...each one is tempted when, by his own evil desire, he is dragged away and enticed. Then, after desire has conceived, it gives birth to sin; and sin, when it is full-grown, gives birth to death." James 1 : 14,15

This can take a sinister turn if you allow evil spirits a foothold in your life through sexual immorality, substance abuse, meddling in the occult, yoga or involvement in other religions and cults. What begins as an 'innocent' interest can later get a real hold on you. Parasites essentially possess their host. Our bodies are to be temples of the Holy Spirit. Intimacy with God requires personal holiness and the denial of anything and everything which grieves the Holy Spirit in our lives. If we choose to give part of our lives over to the worship of other 'gods', holiness and subsequently, intimacy with God, suddenly becomes unattainable, even undesirable. This, in turn, can develop into resentment towards God's standards and his desire for wholehearted commitment. There can be no joy of the Holy Spirit for the man or woman who trifles with sin. In some cases those who

"If we confess our sins, he is faithful and just and will forgive us our sins and purify us from all unrighteousness." 1 John 1 : 9

have been taken over by such 'parasites' begin to defend and fight for the very thing that is destroying their spiritual growth. In the process, they die spiritually.

If you have been poisoned and paralysed by the shame of your sin, you may be tempted to believe that you are no longer worthy to continue your journey towards spiritual metamorphosis, to work effectively for the Lord to bring others to Christ. Read 1 John chapter 1 : 9 and take heart.

# Discouragement

The 'parasite' called discouragement is rampant amongst Christians. Satan knows that God has a purpose for each of us. He fears the potential of those who joyfully recognize their role as Christ's ambassador here on earth. Therefore, as the "Father of lies," he will try to question and cast doubt upon the value of a life surrendered to Christ. Since the beginning of time, he has been plaguing mankind with the lie that life becomes more fulfilling when God's rules are abandoned. He will try to dishearten us by causing us to compare our lives with those who appear to have found happiness and achieved success, without the help of God. Why? Nehemiah 8 : 10 tells us *"...the joy of the Lord is your strength."* If Satan can steal your joy, your strength will be drained at the same time. American pastor and author, John Piper, is committed to teaching people that *"God is most glorified when we are most satisfied in him."* Will people be drawn to follow Christ if we are sour-faced and miserable? Are we even likely to share our faith when unconvinced that following Christ is the best option? Once discouraged, we are far more likely to turn from holy living to seek temporary 'relief'. Once we succumb to temptation, further lies follow, centred around our self-worth and our value to God.

# Self-pity

Self-pity can stem from events in our past, or from current disappointments. Self-pity will seriously limit our spiritual growth and effectiveness in ministry. Brother Andrew, in his book 'The Calling', warns:- *"...no one can be used by God and bring peace anywhere in the world unless he has peace in his heart. We cannot be the solution if we are still part of the problem."*

As I mentioned in my first chapter, if we do not face the issues which cause unrest in our lives, Satan will use them to drain us of both emotional and physical strength. We may give the appearance of growing as Christians, when, in reality, we are struggling with a deep-seated sadness or bitterness. If allowed to feed itself, the 'self-pity parasite' will eventually bring forth a 'wasp', or a 'fly', and will prevent the development of a beautiful butterfly. Questioning the Lord's love and his knowledge of what is best for us can lead to jealousy of others. Beware of taking matters into your own hands in order to secure what you think is best for your life.

# Pathogens

Finally, let us look at the third enemy of our 'winged friends' – disease. Diseases are usually caused by organisms called pathogens. A pathogen is an infectious agent, more commonly known as a germ. The term pathogen is derived from the Greek παθογένεια, - 'that which produces suffering.' Pathogens can be fungi, bacteria, viruses, or single-celled organisms called protozoans.

I do not need to tell you that there will be many things that will cause you suffering in your life. Some of these 'pathogens' will be unavoidable. We live in a fallen world and we are all susceptible to natural diseases and pain. Satan will use these 'pathogens' to try to undermine your faith in God. Most of the time, our diseases are not lethal (as is the case in most naturally-occurring diseases of the caterpillar and the butterfly) but, how we react to such suffering can affect our spiritual growth. (I shall look at this more closely in Chapter 6) Intentionally, or unintentionally, some suffering is self-inflicted. If we over-expose ourselves to these 'pathogens,' we put ourselves at risk of spiritual malfunction or death. Let us take an example from the life of the butterfly.

## Over exposure to harmful agents

Many types of butterfly are susceptible to bacillus bacteria, in particular, Bacillus thuringiensis (Bt). These rod-shaped bacteria are found naturally in soil, on plants, and even in the gut of a caterpillar. The quantities of bacteria present in these environments would not normally be sufficient to kill caterpillars in large numbers. However, these bacteria have been mass-produced as insecticides against pest-caterpillars, in order to prevent crop damage. If a caterpillar eats a leaf covered with the spores of BT, the spores will revive within minutes in the insect's gut and begin to grow and multiply. They then produce a crystalline protein called 'Cry'. 'Cry' molecules have just the right shape to bind to the cells which line the caterpillar's gut. They kill the gut-cells which, in turn, paralyzes the gut wall, allowing the gut contents to enter the caterpillar's body cavity. The symptoms are obvious for all to see. The poisoned caterpillar stops feeding and becomes limp and sluggish. The body starts to turn black as the body of the caterpillar decomposes. Within two to three days the caterpillar will die from starvation or from the effects of septicemia (blood-poisoning).

Can we, as Christians, growing towards maturity in Christ, learn an important lesson from this sobering story? I believe we can. In scripture, we are warned that, although we are in the world, we must not be of the world. There will be 'bacteria' in our immediate surroundings and in our lives, due to our previous lifestyles, or to what we have unwittingly 'ingested' by being in the world.

Spiritually speaking, we have been given the ability to resist and overcome these 'bacteria' in their normal quantities. However, if we carelessly expose ourselves to an environment where these 'bacteria'

"The sorrows of those will increase who run after other gods."

Psalm 16 : 4a

have been deliberately increased, the consequences could be severe. Continuing with this analogy, we must learn to identify the kind of bacteria which attacks our appetite for the "Word of God". How astonishing that the toxic molecules attacking the caterpillar are called CRY molecules. The message is loud and clear - if we allow ourselves to become overwhelmed and overpowered by these 'bacteria', there will be tears and misery in our lives. What's more, subsequent sadness and bitterness can be paralyzing to our spiritual growth. Be careful then what you 'feed' on.

## Turning bad from the inside out

There is another virus called Nuclear polyhedrosis which is probably the most injurious viral pathogen in Monarch butterflies. Both larvae and pupae are vulnerable. The virus actually putrefies the insides of the caterpillar. The caterpillar becomes lethargic, loses its light stripes and then turns from light brown to dark brown and from dark brown to black. The pupa, too, can be affected and turn from light green to black. Once black, if handled, it will break open and a foul-smelling black liquid will spill out.

Nature paints for us a striking picture of the ravages of disease. Spiritual disease can lead to equally distressing consequences. How tragic it is when a Christian, who was once showing all the signs of spiritual growth, suddenly becomes 'infected by the world' or, even worse, directly involved in the occult. Instead of developing as a beautiful new creation, their life, full of potential, becomes corrupted. Their radiance turns to darkness. Instead of making the world a brighter place, they add to its gloom.

## Single-celled but highly infectious

There are parasites that infect caterpillars and butterflies which are not bug-related but protozoans (one-celled microscopic organisms). One such protozoan is Ophryocystis elektroscirrha (OE). OE affects the Monarch and Queen butterflies. Despite starting off as minute, inactive spores, invisible to the naked eye, once ingested by the larva, they multiply rapidly. They are highly infectious and once, in the midst of a certain species of butterfly, affect whole generations because the adult females shower the host plant with spores as they lay their eggs. The emerging caterpillars then eat these spores and the infection is passed on. Both pupae and butterflies can appear normal, even when heavily infected. If examined closely, however, spores can be found all over their wings. The disease has a range of lethal and sub-lethal effects. Infected butterflies have a lower survival rate; smaller adult body size, and shorter life-spans as adults. Butterflies with high spore densities are more likely to struggle to emerge from the chrysalis and, even when successful, have smaller wingspans and lower body masses than uninfected adults.

One website I studied, in relation to this topic, gave me some reason to think deeply about common modern evangelism strategies, and the not uncommon nonchalance, if not aversion, towards doctrine and the systematic study of scripture. University scientists had sent out large numbers of controlled breeding projects to local schools, and other institutions, to promote increased interest and knowledge of butterflies. Sadly, in their enthusiasm, they had, inadvertently, sent out specimens which were infected with OE. As the emerging butterflies were released into the natural eco-system, the disease was spread to the local breeding grounds of milkweed!

Could there be a warning here for us? In our enthusiasm to generate a greater interest in our faith, is there not a danger of disseminating

"Preach the Word: be prepared in season and out of season, correct, rebuke and encourage – with great patience and careful instruction. For the time will come when men will not put up with sound doctrine. Instead to suit their own desires, they will gather around them a great number of teachers to say what their itching ears want to hear. They will turn their ears away from the truth and turn aside to myths."

2 Timothy 4 : 2-4

an 'infected' brand of the gospel – a non-offensive, world-friendly, politically correct, self-help version? Watered-down teaching, with compromised views on moral issues, brushing doctrinal difficulties under the carpet, is sure to produce Christians with inherent weaknesses. Unwittingly perhaps, those weaknesses will then be passed down to the next generation. 'Immature' believers will fail to mature if they are not challenged to move on to learn the doctrinal foundations of our faith. Unable to digest deeper truths, they will only have an appetite for inspiring 'thoughts for the day' and a preference for sermons that merely provide a morale boost for the week ahead. However, if we are to readdress the balance, we must also be careful not to tip too far in the opposite direction and fall prey to another enemy of true spiritual maturity - legalistic religion - which Jesus likened to fungi!

# Fungi

Butterflies are affected by many forms of fungi. Yeast is a fungus. In humans, some species of yeast, such as Candida albicans, are opportunist pathogens which can cause disease. In baking, yeast is used to make the bread rise, and it is well known that it only takes a little yeast to work through the whole dough. Christ referred to yeast to describe the nature of the false teaching of the Pharisees and Sadducees. (Matthew 16 : 11) They were tragically leading people away from a true revelation of the Living God. The fundamentals, as taught by Moses, were swamped by hundreds of burdensome man-made rules and regulations. Over the last two thousand years Christendom has made the same mistakes. Church history traces the injurious departure from apostolic doctrine and practice, as unbiblical doctrines and practices have been handed down and enshrined in denominational traditions. Let us be careful then to ensure that 'religion' does not replace a living and humble personal relationship with our loving Saviour.

## Overcoming our enemies

*"Be self-controlled and alert. Your enemy the devil prowls around like a roaring lion looking for someone to devour. Resist him, standing firm in the faith, because you know that your brothers throughout the world are undergoing the same kind of sufferings." 1 Peter 5 : 8,9*

So, to conclude, we have seen that Satan will use many ways to try and stop our spiritual growth and to stop us from sharing our faith with others. Satan has no concern over lives that *"have a form of godliness but deny its power,"* *"always learning but never able to acknowledge the truth."* (2 Timothy 3 : 5, 7). He will, however, actively seek to destroy those who are pressing on to maturity. Ignorance is no longer a valid excuse. How then must we protect ourselves from these enemies? The answer lies in the importance of guarding our spiritual growth from the moment of 'conception' and on into our spiritual maturity. Reading a website relating to human parasites, I was struck by the terminology used when giving advice for the prevention of infection.

*"**Acknowledge** the existence of the problem. **Cleanse** your body. **Purify** yourself. **Educate yourself** about clean living and regular cleansing."*

Doesn't this sound like spiritual advice too? It could not be more poignant as we seek to rid our lives of the 'parasites and pathogens' that weaken us and stand up to our predators in order to protect our destiny in Christ – complete metamorphosis! Acknowledge the problem, take action to rid yourself of existing problems and, then, do all you can to learn how to sustain a godly life, regularly 'cleansing' your heart through confession and repentance. There is so much teaching in Scripture regarding 'spiritual self-defence'. We need to discipline ourselves to study it. The Lord will also place many 'friends' around us in our spiritual lives to help us to overcome our enemies and grow up spiritually, despite all the odds. Let us ask the Lord to open our eyes to these 'friends'. Above all, may we fix our eyes on him and run the race set before us, keeping sight of that illustrious goal to grow ever more like him and have Christ's glory unveiled through our lives to the praise of his name.

*"Strip down. Start running - and never quit. No extra spiritual fat, no parasitic sins. Keep your eyes on Jesus, who both began and finished this race we're in. Study how he did it. Because he never lost sight of where he was headed – that exhilarating finish in and with God – he could put up with anything along the way; cross, shame, whatever." Hebrews 12 : 1-3 (The Message)*

Larva of the Spicebush Swallowtail (papilio troilus)

Though we have this treasure in jars of clay.. 2 Cor. 4 : 7

Eating till he drops

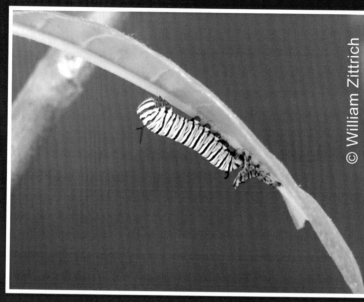

© William Zittrich

© William Zittrich

A Monarch (Danaus plexippus) larva eating and shedding its skin

# Unusual Friends
## and
## Enemies

© Jay Cossey

© Jay Cossey

# God Knows

And I said to the man who stood at the gate of the year:
"Give me a light that I may tread safely into the unknown!"
And he replied:
"Go out into the darkness and put your hand into the Hand of God.
That shall be to you better than light and safer than a known way."

So, I went forth, and finding the Hand of God, trod gladly into the night
And He led me toward the hills and the breaking of day in the lone East.

So, heart, be still!
What need our little life,
Our human life, to know,
If God hath comprehension?
In all the dizzy strife
Of things both high and low
God hideth His intention.

God knows.
His will is best
The stretch of years
Which wind ahead, so dim
To our imperfect vision
Are clear to God
Our fears are premature.
In him
All time hath full provision
Then rest; until
*God moves*
*To lift the veil*
*From our impatient eyes,*
*When as the sweeter features*
*Of life's stern face we hail*
*Fair beyond all surmise*
*God's thought around his creatures*
*Our minds shall fill.*

# Chapter 6

# Symbiosis and Surprises
## Unlikely Friends

*"For my thoughts are not your thoughts, neither are your ways my ways," declares the Lord. "As the heavens are higher than the earth, so are my ways higher than your ways and my thoughts than your thoughts." Isaiah 55 : 8 - 9*

In the light of their many enemies and the subsequent high risk of failing to reach metamorphosis, God has put some 'friends' in place in nature to help the caterpillar and the butterfly. Some of these 'friends' are other creatures; some are the surprising circumstances to which they are led in order to survive.

We have established that we too have many adversaries which threaten our spiritual growth. Nevertheless, it is the Lord's deepest desire for us to grow into his likeness more and more each day to the praise and honour of his glory. To this end, he also gives us many 'friends' to help us. However, the Lord works in mysterious ways. We should not be taken aback, therefore, when his help towards spiritual maturity takes unexpected forms. The Lord will sometimes use the most extraordinary people and situations to provoke and protect both our individual spiritual growth and that of our family, church, or nation. Furthermore, just as the structures and seasons of nature are not in place just to sustain the caterpillar and the butterfly, we must recognise that we too are not the only concern of the Lord. His plans incorporate the working out of his purposes within the lives of all his people and in the world which he created. Our journey towards spiritual maturity is inextricably linked to that of others. Sometimes, the events of our lives, of our families, and even of our countries, will be providing a backdrop in the life-story of someone else. Circumstances may often be bewilderingly beyond our comprehension, but we must

"And we know that in all things. God works for the good of those who love him..."
Romans 8 : 28

have the courage and faith to believe that through it all, the Lord is the author and finisher of both our physical journey through life and of our spiritual journey. He is in control.

Later in the chapter, we will determine why the Lord uses surprising circumstances to bring us to maturity. To begin, however, let us consider the value of symbiosis both in nature and in our spiritual lives.

# Myrmecophily : Ant love!

The caterpillar and the butterfly are both seen to have important, though sometimes curious, symbiotic relationships. Symbiosis[1] (or, strictly speaking, mutualism) is a relationship between two species where both benefit from their relationship with each other. There are several ways this can play out: a service for a service; a resource for a service; or a resource for a resource. Mutualism plays a key role in sustaining life and gives evidence of a Creator who created a universe, fully functioning from the very start, with each organism interlinked with the others. However, some symbiotic relationships are apparently unlikely relationships and may seem to lead to undesirable circumstances. Despite this, mutual associations will work to the benefit of both parties as long as they co-operate. On the other hand, the success of these relationships is threatened if there is a breakdown in this cooperation.

Perhaps one of the most striking examples of unexpected mutualism is between the ant and the caterpillar! Forgive me if I explain this relationship in detail. The mysterious workings of nature to ensure not just its survival, but its optimum development, teach us of the extraordinary, if often surprising, ways in which God promotes growth.

The Lycaenidae (comprising of the coppers, blues and hairstreaks) make up approximately thirty percent of known butterflies. More than half of the species have a relationship with ants during their larval development. This association is known as myrmecophily, which means 'ant-love'. Incredibly, they communicate with the ants using vibrations that are transmitted through the soil in which their host plant is growing. They also use chemical signals. Most of the caterpillars studied possess a honey-gland on the tenth body segment, which exudes a sweet fluid, often described as honeydew. This secretion is extremely attractive to ants. The ants stimulate the production of this food source by stroking their legs and antennae against the caterpillar's body. It is thought that some caterpillars are even able to distinguish differences in the way varying species of ants will use their antennae and will hence only provide food to the particular ants with which they have established a mutualistic relationship. In return for food, these belligerent insects protect the larvae and pupae from natural predators and parasites such as Braconid wasps and Tachinid flies. Without a tending ant to help fight off these parasites, the caterpillar would be almost defenceless. Some caterpillars seem almost dependent on the ants; their development is impaired if the ants are absent. In the case of the Lucia limbaria (Small Copper), the female will only lay her eggs in the presence of attendant ants! If an ant-chamber is not already present at the base of the chosen plant, then the ants will quickly construct one to receive the newly-hatched caterpillars.

Populations of the G. lygdamu, more commonly known as the Silvery Blue, also benefit significantly from their relationship with ants. *"Larvae whose ants have been*

---

[1] Please note: I interchange the term "symbiosis" with "mutualism" throughout the chapter, in light of the commonly accepted usage of the word as "a relationship between two organisms which benefits both parties." However, I acknowledge that the strict scientific use of the word "symbiosis" can signify all relationships between two organisms and thus includes parasitism.

*experimentally excluded are far more likely to disappear from host plants than larvae with ants, simply because larvae drop off plants without ants. Taking into account parasitism, predation and drop-off, a cohort of ant-tended larvae is four to twelve times more likely to survive to pupation than a similar group of untended larvae. Most of this difference in survivorship occurs during the final two larval instars."*

Studies carried out on the lycaenid butterfly, Paralucia aurifera, in south-eastern Australia show the benefits of mutualism both to the caterpillar and to the ant. The larvae spend daylight hours in the ants' chambers, located at the base of their host plants. They then come out to feed at dusk! Amazingly, the larvae develop faster and stronger, spending more time feeding, than larvae which are not attended by ants. These experiments show then that the caterpillars can benefit from their association with ants in ways other than, or in addition to, protection from natural enemies. In turn, the ants appear to benefit just as much. Laboratory experiments showed that forty percent more ant-workers survived when lycaenid larvae were present than when they were absent. This is probably due to the ants eating the lycaenid's nutrient rich "honeydew" which contains considerable amounts of glucose and amino acids.

# The relevance of symbiosis in spiritual growth

Through mutualism, nature reflects God's will and purpose that we should all work together to help each other lovingly towards spiritual maturity. We have been designed to be dependent upon one another, not just for reproduction but also in a trade of skills, creativity and information that make our lives richer. As a result, our lives are woven together with those of others in the most complex and fascinating way. Relationships give life its depth, meaning and beauty. Through living, working and playing together, God intends us to understand his attributes, the fruit of the Holy Spirit – love, joy, peace, patience, kindness, goodness, faithfulness, humility and self control. Imagine trying to understand those concepts without

"As iron sharpens iron, so one man sharpens another"
Proverbs 27 : 17

relationships. However, it is often not until we are in danger or need that we actually acknowledge our need of each other. Caused to turn to others, our eyes are opened to the amazing tool relationships are, in the Lord's hand, to mould our characters and bring us to maturity. The Lord will often choose to use the most unusual people to create the beautiful designs he wants to display through our lives, to his glory. Some will bring dark colours, others gloriously bright colours; some will leave a dash of colour, others will draw bold defining lines around our 'wings'. All will serve the Lord's purpose. Equally, the Lord will use our lives – our characters, our choices and our attitudes - to paint his pattern in the lives of others.

But, how do we respond to the Lord's design and command to be interlinked, especially as he so often uses 'unlikely friends'? Would we prefer to be independent, to insist that everyone else 'mind their own business'? Are we guilty of wanting others to serve our needs without wishing to be part of serving theirs? Christ taught his disciples to serve one another. Washing their feet, he urged them to follow his example. We grow and mature spiritually because Christ serves us. He often does this through his servants. When we serve, we become Christ's hands and feet to serve others and thus enhance their spiritual growth towards maturity. This is costly and requires many sacrifices but Christ promised it would bring many blessings. (John 13 : 14 - 17)

The first disciples remembered the teaching of Christ. The early church lived as a community - meeting every day, sharing everything, helping the poor and teaching each other. As a result, everyone prospered and the church grew in numbers every day! (Acts 2 : 43-47) Sadly, this model of community has been lost and, with it, the blessings of spiritual growth – both of the individual and of the congregation.

One Sunday, a few years ago, one of the elders of my church presented the congregation with a shocking challenge. He asked us how we would feel if the church leadership announced that, as of the following week, we would all be kindly requested to pay our salaries into the general church fund. Our needs would then be met accordingly, with any spare cash to be used to help local homeless or suffering people. I can personally remember my reaction. It literally sent a shiver down my spine. I felt my hand close over my possessions with thoughts such as, "No way! That is not fair! I am not letting my hard-earned salary subsidise those who have got a far less stressful job than mine!" The elder was not being serious but he had made his point! Such a notion is now far from acceptable. I would imagine that many realised that day just how possessive they had become over their possessions. I was deeply challenged that I valued independence, afforded to me by my salary, above the desire to live like the early church, despite the huge blessings and spiritual growth which resulted from their sacrifices. In other words, I rejected interdependence with others despite the fact that these 'mutual associations' would have indeed greatly accelerated and enriched my journey, and that of many others, towards spiritual metamorphosis and maturity. Sadly, I don't believe I was the only one who failed to see this 'unlikely friend.' Perhaps it will take the visit of another 'unlikely friend', that of great need or tragedy, for the Lord to be able to lead our community to the blessings of mutualism. As for living as a community, 'other priorities' ensure that the majority of us are too busy to commit time to serve each other or the church. Even when we do serve, we are often so tired that we help almost begrudging the 'loss' of our personal time and energy. If the truth be known, we would rather pay others to feed, serve and minister to us. Tragically, in avoiding servanthood, we miss the promised blessing attached to Christ's teaching: *"Now that you know these things, you will be blessed if you do them."* (John 13 : 17). Instead, we become more like 'parasites' and those we expect to serve us often become the victims of the breakdown of what should be a mutual relationship to the benefit of all.

## The Breakdown of Symbiosis

Most of the lycaenidae that associate with ants have a mutualistic relationship with them. However, the Alcon blue and other large blue butterflies (butterflies in the genus Maculinea) have also become parasites of ant colonies. It has been discovered that they trick the ants into sheltering them in their nests by emitting a smell that makes the ants believe they are ant larvae. The ants will then often give up looking after their own brood and focus on feeding the caterpillar! In some cases, rather than rewarding the ants by feeding them from their honey-glands, the caterpillars have been known to eat the ant larvae or, worse still, other caterpillars sheltered in the same chambers!

The failure to appreciate the friends or circumstances which God has given us for our mutual spiritual development will result in bad attitudes and selfish behaviour. If we neglect our personal responsibility to serve in the church - to play our part in the intended symbiotic relationships God has provided for our spiritual growth - we may start to take advantage of those who are feeding us and fail to give anything back.

> "I am among you as one who serves."
> Luke 22 : 27b

Looking solely after our own interests, we may even begin, like the Alcon blue larvae, to assassinate the characters of those who are actually in place to protect us, especially if we feel our needs are not being met adequately! When there is a breakdown in the symbiotic nature of a relationship, one party usually continues to give at their expense. How many of our leaders and servant-hearted people within the church have suffered the same fate as the protective ants? Do you know people who have been 'tricked' into believing they should feed and attend to their congregations, or to other Christians, at the expense of their own families or indeed, their own development? Yes, we are meant to serve but many people misinterpret Scripture in this area. Much of Paul's teachings to the early churches records that the Lord expects the serving to be mutual and beneficial to both parties. When it is not, an aberration from God's divinely-created order has taken place and this is not the will of God.

## God works in mysterious ways

We have established the significance of mutualism to our spiritual growth as well as its costs. Let us now look more closely at the unusual nature of the 'friends' and circumstances God often uses - both in nature and in our lives. Can we learn to look expectantly for the Lord's hand even in the most surprising, and perhaps even difficult, of circumstances? Who would have thought an ant would be of any use to a caterpillar? Not only are the insects so different but the larvae of the various myrmecophilious (ant-loving) species find themselves in seemingly undesirable circumstances because of this symbiotic relationship.

The Alcon Blue starts its days inside the beautiful flower-head of the Marsh Gentian. Life is almost quite literally a 'bed of roses'. However, it grows very little during its first three instars inside the flower-head. Once in the ants' nest, however, it really develops, increasing in weight a hundred fold in the first month! The chambers of an ants' nest might not seem like a fitting start for a beautiful butterfly but it finds the greatest protection and growth there. The larva remains protected in the nest throughout the autumn, winter and spring, turning into a pupa in the early summer.

Our Lord left the glories of heaven, and chose the most unlikely life and surroundings for the King of Kings, in order to fulfil God's purposes! (Philippians 2) We may be asked to follow his example. Perhaps you are currently in a 'beautiful place,' feeling as if you are getting along just fine, feeding yourself. However, God may be about to change your circumstances or the people in your life dramatically. He might cause you to be dependent on someone else. This may be only for a season but you can be sure that your spiritual growth and protection will, in some way, be the reason. Your response to such situations is crucial. I encourage you to respond in faith. Ask the Lord to let you see through his eyes and take every opportunity to grow.

When ants attend to the larvae, it is described as 'adopting' the caterpillar. Seeing a group of ants tending to a caterpillar, one would be forgiven for thinking they were attacking or exploiting the caterpillar. Sometimes in our spiritual walk, the Lord will cause us to be 'adopted' for various seasons. As in the case of the larvae, it will be beneficial to our spiritual development, even if it may seem as if we are being over-protected. During my time on MV Logos 2 I was under the 'adoption' of OM Ships' leaders. The rules they put in place seemed restrictive but they were for our protection and growth. In return for the opportunity to grow in a protective environment, we served the Lord, reaching out through the organization to the local people.

Most men and women regard ants as pests. We perhaps overlook their hard-working nature and their importance in the ecological system. With this in mind, I am going to suggest that the very people the Lord has chosen to use to enhance your spiritual growth will appear to you as the most unlikely candidates! The Lord may place people around you who seem to be like irritating ants – over-attentive or always trying to get something out of you. It is all too easy to fail to see how others provide for us, when blinded by our own fixation with what we appear to give to them! This can be especially true when involved in ministry. You may feel as if you are doing all the 'feeding' to produce the 'honeydew' for the 'little ants' around you. Are there people who make you feel that you are in a dark 'ants' nest' rather than in a 'bed of roses'? Ask the Lord to show you his purpose in placing you where you are. Look for the God-given potential to mature spiritually by befriending those you initially find difficult. It is easy to connect with, and to work alongside, amenable people with similar views but you will probably develop more around those who challenge you! We are usually reluctant to make that choice for ourselves. Therefore, the Lord often has to take us out of our comfort zone and bring us to the end of our own resources, in order to change our perspective and recognize the value of the 'ants' and the great benefits of symbiosis, even with the most unusual of 'friends'! Corrie Ten Boom recounts a touching story in her book, 'The Hiding Place'. Whilst in solitary confinement in Scheveningen Prison, she craved company. Amazingly, the Lord sent some ants, literally! She could have simply overlooked the ants. Indeed, she talks of almost stepping on the first one she saw. However, she recognised them as something precious. The ants became her companions - their presence stopped her from going mad. During her times of loneliness the little ants would appear on a regular basis. She would feed them tiny crumbs of the little she was given to eat and talk to them. I feel sure that, once out of that cell, she never looked at an ant in the same way again!

# Unfamiliar paths

*"I will lead the blind by ways they have not known, along unfamiliar paths I will guide
them ..." Isaiah 42 : 16*

Symbiotic relationships normally consist of two organisms. However, it is also
not unknown for the Lord to use challenging circumstances as 'unlikely friends' in
order to develop certain qualities in our lives. To establish a deepening relationship
with someone, we must learn to trust them. Trust is most deeply-tested in situations
which are outside of our control or our comfort zone. Those who aspire to increase
their faith should, therefore, expect to be stretched. The Lord knows that we would not
choose these ways for ourselves, even if we knew their benefit to our spiritual growth.
Consequently, these 'friends' are usually deliberately brought into our lives, beyond our
control. Like a caterpillar being transported into an ants' nest, we may feel we are being
led, blind, to somewhere rather dark and foreboding. Furthermore, the Lord may, at
times, conceal his presence, asking us to grow in faith by simply trusting his good will
until the unlikely friends have fulfilled their role. At other times, our 'blindness' to his
presence, in the midst of our unusual circumstances, is caused by our own condition of
heart. Either way, the Lord can use these difficult times to provoke spiritual growth and
bring us a step closer to himself.

The two disciples on the road to Emmaus were devastated. Having witnessed faith-
shattering events, they had lost heart. The man to whom they had dedicated their lives,
was dead, crucified as a common criminal. They assumed that all the promises of Jesus
were now impossible. In this desperate hour of doubt, grief and disillusionment, the
Lord did not leave them to walk alone. He came and
walked the road with them. Yet he did not reveal    "And surely I am with you
his identity. (Luke 24 : 16) Instead, he gave them    always, to the very end of the
the opportunity to pour out their hearts to him. In    age."
recounting the recent events to this 'stranger', the                   Matthew 28 : 20
two disciples must have discovered the true state of
their hearts – not just how much the Lord and his promises had come to mean to them
– but also their lack of faith now that he had, apparently, let them down. Jesus exposed
their ignorance of the Scriptures concerning the Messiah, thereby indirectly revealing
that whilst Jesus had been with them, they had never fully grasped the greatness of
the Messiah, nor that he would victoriously redeem them with his own death. This
extraordinary encounter with Jesus changed their entire understanding of Scripture and
God's eternal purposes. It would surely have stayed with them for the rest of their lives.
The next time they were tempted to doubt the Lord's promises, or purposes, the memory
of the Emmaus walk would remind them to look expectantly into God's word, with the
eyes of faith, to comprehend his intentions. Their faith had indeed been stretched but
now they had room to grow even further!

Do you feel you are on a dark road of doubt or despair? Turn and look at your travelling companions. Could it be that those around you, even your circumstances or emotions, are in fact being used by the Lord to give you an opportunity to discover something about your faith? Have you been placed in a certain situation to reveal your underestimation, or ignorance, of your Saviour?

Mary and Martha experienced a great time of testing when their brother Lazarus fell ill. (John 11) They sent for the Lord. He sent word back assuring them their brother's sickness would not end in death. Then Lazarus died. What must they have felt towards the Lord? What did his promises mean now? We get a notion of Mary's disappointment through John's account of Jesus' arrival. Mary would normally have rushed out to see the Lord. But only Martha went to face the Lord. Martha had to call Mary and tell her the Lord was asking for her! Why did the Lord allow the 'unlikely friend' of death, and days of grief and doubting, in the lives of his beloved friends? Through this experience, their understanding of the greatness of their Saviour grew in a far greater way than if the Lord had simply come and healed their brother. They had seen Jesus heal people many times. Now, he was giving them the opportunity to trust him for a far greater miracle – resurrection from the dead! Had their hearts yearned to grow in faith and to know him in an even deeper way? I am sure they had; they loved the Lord. So the Lord responded to their hearts' cry ….. but by taking them blind along a way they had previously not known.

There have been many periods of my life in which I have felt I was being led blind along a rough, unfamiliar route. I have to confess that my initial reaction towards the Lord, in those times, has usually been one of frustration. After all, surely, the one thing that is imperative when you are caring for a blind person is to follow familiar routes, in order to help them have some level of independence and avoid accidents. Why would God, when we are 'blind' and struggling, make life harder not easier? In my annoyance, I have so often missed the point. The Lord is not trying to encourage independence – quite the opposite. He wants us to learn to be dependent on him and trust him, even when we don't know where we are going! The Lord is not cruel. The scriptures do not say that he will abandon us in strange places but rather that he will lead and guide us through unfamiliar routes. However, his guides may come in very unlikely, even undesirable, forms.

## Unlikely friends

"Hinds' Feet on High Places" by Hannah Hurnard is one of my favourite books. I read it just as I was preparing to leave for the ship, and many times during my ship-life. How I related to the main character, 'Much-Afraid'. In trembling obedience to the Lord, she starts her journey to the 'High Places'. She longs to please the 'Chief Shepherd'. Yet, she knows her weaknesses. She fears her enemies, 'Pride' and 'Self Pity', will attack her. She doubts she will ever make it to the 'High Places'. So she asks the Lord for help, hoping for companions such as 'Joy' and 'Peace.' To her horror, the 'Chief Shepherd' puts 'Sorrow' and 'Suffering' alongside her. The Lord challenges her to trust that he has chosen the best possible guides for her so, albeit reluctantly, 'Much-Afraid' accepts her veiled guides. Through many trials, the three-some reach the 'High Places'. No longer 'Much-Afraid', she is given the new name 'Grace and Glory'. The veils of her guides are removed and lo and behold, they too are completely transformed into 'Joy' and 'Peace'! In wonder, 'Grace and Glory' hears how, ironically, 'Sorrow' and 'Suffering' had despaired when they saw that they had been given 'Much Afraid' as their companion! But, each time 'Much Afraid' accepted their help, they too had begun to change. Had she rejected their help, none of them would have ever made it to the 'High Places'. The Lord had graciously arranged for this unlikely set of companions to help each other to the 'High Places' to the glory of his name!

Hannah Hurnard's analogy perfectly illustrates the beauty and mystery of the surprising symbiotic relationships the Lord chooses for us, in order for us to help one another to the "High Places". As we serve each other, we indeed are guided ourselves and grow in faith and spiritual maturity. But we must trust the "Chief Shepherd" and accept the 'guides' he has chosen, even when they initially seem undesirable and lead us in ways we have not known. We must prioritise spiritual growth and maturity over independence and ease for, if we could choose 'Joy' and 'Peace' to attend us all the way through life, it is doubtful we would even attempt the journey to reach the "High Places". More than likely, we would settle for earthly 'happiness'.

The Lord will often give us difficult 'companions' in answer to our prayers for spiritual growth. Prayers for patience and perseverance may bring times of testing and a long, uphill struggle. Prayers for integrity may bring temptations. Prayers for passion might bring the experience of unrequited love in order that you can identify with the sorrow of the Lord over our indifference to his love. Some of you may experience crushing loneliness as you are drawn into a secret place to learn to rely on the Lord only, instead of on your own strength or that of your friends.

Above all, however painful the problems, heartache and convictions the Lord allows as our 'unlikely friends', if we will but trust him, they will always lead us to a deeper understanding of him and of ourselves. Even the things that we dread the most can become unlikely guides, sent to bring us to spiritual maturity. Let me share with you my own testimony of spiritual growth as I was led 'blind', or should I say, left 'blind' - hanging in mid-air from God's finger. The loss of all my own strength and courage became my undesired 'guide'.

# Girl on a Swing

Whilst preparing to leave the ship, MV Logos 2, in September 2007, I was praying for guidance as to the future. Two years previously I had faced the challenge of leaving my old, familiar, 'safe' life to go towards the unknown. Although it was stressful, I had at least known it was for a two year period and I would have a community around me with a clear structure and purpose. By contrast, I was now leaving the ship, not to move to another structured life but to face a totally blank canvas. I longed for a path ahead, or even just a light to show the next step. Instead, I was given a picture of the Lord standing at the end of the gangway reaching up his hand, like a bridegroom waiting to take his bride to the place he has prepared for her. This vision was confirmed with many words of reassurance that the Lord had gone ahead of me and would lovingly guide my steps.

Despite this encouragement, the 'blindness' – the uncertainty of my future - was still very hard to bear. A flood of memories from my two years aboard MV Logos 2 should have provided a feeling of exhilaration - the privilege of having seen the Lord's amazing work in nearly forty countries, not to mention his work within my own life, and that of others. But I was tired – physically, emotionally and spiritually - and, in my exhaustion, I became very vulnerable. Satan attacked my identity and my ministry, slowly persuading me that my time onboard had been a monumental display of my weaknesses instead of my strengths. On the one hand, my heart's desire was to continue in ministry, especially in discipleship, through writing and teaching about the Bible. On the other hand, struggling with crushing disappointment and anxiety, I questioned the validity of any ministry I might do. How could I minister to others about the purpose of God in their lives, when my own faith did not seem to bring me any peace about the purpose of God in my own life? I could not sleep. I wrote, or rather etched, in my journal, remonstrating with the Lord, arguing that there was no point in having knowledge of the Bible, if it did not help me to overcome my disappointments and fears.

I was uncertain about the future; about the world I lived in; about my own abilities; about my personality; about my ministry; about my own health; even about my mental health, as a decade-long battle with irritable bowel syndrome drained me of so much mental energy and enthusiasm for the future. Above all, I was uncertain that I would ever be truly happy whilst I felt so hopeless.

As I tried to settle into life back home, I felt very uncomfortable. My future seemed like a deep black hole. Prior to the ship, I had lived for seven years with Rhona, an inspiring lady who lives by faith, serving the Lord in our church and playing a key role in charity work in Uganda. I had always viewed her day-to-day life through rose-coloured spectacles – maybe even "green" spectacles on occasions. As a full-time teacher and middle-manager, I seemed to be permanently stressed, coming in most evenings just before 7pm, with marking still to be done. Rhona would be off to her next meeting and I would naively think how nice it must be just to do the Lord's work, to have time to do your quiet time, to be available to people… The reality of my post-ship circumstances did not allow much time for wishful thinking. My life lacked structure - no term schedule; no fixed salary coming in reliably every month; no pension scheme; no knowing what the future held. I hated it! I was stressed. I wanted out! Although in my heart I wanted to stay in ministry, I just could not face the uncertainty of it all. Remarkably, only six weeks after leaving the ship, a job came up in my old department in the local school. I applied.

During the following two weeks, I attended a course especially designed to counsel missionaries. During one evening session, I was sharing with my group how difficult re-entry had been and that I had decided to go back to teaching. However, having been given a date for interview, I was now feeling uneasy, if not anxious, doubting my decision! They gathered around me to pray. Marianne from South Africa began, *"I see you sitting on a swing but there is no frame to the swing – rather the swing is hanging high up from God's finger. He is leaning over you and asking, "Can I swing with you yet?"*

There were quiet murmurs in the group. I looked up and smiled weakly. If only they could have heard my thoughts. *"No, you cannot swing with me! I am hanging in mid-air and I am absolutely freaked out! Give me a break!"*

That night I could not sleep - in fact, I had a panic attack. Full-time teaching was definitely not synonymous with swinging from God's finger! It was going back to structure and security with both feet firmly on the ground. But to withdraw meant utter nothingness. There was nothing else in the pipeline for me – just a dream to write a book and to minister to others, and that was lying in tatters as I faced my own despair and anxiety. Just as the bewildered Simon Peter found some relief in returning to fishing for a livelihood (John 21), I was at the point of persuading myself that a return to full-time teaching would be less stressful than following the Lord into the unknown! What was I thinking?

*"Will you leave me too?"* Jesus asked. The words of the disciples echoed in my ears – *"Lord, to whom shall we go? You have the words of eternal life. We believe and know that you are the Holy One of God"* (John 6 : 68).

The next day I contacted the school to withdraw my application. The Head of Department was so kind and understanding. I clung tightly to the 'ropes of the swing' and tried not to look down!

It took weeks until I felt at peace on that 'swing'. The Lord counselled me in my exhaustion and used my family, friends and church leaders to build a high wall around me to protect me from Satan's lies about my time on board, and my future. As I started to relax, I heard the Lord's reassurance. He had promised he would lovingly guide me. He was the shepherd of my soul. He would lead me in green pastures and beside still waters to restore my soul and then lead me in the ways of righteousness for his glorious name's sake.

The New Year turned with me in bed, full of a cold. I cast my mind back to the same scenario in December, 2004. I had cried myself to sleep, depressed at the thought of turning thirty that year, not seeing anything new, or exciting, on the horizon for me. A year later, surrounded by new friends, I had shouted in the New Year aboard the MV Logos 2 in Bermuda! This time I decided, resolutely, I would bypass the tears and hopelessness. God had been so faithful. Why would 2008 be any different?

On the second of January my Oswald Chambers' calendar read : *"Will you go out without knowing?" "One of the most difficult questions to answer in Christian work is, "What do you expect to do?" You don't know what you are going to do. The only thing you know is that God knows what He is doing."*

I stood in my room and said aloud to the Lord, "Yes, Lord, I will go out without knowing." Hope rose in my heart. My circumstances had not changed but my relationship with the Lord had. The swing had started to swing. That very week, I received a cheque that covered three months rent. I began to write this book.

Around this time, I was asked to look after Toby, my friend's two year old son, for a few hours. He had never been out with me alone before as I had always visited him at his home. Furthermore, coming to my home, he was going to be in a strange place, meeting people with whom he was not that familiar. As we entered the house, he suddenly clung onto my hand and moved in close to me to hide behind my leg. This response of trust, believing in my protection and love filled my heart. I knew it signified a growth in our relationship. He was a little overwhelmed but he did not cry because I was there.

This small incident blessed me with such a loving insight into the Lord's dealings with me over those first few months after my leaving the ship. He had wanted me to grow up in my faith – to be introduced to new situations, to be led in unfamiliar ways. Far from disappointing him with my fear, he'd expected it, much as I had for Toby. When I had hung on tightly to him, it had delighted his heart that I had turned to him, just as it had touched me when Toby clung to me. I had braved a very new situation with my Lord beside me. Furthermore, he had been even more thrilled when, like young Toby, I had begun to lose some of my fears, even to enjoy the change before allowing him to push the swing!

# Treasures of Darkness

*"I will give you the treasures of darkness, riches stored in secret places, so that you may know that I am the Lord, the God of Israel, who summons you by name."*
*Isaiah 45 : 3*

Darkness – the total uncertainty of the future - had become to me an 'unlikely friend' that, like the presence of the ant to the caterpillar, helped me to grow spiritually far more than if it had been dispelled. The Lord had deliberately withheld his plan and long-term leading so that I would learn to trust him on a daily basis and be more interested in the relationship I was developing with him on my spiritual journey than in the destination itself. I learnt through this season of darkness that we actually face the unknown all the time in life. None of us knows what the next day holds. However, we don't often face this reality because most of us have frameworks through our jobs, our relationships or our finances that make us feel the future is more secure, more in our control, more predictable. When these familiar frameworks are removed, we suddenly realize how 'blind' we are. The Lord shows us the true extent of our faith and whether we have our hope in earthly securities or truly in him. The treasure of darkness is to find that there is something more certain, trustworthy and secure than a light or a known way – there is the hand of God. To have peace simply by knowing our hand is in the hand of God is better than any worldly security. It is even better than having the answers to all our anxious questions about the future. We are truly blessed if we can peacefully swing from God's finger, without demanding guarantees for all of life's unknowns. We can rest content that our Heavenly Father knows everything and he will reveal all to us as and when it is necessary. Such faith is a gift that can never be taken away by any person or even through the loss of a loved one; such faith can not be upset by any difficult circumstances either, nor through the loss of a particularly good set of circumstances.

However, the darkness of the dark days which the Lord allows is still very real. You will face your own weaknesses and, probably, like me, the distressing reality of your need for answers, health, security and rewards rather than for the presence of God. You may realise how little you walked by faith before. You may even discover how little faith you actually have and how much fear and doubt that can produce. As you attempt to move forward in the dark, do not be surprised if you suffer the terror of the 'darkness' even more. Satan will be angry! As you stumble forward reaching out for the hand of God, your enemy will try to persuade you that there is still time

> "Look around and be distressed, look inside and be depressed, look at Christ and be at rest."
>
> Corrie Ten Boom

to return to the 'safety' of familiar ground. It will often be very hard to grow in the darkness, trusting in his unfailing love. Satan will try and persuade you to light your own way - to take matters into your own hands; to put 'security' and familiarity back into your life, in place of faith. However, I urge you to heed the warnings of Isaiah 50; I know from personal experience, that if you attempt to second-guess God - trying to figure out the future for yourself, you will be in torment.

*"Let him who walks in the dark, who has no light, trust in the name of the Lord and rely on his God. But now, all you who light fires and provide yourselves with flaming torches, go, walk in the light of your fires and of the torches you have set ablaze. This is what you shall receive from my hand: you will lie down in torment."* Isaiah 50 : 10,11

# The point of it all

*"My God turns my darkness into light." Psalm 18 : 28b*

If we are to compare our spiritual journey to that of the caterpillar becoming a butterfly, at least half our lives will be spent alongside 'unlikely friends'. It will be easy to lose heart and forget, somewhere along the way, the point of submitting to all these unusual symbiotic relationships in order to grow. Let us then look back frequently at the caterpillars and ask ourselves, "Why does the Lord give them such unlikely friends as an ant and a dark ants' nest? Why is it so important to protect their growth even in the strangest of ways?" The answer, of course, is to afford to them the highest possibility of reaching the point of metamorphosis, and so the marvellous opportunity to move from an earthbound world of blind darkness, to a life of flight and vision and purpose. All the eating; all the struggles to grow through the marvellous process of apolysis and ecdysis; all the efforts and unusual defence strategies to avoid danger and to protect its continual growth – all of these things are to bring the little caterpillar to this one crucial point – metamorphosis. The caterpillar is then faced with an extraordinary challenge – to surrender itself to the darkness of the chrysalis.

In our struggles to grow, may we remember that the Lord has the same aim. He works to protect our spiritual growth at all costs until, through our acceptance of all the unusual guides and circumstances deemed to be a necessary part of our maturing process, we too are prepared to lay everything down in order to become a new creation. This is the final border between spiritual immaturity and spiritual maturity.

Let us move on to look at the caterpillar's preparation for this dramatic act of self-surrender, determined to reach that same point of faith in our own lives, trusting God to lead us to a new life of revelation and purpose in the high places.

Lord, may Thy blood now cleanse me,
Wash all my sins away,
That with Thy Holy Spirit
Thou may anoint, I pray.
My service, I confess, Lord,
Is failure-full and weak;
The filling of Thy Spirit
To live for Thee I seek.

Chorus
Oh, from myself deliver,
From all its misery;
I'd henceforth be forever
Completely filled with Thee.

Oh, Lord, how dry my heart is,
It yearns and pants for Thee;
The filling of Thy Spirit
Is now my fervent plea
Within the smitten Rock, Lord,
I would entirely hide;
Pour through Thy living water,
Till I am satisfied.

*How cold my heart has been, Lord*
*How slow obeying Thee;*
*So fill me with Thy Spirit,*
*I'll ne'er rebellious be*
*I lie upon Thy altar*
*And dare not move away;*
*Oh, may Thy flame descending*
*Consume my all, I pray*

*Oh, may Thy Cross within me*
*Deepen its work and burn*
*In me enlarge Thy measure,*
*And me to ashes turn.*
*Oh, may Thy Spirit fill me*
*Each day more than before,*
*And may Thy living water*
*On me and through me pour*

Watchman Nee
(1903-1972)

# Chapter 7

# Restless Wandering Stage
## Facing the Stress of Surrender and Change

*"Circumcise yourselves to the Lord, circumcise your hearts." Jeremiah 4 : 4a*

As the caterpillar reaches its fifth instar, it enters "The Restless Wandering Stage" – a term coined by naturalists in an attempt to describe the behaviour of the caterpillar in this final stage of its life. In apparent anticipation of great change, the caterpillar begins to prepare itself for the chrysalis - the turning point of its life.

The one thing that is certain in life is change. Every one of us will come to major crossroads in our lives; we shall have to make crucial decisions that we know will invoke great change. However, there are no greater choices than the ones the Lord lays before us at various stages of our spiritual development. The prerequisite of spiritual maturity is to leave any self-centred, or immature, ways of thinking behind. This usually entails the wholehearted surrender of any particular issue, or area of our lives, which questions Christ's sovereignty. This will be beyond merely 'shedding a skin' as it insinuates that we must pass through a point of no return, committed to leaving our old nature behind. Whichever area of life we are being asked to address, the time immediately preceding surrender can often be stressful. Have you ever felt agitated and uneasy, as the caterpillar appears to be, when considering obedient surrender to the Lord's will over a certain issue? Did your restless thoughts seem to go over and over the various consequences of such an act of surrender, until, at last, you reached a decision and took some action? In many ways, this could be considered then as a time of 'spiritual restless wandering' as we sense the conviction of the Holy Spirit, drawing us ever closer to 'spiritual metamorphosis' in all the key areas of our lives.

This transitional phase of the caterpillar's life is marked by clear changes in behaviour (provoked by hormones) which signify the end of one part of its life and the preparation for the next. Let us look at each of these changes and ask ourselves whether we too will take the necessary steps in times of "spiritual restless wandering" to prepare actively the way for spiritual transformation within our own lives. The caterpillar passes through this stage only once. We, on the other hand, may have to mature spiritually in various areas of our lives at different stages in our lives. We may, for example, be spiritually mature in the way we view and handle our finances, yet remain immature in our relationships.

However, as and when we are challenged by the Lord to face, and traverse, the difficult transitional seasons of ' spiritual metamorphosis', there are valuable lessons to be drawn from the actions of the caterpillar.

## The end of the old way of life

The caterpillar does not continue in its old way of life, hoping that somehow it will, one day, just automatically metamorphose. Rather, when it reaches the fifth instar, it begins an evident process of change. First of all, it stops feeding. This may seem insignificant but, up until now, that has been the singular, self-centred focus of its life! Now the caterpillar has reached the point where it is time to fulfil the purpose of eating all that food.

This first observation may seem very obvious, but it is a point each one of us must reach for ourselves. We must come to recognise the purpose of spiritual growth and then pursue it. We cannot hope to drift into spiritual maturity. Christ taught in Matthew 6 that the way to God is a narrow road, through a small gate, and there are few that find it. Unless a decisive choice is made to seek first the Kingdom of God, you are more likely to wander onto the broad highway. Sadly, the very people who are perceived to be closest to spiritual transformation, those sitting in churches and Bible studies, as opposed to those living an outwardly sinful life, are probably the most likely to stall at this stage, failing to recognise the continuous need to take decisive action to go deeper with the Lord. They may seek to justify their inaction either by counting the personal changes already made on their spiritual journey ('shedding skins') or by comparing their "progress" with less committed disciples. Jesus was aware of this problem. In telling the parable of the Pharisee and the tax collector (see Luke 18 : 9), he was warning those who were confident of their own righteousness to the point of complacency and even self-congratulation. Jesus did not hesitate to condemn the common religious customs by which proud men sought to establish their own righteousness. He was particularly scathing of the merely outward religiosity of the Pharisees. Calling them "blind guides", "blind fools", "blind men" (see Matthew 23), he accused them of loading burdens on their fellow men. The Pharisees, although deeply religious, remained 'blind caterpillars', for they refused to humble themselves and allow their hearts to be circumcised by the hands of God. Instead, they chose to trust in the circumcision done by the hands of men, in tradition and in the righteousness of Law-keeping.

> "Not everyone who says to me, "Lord, Lord," will enter the kingdom of heaven, but only he who does the will of my Father who is in heaven."
>
> Matthew 7 : 21

With these things in mind, perhaps we ought to ask ourselves whether we, too, are actually more comfortable with a 'religious lifestyle' we can control, than with the total surrender of our lives to the Lord Jesus. His will is for each one of us to be become a new creation in Christ and to move on to spiritual maturity. This can only come through spiritual metamorphosis and therein lies the problem. Metamorphosis - as the caterpillar's life-story illustrates - signifies giving up control of our lives and moving out of our comfort zone to die to self. As Jesus himself said, it means "taking up our own cross" and following the voice of the Lord as he calls us into a deeper and deeper relationship. As a result, many of us try to 'manage' our faith in such a way as to avoid surrender, with all its risks, convincing ourselves that reaching the 'fifth and final instar' is surely good enough. At such times, we need to recognise the good as the enemy of the best.

Satan's persuasions can sound so plausible – a daily quiet time; church attendance; giving to mission; a moral life. Anything more would be extremism, wouldn't it? Do we really need total surrender? Do we really need to give up that final 'old skin' - whatever it constitutes in our lives? Is becoming a 'butterfly' so special anyway?

## Tie-on wings

There once was a caterpillar just entering into his final instar. He was so close to becoming a butterfly. The only problem was that he resented the fact that he must now give up his current self in order to become a butterfly. Not only that but, if he were totally honest, he was afraid to die to self. He crawled along the undergrowth noticeably dissatisfied. The snake was lurking in the background. He hated caterpillars because he was so envious of their hidden treasure within – the chance to become a beautiful butterfly. "Oh, to be airborne and beautiful!" he thought to himself. He snapped out of his daydreaming. Seeing his opportunity to deceive the fearful, weakened caterpillar, the sly snake slithered up to the caterpillar and questioned his downcast appearance, pretending to be concerned about his welfare. The caterpillar muttered his self-pitying objections to the process of change required of him to fulfil his destiny. The snake laughed and produced a pair of attractive wings saying, "My friend, you are deceived. You do not need to die to be like a butterfly. Here, I have these wings for you. I know you don't see so well, so I shall describe them to you. They are decoratively patterned with self-righteousness and good works. I can assure you that if you wear them correctly, you will be just like a butterfly and, best of all, you will have avoided all the pain and misery of death to self!"

The caterpillar seemed delighted and carried his new wings to the top of the nearest plant and tied them around his waist. Very satisfied with himself, he called down to his fellow caterpillars and the surrounding wildlife, "Hey, look at me. I have managed to become a butterfly without undergoing the fearful and vulnerable chrysalis stage! Don't be tricked anymore, fellow larvae – you don't need to bother with metamorphosis! You can stay yourself this way and still get wings! Go and see the snake! Furthermore, these wings don't seem half so fragile as the wings of our ancestors."

At first, some of the caterpillars were interested but as the boasting went on, they began to resent this pretentious caterpillar. The wings made him proud although he never managed to fly. The deceived caterpillar had put himself on a rigorous diet, determined not to eat leaves, but he could not resist them because he consistently failed to extract nectar from the flowers. As time passed, the caterpillar became more and more grumpy and irritable, weary of carrying his fake wings around. The wings began to drag limply behind him through the mud and the undergrowth, spoiling their crafted beauty. When he had the energy to drag himself to the top of a flower stalk, he would try and remind himself why he went to such trouble. He watched the butterflies wistfully, wishing that he could truly fly and be free of this heavy body and fake wings. All the other caterpillars no longer wanted to be friends with him because he'd thought he was better than they, declaring that, at least, he had some form of wings and wasn't just a plain old worm. Worse still, most of his old friends had moved on and were now flying gaily around somewhere. As for the other wildlife, they would look on him thinking, "Well, if that is what it means to be a butterfly, I am glad I am not one!" A butterfly had once landed beside and offered to untie the wings, and encourage him through the restless wandering stage, but he was too proud to admit he had been wrong. Then, one awful day, so conspicuous sitting on the top of a flower, he was eaten by a bird. Handicapped by his heavy wings, he was unable to escape and made easy prey for the hungry bird!

# A form of godliness

Clearly, like any analogy, this story has its short-comings. However, the story is to illustrate the failings of self-righteousness and how much we miss when we try to bypass 'the chrysalis stage!' Surrendering to the Lord is the only way through which we can become spiritually mature in any area of our lives. As we grow in Christ's likeness, we are given a new nature of holiness with which to serve the King of Kings, empowered by the Holy Spirit within us. This life is as superior as that of a butterfly's to a worm's. Yes, it will require discipline and commitment for, as in the life of the butterfly, there is a lot to be done in a short lifespan and we have many enemies. However, it will not be a life of drudgery and duty, striving like a caterpillar with fake wings tied around its waist. Did you ever see a butterfly that looked burdened? Spiritual maturity brings an abundant life. This is why we should set our hearts on holiness, despite the sacrifices it will entail. Christ came to establish a relationship with us, and give us life to the full now, not just in eternity.

Are you trying to become a butterfly without dying to self? Why? Are you doubting the Lord and his potential dealings in your life? So often we fail to believe in the powerful attributes of the Holy Spirit to deliver us from our old nature and transform us. Other times, we do not even have the desire to entrust our lives to the Lord for such a transformation. Instead, as a result of our evasive behaviour, we end up like the near-blind, earthbound caterpillar with fake wings, *"having a form of godliness but denying its power"* (2 Timothy 3 : 5), unable to rise above our limitations and be used by God.

At a closer look at 2 Timothy chapter 3, the list of characteristics, attributed to those who have a "form of godliness," may surprise you. There seems to be nothing godly about them at all and yet they are described in the New Living Translation as those who "act as if they are religious." 2 Timothy 3 :1 - 5 reads, *"But mark this: there will be terrible times in the last days. People will be lovers of themselves, lovers of money, boastful, proud, abusive, disobedient to their parents, ungrateful, unholy, without love, unforgiving, slanderous, without self-control, brutal, not lovers of the good, treacherous, rash, conceited, lovers of pleasure rather than of God – having a form of godliness but denying its power."*

A form of godliness may be used to mask many undesirable characteristics but it never removes them. If, up to this point, we have been 'shedding skins' just to feel better in 'our new skin' and never really intending to surrender our lives to the Lord, we shall never be truly free. We shall never 'fly' in newness of life. Instead, in our self-deception, we will determine to cover up our weaknesses by means of greater personal discipline and dress up our old nature

> You Christians seem to have a religion that makes you miserable. You are like a man with a headache. He does not want to get rid of his head, but it hurts him to keep it. You cannot expect outsiders to earnestly seek anything so uncomfortable.
>
> "The Christian's Secret of a Happy Life."

in an attempt to become new creations in our own way. Self-effort manifests itself in laudable good works; self denial; attending church; reading Christian books or studying the Scriptures religiously, like the Pharisees. Such a way of life will indeed weigh heavy on us. Self-righteousness, like a destructive parasite, prevents the life-transforming grace of God. Regrettably, self-righteousness can be as much a church problem as an individual problem. Any attempt to portray the beauty of holiness with the 'fake wings' of self-righteousness will soon be exposed as hypocrisy. Whatever form self-effort takes, it will lead to disillusionment. Nothing short of total transformation – spiritual metamorphosis – will avail. In Galatians 6 : 15 we read, *"Neither circumcision nor un-circumcision means anything; what counts is a NEW CREATION."*

## Actively preparing for change

*"So here's what I want you to do, God helping you:.* **Take your everyday ordinary life – your sleeping, eating, going-to-work, and walking-around-life and place it before God as an offering.** *Embracing what God does for you is the best thing you can do for him. Don't become so well-adjusted to your culture that you fit into it without even thinking. Instead, fix your attention on God.* **You'll be changed from the inside out.** *Readily recognise what he wants from you and quickly respond to it. Unlike the culture around you,* **always dragging you down to its level of immaturity,** *God brings the best out of you,* **develops well-formed maturity in you."** (The Message - emphasis mine)

This twentieth century paraphrase of Romans chapter 12 : 1,2 compares the effects pagan culture has upon our lives – dragging us down to its level of immaturity – with the effect the Word and will of God has upon our lives – bringing out the best and developing maturity. Its practical application, referring to every area of our lives, indicates how comprehensive our surrender and transformation must be. We must reject the stubborn desire to stay in a spiritual rut. This passage exhorts us to make, soberly and responsibly, the kind of long-term decisions which will determine the future course of our lives. The Apostle Paul presses home his exhortation with an urgency which demands decisive action in the here and now, and allows no room for procrastination. We are to prepare ourselves for a change no less radical than the caterpillar's fifth and final instar, with additional dangers to which we are not accustomed.

The caterpillar, in its bid to survive the most important phase of its journey to maturity, begins to wander around restlessly, making it a priority to seek out a suitable and safe place to undergo metamorphosis. This wandering has a two fold purpose: -

a) Move away from the host plant
b) Move into a place where changes are safe(r)

Relative to its size, the caterpillar often covers huge areas during this time of wandering, such is the importance to ensure, as much as possible, the survival of the larva once it enters the vulnerable pupal stage. The predators and parasites of the caterpillar are drawn to the host plant by the presence of butterfly eggs and larvae. By moving away from the larval food-plant, it minimises the risk of being attacked by any enemies which would endanger, or prevent, change.

# Moving away from those who might jeopardise change

In light of this, we who aspire to spiritual metamorphosis need to give some thought to the subject of spiritual predators and parasites. It is our responsibility to distance ourselves from every potentially harmful, ungodly influence. Personal discipline will be needed, especially in the area of recreation. We must reject a lifestyle which desensitises our spiritual consciences. Instead of immersing ourselves in hours of television shows, films, literature or social company that does not encourage holiness, let us make ourselves more sensitive to the required changes by reading God's word and listening to godly preaching. Let us

"So let us stop going over the basics of Christianity again and again. Let us go on instead and become mature in our understanding." Hebrews 6 : 1 (NLT)

pray and ask the Lord to search our hearts, and reveal anything which is holding us back. If we will not fully surrender in this way, the culture around us will drag us back to immaturity, just as chapter twelve of Romans states.

The caterpillar, in moving away from the host plant, is not just moving away from its enemies but, also, away from its former diet – the leaves of the host plant. This is perhaps a harder part of the analogy to recognise within our spiritual lives. After all, the leaves of the host plant were formally God-ordained as its legitimate food source for growth. Now, however, the caterpillar needs to stop feeding and prepare for a completely different diet. This time of fasting, during the 'restless wandering stage', gives its body an opportunity to let go of its former way of life, as well as to establish its position for the process of metamorphosis. What could this process equate to in our spiritual life?

The most crucial seasons of change in our spiritual lives may also be best aided by periods of fasting. Fasting can help to focus the mind and empower us, through prayer, to let go of parts of our old nature and move into a place of desiring to meet with God on a much deeper level.

As we discussed in Chapter 3, different diets are also appropriate at different points of our spiritual growth. Part of our 'restless wandering stage' may well incorporate building up an appetite for, and preparing to assimilate, a new diet of deeper spiritual truths, once through the process of 'spiritual metamorphosis'.

## Move towards those who will protect and encourage change

Interestingly enough, for larvae that have been parasited, the 'restless wandering stage' is the most dangerous. It is the point at which most parasitoids will finally attack and kill off the larvae. May this unpleasant fact of nature serve as a reminder of our own potential vulnerability. When we reach the point of surrendering ourselves to 'spiritual metamorphosis', we dispossess our former parasitical sins and habits of their 'host'. For this very reason, Satan will do his utmost to prevent us from reaching this life-transforming stage. We must anticipate therefore, and be on guard against, subtle attacks from Satan by which he will try to keep us from going through with the process of change. He will use all manner of deception and intimidation to prevent our making the necessary changes to go into the 'chrysalis.' He will dig up issues in our lives that we have left unaddressed to delay or abort 'spiritual metamorphosis'. He will cause all sorts of fears and protests to arise within us. Having previously encountered the opposition of the evil one at each stage of our 'skin-shedding', we should, at this final stage, know how, with the Lord's help, to answer and resist him.

For the caterpillar, the 'restless wandering stage' is a longer than normal period of vulnerability as the changes are much more radical and extensive than were the shedding of a skin. The caterpillar must, therefore, find a safe place to undergo both internal and external changes. We, too, need to bear in mind that the life-transforming stages in our spiritual development, leading to what we shall call 'spiritual metamorphosis', will be more radical than all earlier stages, and so we may also require a 'safe-haven' to shield our vulnerability. Just as some species of caterpillars use ants at this transitional stage to protect them, seeking refuge in the ants' chambers, you may find it safer to work through the challenges of 'spiritual metamorphosis' in the shelter of a supporting home-group, or in a one-to-one accountability relationship.

## Cleansing makes way for Change

The restless wandering to find a safe(r) environment for metamorphosis is not the end of the caterpillar's stress. Once in its chosen place for metamorphosis, the caterpillar appears to become very agitated. It starts to excrete all the dirt within its body as it empties its stomach. Enzymes are secreted internally that literally turn its entire innards into a 'soup', disintegrating its old stomach to make way for a smaller mid-gut. This part of the 'restless wandering stage', therefore, becomes a unique time of stripping away the products of the old nature and cleansing, as the caterpillar rids itself of all the wet frass produced by the breaking down of the defunct large gut and its contents. The caterpillar will then be ready to remove its old 'garment' and become a chrysalis. During the chrysalis stage, it will be transformed into a 'sun-worshipper', marvellously clothed with beautiful new 'garments.'

'Spiritual metamorphosis' must be preceded by times of repentance and cleansing. The Holy Spirit will reveal to us parts of our old nature that are no longer appropriate, as well as prompting the huge internal changes required for spiritual transformation. Let us revisit the story of Jacob we covered in Chapter 3 to see an example of this process worked out in real life. Jacob recognised his old nature as he gave his name to the Lord, revealing his true identity. He then went on to grow into his new nature, beginning by humbly restoring his relationship with his brother. But, as he worked through that growing and 'shedding skins' process, his family still got into a real mess. Finally, the Lord said, *"Go back to Bethel"*; in other words – "Go back to the house of God." *"Get rid of the foreign gods you have with you, and purify yourselves and change your clothes."* (Genesis 35 : 2)

Jacob and his family obeyed. In a process not unlike that of the caterpillar, they dismantled their old ways, ridding their household of idols; they purified themselves and put on new garments to worship the Lord at Bethel.

Need I say, this process requires resolve and perseverance? As we break down and get rid of everything belonging to our old nature, the cast-off evidence may be just as ugly as the caterpillar's 'frass'. We will have to come to terms with having to oust the dirt visibly! (see Chapter 4) This can be a stressful thing to face especially as it is accompanied by huge internal changes! It may be advisable, therefore, to enlist the support of another mature Christian.

# Do not disturb!

Eventually, the caterpillar, now deliberately positioned for death to self, becomes quiescent. Those who raise butterflies in captivity must never disturb the caterpillar at this crucial stage. Why is it so important to leave the caterpillar undisturbed during this period? As we have seen, the 'restless wandering stage' is a time of change. It may appear to be dormant for hours but internally many things are beginning to take place. The caterpillar is making its preparations to moult for the last time, leaving itself entombed within the final layer of skin – the pupal skin. There is such internal change physiologically that there may be a noticeable change in the colouration of the larva. Though it still looks like a caterpillar, it will now no longer be able to do what it could before, for example, its feet will become useless. This means it has become highly vulnerable. Disturbing the caterpillar, or in any way causing stress by giving the impression it is under attack, could jeopardize the whole process of metamorphosis.

I find this observation from nature to be not only interesting, but also instructive. It contains a lesson which we need to apply at important stages in our spiritual development. In Ecclesiastes 3 : 11 it states that the Lord makes all things beautiful in its time. These words "in its time" must not be overlooked. Transformation takes time. God takes time in his dealings with each individual. Let us share in the confidence expressed by the Apostle Paul .... *"that he who began a good work in you will carry it on to completion until the day of Christ Jesus."* (Philippians 1 : 6) In so doing, we should refrain from interfering when we see a fellow-Christian working through a period of transformation in their lives. Any attempt to speed up the process will do more harm than good. I am so grateful that my church elders advised me to take adequate time to be sure of the Lord's leading in the months immediately following my leaving the ship. Weeks became months, and months became a year, as the Lord led me to the point of trusting him to live by faith for as long as it took to write this book and develop my ministry. That period, in which I was left undisturbed, was a season of spiritual growth. Whilst going through that transitional phase, and needing time in secret with the Lord, I may have appeared quiescent to onlookers. In reality, I was far from being inactive internally. I could not have moved forward spiritually if I had felt under pressure to be involved in all sorts of commitments at the church. Wise leaders will recognize those special times when someone needs to be given both time and space to become sensitive to the leading of the Holy Spirit and responsive to what is revealed.

## Will we reprogramme?

The quiescent caterpillar begins to reprogramme its cellular physiology ready to metamorphose into a butterfly inside the pupal skin, the chrysalis. It creates a smaller mid-gut for its life as a butterfly in which it will drink only nectar and will not require a large stomach. When the pupa later forms, the organism will consume the larval stomach to create energy and carry it through the pupa stage. This will be noticeable as the pupa becomes about half the length of the original larva, due to the fact that about half of the larva's body consisted of just its gut!

This re-programming is the point of no return. It is destroying both its appetite and capacity to live in the ways of its old nature. It then actively recreates a new nature that will no longer accommodate the old lifestyle. The new nature requires a new habitat, behaviour, form of nourishment and preservation. Take note! The caterpillar does not try to handle the appetite belonging to the old way of life. It destroys the very source of that appetite – its gut! In other words, it burns *"Without faith it is impossible to please God."* Hebrews 11 : 6a its bridges! Does that say anything to you? If the wise king Solomon was inspired to recommend that we learn something from the ant (Proverbs 6 : 6 and 30 : 25), should we not be prepared to learn something from the caterpillar? Surely, here we can learn the importance of not trying to accommodate the appetite belonging to our old nature. In the words of the Apostle Paul, *"Put to death, therefore, whatever belongs to your earthly nature."* (Colossians 3 : 5) We are called to 'reprogramme' completely. If we are not prepared to do this, we shall never experience true transformation.

Let us look at an example in the Gospels of a religious young man who came so close to a life-transforming experience and yet missed the opportunity to experience 'spiritual metamorphosis' because he shrank from surrendering everything to the Lord. The rich young ruler could perhaps be compared to a religious person of today. He almost certainly attended the synagogue and, perhaps, gave many gifts to the temple. He was a "good man". From childhood, he respected and obeyed the Ten Commandments. Indeed, Mark chapter

*"Does the Lord delight in burnt offerings and sacrifices as much as in obeying the voice of the Lord? To obey is better than sacrifice, and to heed is better than the fat of rams. For rebellion is like the sin of divination and arrogance like the evil of idolatry."* 1 Samuel 15 : 22-23a

10 : 21 says, *"Jesus looked at him and loved him."* In terms of our analogy, we might say he was a man who had 'shed many skins' and reached a respectable level of spiritual maturity. Yet, when it came to the ultimate test of faith, to "lose one's life" (and burn any bridges back to it) in order to follow the Lord and truly gain life, he had neither the will nor the faith. He went away sad!

God reveals many times in Scripture that adherence to the Jewish law and religious ceremonies – ie:- religious effort – was meant to be an outward expression of our inward obedience and utter devotion to the Lord. Religious adherence to God's laws was not and still is not enough, in and of itself, to enable us to reach spiritual maturity, for none of us would ever attain to righteousness. Furthermore, reaching for spiritual maturity should never become like a bid to guarantee our eternal security. Rather, we should be driven by a passion to move into a deeper level in our personal relationship with the Lord, whatever the cost. It would seem that the rich young ruler was aware of this. His enquiry, *"What must I do to inherit eternal life?"* indicates that his keeping of the commandments had indeed given him no assurance of salvation. He gave the impression of being ready to do whatever else was necessary in order to be sure of inheriting eternal life but he recoiled as soon as Jesus revealed the one thing that was preventing him. *"One thing you lack. Go, sell everything you have and give to the poor, and you will have treasure in heaven. Then come, follow me." At this the man's face fell. He went away sad, because he had great wealth."* (Mark 10 : 21,22)

There will come a point in our walk with the Lord where the Lord will lay his finger on the very issue which is hindering our spiritual growth. We will be faced with a decision, a personal response. Will we worship him unreservedly, laying our lives as a living sacrifice before him, or will we hold back, wanting to keep one foot in the world?

## Losing the old skin

The Lord's challenge will be different for each of us but we can be sure that the Lord will identify whatever constitutes the final restrictive skin of our old nature. This is not because the Lord is deliberately trying to make it difficult for us. Rather, he knows that without surrender, we are left unfulfilled. Just as the butterfly cannot come forth unless the caterpillar surrenders its old nature to transformation, so the Lord cannot give us a new nature in him until we fully let go of our old nature, the old skin.

The Gospels, Matthew, Mark and Luke, all tell of one occasion when a question about fasting betrayed ignorance of the difference between the old covenant (Mosaic ceremony) and the new covenant ( life indwelt by the Spirit). Jesus answered with two brief analogies. *"No-one sews a patch of unshrunk cloth on an old garment, for the patch would pull away from the garment, making the tear worse. Neither do men pour new wine into old wineskins. If they do, the skins will burst, the wine will run out and the wineskins will be ruined. No, they pour new wine into new wineskins, and both are preserved."* (Matthew 9 : 16,17)

New animal skins, because of their elasticity, were used for the fermentation of wine. Old skins, previously stretched, lost their elasticity and became redundant. By this analogy, Jesus was teaching that the Mosaic ceremonies and practices had served their purposes for a time but they were now exhausted and redundant. The problem peculiar to the Pharisees was that their clinging to 'the redundant skin' was preventing them from recognising Jesus as their Messiah and receiving the abundant life of the new covenant. Whilst waiting for the Messiah, the Jews had become so comfortable and self-righteous in their religion, that they did not receive the Messiah when he came. They were stuck in the 'old skin' of legalism which left them feeling proud and superior. They did not want to acknowledge their personal need of a Saviour. They preferred to believe that the Messiah would not be coming to rescue them from their own sinful nature but, rather, from the occupying forces of the gentile Roman army. Jesus Christ came with new wine - a new covenant; the gift of saving grace and mercy for all sinners, as well as the indwelling power of the Holy Spirit to help the saints to continue to walk in obedience to the Lord. Tragically, as the Jews would not accept they were sinners and shed the 'old skin' to accept a new skin, neither could they receive the new wine.

> But we never can prove
> The delights of His love
> Until all on the altar we lay:
> For the favor He shows.
> And the joy He bestows.
> Are for them who will
> trust and obey.
>
> John H. Sammis

New wine cannot be poured into old wineskins, otherwise both the wine and the wineskin will be ruined. Rather, the new wine has to go into a new wineskin. Christ came to lay down his own life so that we could cast down ours before him and take up a new life in him, eternal life with purpose, distinguished by a beautifying and fulfilling holiness. Will you accept his sacrifice as motivation and courage for yours? The Lord will not strip you; he will only tell you,

> It is not death or pain that is to be dreaded. but the fear of pain or death.
>
> Epictetus

through the conviction of his Holy Spirit, that he needs to 'undress' you of your old nature, in order to reclothe you in himself. Then he will await your response.

# Can I undress you?

C. S Lewis, in his book, "The Voyage of the Dawn Treader", tells of the adventures and misadventures experienced by a group of friends as they sail, in an earnest quest, to discover Aslan's country. Eustace's life lesson takes place on the aptly named Dragon Island. Falling prey to his old disagreeable nature, he wanders away from his friends and is enchanted when he discovers a cave full of gold. Immediately, he seizes a golden bangle and pushes it onto his arm to take away with him. However, he falls asleep in the cave and on awakening, discovers to his horror that he has turned into a dragon. When reunited with friends, they form the opinion that Eustace's character is much improved by virtue of the fact that he now sees himself as a dragon. Eustace, however, becomes weary and miserable, wondering what will become of him. At this point, Aslan the Lion comes to him and leads Eustace to a garden on the top of a mountain filled with fruit and trees. In the middle of the garden, he sees a well of water with steps going down into it. He longs to bathe in the water to ease his pain but Aslan tells him if he wishes to bathe, he must first undress. Not fully understanding, he determines to try and scratch the old dragon skin off. He finds the skin peels away, but each time he succeeds in scratching an old skin away, there is a new dragon skin underneath. Three times he tries unsuccessfully to free himself until Aslan says, "You will have to let me undress you".

*"I was afraid of his claws, I can tell you, but I was pretty nearly desperate now. So I just lay flat down on my back to let him do it. The very first tear he made was so deep that I thought it had gone right into my heart. And when he began pulling the skin off, it hurt worse than anything I've ever felt. The only thing that made me able to bear it was just the pleasure of feeling the stuff peel off ......."*

*" ...... he peeled the beastly stuff right off just as I thought I'd done myself the other three times, only they hadn't hurt – and there it was, lying on the grass, only ever so much thicker, and darker, and more knobbly-looking, than the others had been. And there was I, as smooth and soft as a peeled switch and smaller than I had been. Then he caught hold of me – I didn't like that much for I was very tender underneath now that I'd no skin on – and threw me into the water. It smarted like anything but only for a moment. After that it became perfectly delicious and as soon as I started swimming and splashing I found that all the pain had gone from my arm. And then I saw why. I'd turned into a boy again."*

Aslan then takes Eustace and dresses him in new clothes.

This clever children's story parallels the Lord's dealings with us as shown through the caterpillar's life and final surrender. We need to be led to a deeper place where we realise that only the Lord can take away the old nature and baptise us with the healing streams of the Holy Spirit, before raising us to new life in Christ. There must be no more self-righteous efforts to scratch off old skins. In the pre-pupa stage, the caterpillar faces a similar final stripping. There is no new caterpillar skin underneath, as previously. This time, they become smaller, protected by a smooth pupal skin. Inside this chrysalis, they will be brought to a watery grave of the old body, like Eustace, only to be brought out again with beautiful new garments.

An important point to take from the story is that Eustace, underneath the dragon skin, was a boy, the boy he had always been, yet now brought to maturity, stripped of his selfish, immature nature, changed by Aslan's intervention. This may seem obvious, but we often forget that through metamorphosis, we are being restored spiritually to our original glory. Believe it or not, the caterpillar

The delight of sacrifice is that I lay down my life for my Friend. Jesus (see John 15 : 13) I don't throw my life away, but I willingly and deliberately lay it down for Him and His interests in other people.

Oswald Chambers: My Utmost for his Highest

has actually always been a butterfly. As mentioned earlier, there are imaginal disks within the caterpillar's body from the early instars. These disks are like little groups of embryonic cells that hold the genetic information for the wings, legs, antennae and all the organs of the butterfly. Initially they lie dormant, but as soon as the caterpillar enters the 'restless wandering stage' and begins the process of metamorphosis, they start to develop very rapidly once the final larval skin is shed. Evidence of this development can be seen immediately. The shape of wings becomes apparent within the pupal skin within minutes of the caterpillar becoming a pupa.

Is it not even more wonderful that we were made in the image of God? We were made to be Son-worshippers. However, as with the caterpillar, God can only bring us to maturity and restore us to what he originally intended, as and when we actively begin the process of surrender to spiritual metamorphosis. Christ promised, "Whoever loses his life for me will find it." (Matthew 16 : 25b) Christ will not take our lives from us. We must lay them down. Like the caterpillar, we must entomb ourselves, so to speak. He will call us to make visible changes in our lives and position ourselves for the surrender that will lead us into metamorphosis. Once we are "in position" to allow God to change us fully in order to be ready for his purposes, he will not be slow to respond. Indeed, in my experience, God's desire to bring us to maturity, and bless us with a new nature and purpose, begins to reveal itself right from the moment of the first step of faith towards complete surrender.

## Position of surrender

There are a number of places in which the various species of butterfly pupate. Some species pupate inside an ants' nest, buried under the ground; others camouflage themselves in a pile of dead leaves. Most will use their silk glands (spinnerets) to spin a silk pad, or a silk thread, which will hold the chrysalis securely whilst fastened against a branch, or hanging upside down from a leaf. In the case of those hanging upside-down, the caterpillar will turn its head up and form a J position. Whilst slowly condensing its body, the larva will form the outer layer of the pupa beneath its exoskeleton. (see Chapter 4) When the larva moults for the final time, the pupal skin is exposed beneath.

The shedding of the final skin can be completed in minutes but requires real physical exertion! The caterpillar can be seen jerking violently to release itself from the skin. The skin will be shed from the head to tail requiring the caterpillar to master a split-second release of the prolegs to flick the old skin away, before re-attaching itself securely into the silk pad on the branch. Once the barbed cremaster ( a hook at the end of the body) is fixed into the silk, it cannot be removed.

No matter how hidden, or camouflaged, the position they choose, all caterpillars face a time of great vulnerability. They are totally incapable of self-defence, or escape, as they shed their final skin and surrender to the metamorphic breakdown of all the caterpillar has formerly known.

It seems a biological mystery; a very strange act of nature, to peel one's skin back and then become vulnerable and defenceless in the pupal skin of the chrysalis. But, once again, nature reveals spiritual truths in a beautifully visual way. In our individual spiritual development it is common, at the stage of our counting the cost and surrendering to the Lord, to feel as if our fate is hanging from a single thread, with our lives turned upside down and about to go through some kind of meltdown! This is often accompanied by a feeling of unprecedented vulnerability. It can almost appear as if the Lord is deliberately making us weaker, rather than stronger, for the task that lies ahead. In reality, God is using these baffling times of pain and vulnerability as part of the process of 'spiritual circumcision' to bring us into the secret place of 'spiritual metamorphosis' from which we will emerge transformed, victorious, and set free from our old nature!

> "In him you were also circumcised, in the putting off of the sinful nature, not with a circumcision done by the hands of men but by Christ...."
> Colossians 2 : 11

# Spiritual circumcision

Both the Old Testament and the New Testament speak about circumcision as a requirement, but with different meanings. We need to understand the difference. Circumcision in the Old Testament was mainly - not exclusively - physical. In the New Testament, the emphasis was on spiritual circumcision. Initially, the rite was introduced by God in the days of Abraham and was intended to be the sign of the covenant God made with Abraham and his descendants. As such, the rite was to remain in force throughout succeeding generations, identifying the circumcised as belonging to the lineage of Abraham and making the keeping of God's commandments incumbent upon them. However, during their grievous, disastrous forty years of wandering in the desert – a divine judgement because of their unbelief and grumbling spirit – the rite of circumcision was neglected. A whole generation with the exception of just two men, Joshua and Caleb, failed to reach their Promised Land. Due to their rebellion, they perished in the wilderness.

A new generation of Israelites, who had only ever known an existence of restless wandering, now stood on the edge of Canaan under the command of their new leader,

Joshua. By trusting the Lord to help them cross the Jordan, they had shown that they were prepared to obey the Lord and move forward to fulfil their destiny and claim the Promised Land. They were now awaiting the Lord's commands, about to face the formidable Canaanite armies.

How would the Lord prepare them? Perhaps you would expect God to command them to eat good food to build themselves up and to come together as tribes to create a strategy and train for battle. Instead, Joshua received the following order from the Lord: *"Make flint knives and circumcise the Israelites again."* (Joshua 5 : 2)

Evidently, men of this generation had not been circumcised in childhood. But why reinstate circumcision at a time when the men needed maximum fitness and strength? Circumcision would seriously weaken them. They would be in considerable pain and vulnerable, unable to defend themselves if attacked. They would also need to rest after circumcision, thus delaying the start of the military campaign.

Why does God sometimes appear to weaken us, or bring us to our knees in pain, brokenness and contrition, when we most want to move on into spiritual maturity? Amanda and Roland Buys of the South African "Kanaan Ministries" teach that we cannot be effective warriors, holy unto the Lord, who can press through to the Promised Land, until we have been spiritually circumcised and taken the time to recover. Unclean (uncircumcised) soldiers are not eligible to enter the Promised Land.

Physical circumcision symbolized spiritual circumcision – a cutting away of the flesh, the old carnal life, In Joshua 5, the place of circumcision was given the name Gilgal which sounds like the Hebrew for "rolled away." The Lord said to the Israelites *"Today I have rolled away the reproach of Egypt from you"*. (v9) Egypt symbolised the land of slavery - the flesh. In our case, spiritual circumcision removes "Egypt", representing the world, the flesh and the devil, from our hearts. Even the caterpillar's final ecdysis can be viewed as its ultimate release from bondage to its old nature. In its determination to throw off the old skin completely, in order to avoid any deformity of the metamorphosis or obstacle to the later eclosion of the butterfly, the caterpillar will wriggle violently and even risk falling to its death. If we wish to develop effectively in our spiritual growth, we, too, must make every effort to ensure that our 'spiritual circumcision' is complete and that spiritual metamorphosis is not restricted in any way.

The Passover is always associated with Israel's deliverance from Egyptian bondage. When it was first instituted, the Lord insisted that no un-circumcised male should eat of it. On their arrival in the Promised Land, the Israelites first celebrated the Passover, immediately following the circumcision of the men. The very next day, they ate of the produce of the Promised Land. God changed their diet permanently. There was no further need of manna. The Promised Land was the land of milk and honey. Here again we see a remarkable similarity with the caterpillar's change of circumstances. Once the caterpillar commits to the process of metamorphosis, it will never eat the diet of the caterpillar again. As a butterfly, it will drink nectar – the sweet liquid used by the bees to make honey, known in fables as the drink of the Gods. It derives its name from the Latin "nectar" which in turn has its origins in the Greek word νέκταρ (néktar), presumed to be a compound of the elements nek- "death" and -tar "overcoming". What a testimony to the diet of the spiritually mature - the Word – who in overcoming death himself, won eternal life for us and made us also those who overcome death!

A final thought. A man can be circumcised only once. Once he has been circumcised, there is no turning back. Similarly, once the caterpillar has rolled back its final skin and entered into the chrysalis mode, there is no turning back! The process of becoming the imago - the adult butterfly - has begun. In the same way, when we yield to 'spiritual circumcision' done by the hands of God, it is a sign of our commitment to pursue spiritual maturity wholeheartedly for the rest of our days.

*No one experiences complete sanctification without going through the burial of the old life. Death means you stop being. You must agree with God and stop being the intensely striving kind of Christian you have been. Has there been a point in your life which you now mark as your last day?*     Oswald Chambers

"I want to know Christ and the power of his resurrection an
the fellowship of sharing in his suffering, becoming like him
his death, and so somehow to attain the resurrection"
Philippians 3 : 10,11

Monarch larva (Danaus
plexippus) jerking from
side to side to shed its
final skin and reveal the
pupal skin

© William Zittrich

© William Zittrich

© William Zittrich

No-one pours new wine into old wineskins ... New wine
must be poured into new wineskins.   Luke 5 : 37-39

The wonder of metamorphosis

© William Zittrich

Therefore, we do not lose heart. Though outwardly we are wasting away, yet inwardly we are being renewed day by day. For our light and momentary troubles are achieving for us an eternal glory that far outweighs them all. 2 Cor 4:16-17

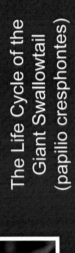

# The Life Cycle of the Giant Swallowtail (papilio cresphontes)

# *Found*

*Amazing love,*
*now what else shall I need?*
*Your name brings life*
*It's more than the air I breathe*

*My world was changed*
*When your life you gave for me*
*My purpose found*
*And all that you want for me*

*And I've found myself in you, Lord*
*And I've found myself in you*

*So take me to a place*
*Where I can see you face to face*
*All I wanna do, all I wanna do*
*Is worship you*

By Dave George

# Chapter 8

# Chrysalis: Intimacy with God
## The Beauty and Pain of Metamorphosis

*Love slays what we have been that we may be what we were not. St. Augustine*

The chrysalis is perhaps one of the most vulnerable, yet fascinating, aspects of nature. Within the secrecy of its hidden chambers, the caterpillar - an earthbound, often frightful-looking, wormlike creature - is transformed into a beautiful, delicate, winged insect. The biological process that enables this awesome metamorphosis is nothing short of a miracle. Without wishing to overwhelm you with a complicated scientific explanation of the workings within the chrysalis, I ask you to ponder over the following sentences and marvel at the amazing transformation of the caterpillar. If God performs such an amazing work of metamorphosis in the life of a wormlike creature, will he not work all the more wondrously in our hearts to bring forth new creations unveiling the glory of Christ as we are transformed to reflect his likeness?

The chrysalis stage could easily be mistaken as a time of dormancy and inactivity because, to the outside world, the pupa seems lifeless. However, it is far from that. The chrysalis is a place of great change and this change requires a tremendous amount of energy. (The chrysalid of the Monarch species, for example, has been shown to lose nearly half its weight using up fat to metamorphose.) The importance of the caterpillar's appetite now becomes apparent. Larvae store fat and nutrients for conversion into the adult parts, and for energy to carry them through this non-feeding pupal stage. The genes for change have all been held in the caterpillar since emerging from the egg but have lain in wait whilst the caterpillar prepared itself to be physically capable of such a change.

Metamorphosis is a combination of two processes – histolysis and histogenesis. They take place simultaneously and one is dependent on the other. The first is the breaking down of the caterpillar and the latter, the creation of the butterfly. Within the first few days of being enclosed in the pupal skin, the caterpillar disintegrates into a rich fluid media which is then carried by the open blood system to the forming adult tissues. This catabolic process, breaking down complex molecules into simple ones, is called histolysis. Conversely, the building up of the adult butterfly is an anabolic process called histogenesis. This means that body tissues are synthesized from food. The miniature wings, which began to develop even within the larva before it shed its final larval skin to reveal the pupal skin and so become the chrysalis, can now be seen on the outside of the pupa. The outer layer of the chrysalis contains the cells which will become the future wings of the butterfly. They undergo rapid cell division (mitosis) and absorb the rich nutrients. As they develop, the wings are in a compressed format. When the butterfly emerges (eclosion), they will be gradually inflated to their full size. This outer layer – the pupal skin - also contains the cells which will become the legs, antennae, proboscis and spiracles (air breathing holes) of the future butterfly.

Within the chrysalis lies a truly breathtaking discovery. Mr. Jules Poirier, in his book, "From darkness to light to flight" describes his amazement on performing a form of micro-surgery on the chrysalis of Monarch butterflies, to discover that although most of the internal parts of the caterpillar are all turned into a green fluid within several hours, the heart of the caterpillar is retained intact. A tiny 0.1 inch diameter red heart is to be found beating within the golden crown region of the Monarch chrysalis.

The length of time spent as the chrysalis varies between the different butterfly species and also depends on the time of year. Some butterflies will spend several months as the pupa. However, most species spend eight to fourteen days in the chrysalis stage. In the case of the Monarch butterfly, there are few visible changes within the chrysalis for up to six days. Then on the seventh day, eyes and antennae appear. By the eighth day, the entire nature of the caterpillar has undergone change. Its heart has been enlarged; it has developed seeing-eyes, a new nervous and tracheal system for breathing, and a digestive tract suited to the future liquid diet of the adult butterfly. Nothing has been added to the chrysalis from the outside. The butterfly has been brought forth solely from the former caterpillar.

Prof. Lincoln Brower of Sweet Brier College, VA describes the totality of the transformation in the following way: *"(the imaginal disks) ... start growing really rapidly and differentiating into the different tissues, so that literally the entire internal contents of the caterpillar---the muscles, the entire digestive system, even the heart, even the nervous system--are totally rebuilt. It's like you took your car, a Ford,into the shop and left it there for a week and it came out as a Cadillac."* He goes on, *"It truly is a miraculous biological process of transformation."*

## Spiritual transformation

Do you long for 'spiritual metamorphosis' - to see your nature as magnificently transformed as that of the caterpillar? I certainly do! Oswald Chambers once said that we need to come to the point where we are "sick to death of ourselves" – in other words, to so desire change that we are prepared to die to self, take up our cross and follow the Lord. I need my nature to be so changed that, like the caterpillar, my habitat, vision, behaviour and even my life purposes will be totally altered as a result. Metamorphosis, therefore, brings me great hope for it speaks of a Creator-God who is in the business of total transformation! David, the Psalmist, said that all creation speaks of the glory of God. The breathtaking process of metamorphosis – both in the natural world and in the spiritual sense – is a powerful testimony to the redemptive power of God. Coming from the combination of two Greek words "meta" - form - and "morpho" – to change, the word "metamorphosis" signifies a change in character or form. The same creative power that transforms the caterpillar lives and works within us - in the form of the Holy Spirit. By the miracle of regeneration and the process of sanctification, God transforms our characters into his likeness. *"I will sprinkle clean water on you and you will be clean; I will cleanse you from all your impurities and from all your idols. I will give you a new heart and put a new spirit in you; I will remove from you your heart of stone and give you a heart of flesh. And I will put my spirit in you and move you to follow my decrees and be careful to keep my laws."* (Ezekiel 36 : 25-27)

Our weaknesses, doubts and fears can be converted into the fruit of the spirit (Galatians 5 : 22,23) thus changing our nature to bless, restore and heal others – the very promise held out through the butterfly vision to all those who will obediently surrender themselves into the hands of the Creator-God.

How does such a personal transformation come about? As ever, there is a process to undergo and, although wondrous, it can, at times, pass through apparently disheartening phases. A closer study of the chrysalis leads to some valuable insights to prepare us for, and encourage us through, our times of transformation - our spiritual 'chrysalis' seasons.

## Changing my perspective of the chrysalis

When I first began to write this book, I imagined that Chapter 8 would discuss God's use of seasons of darkness and trials to bring his people to spiritual maturity in the various aspects of their lives. The demise of the caterpillar in the isolation of the chrysalis seemed to speak of being so comprehensively broken down that I presumptuously equated it to a painful trial. Discovering that the word "chrysalis" has its roots in the Greek word "golden" (due to the golden brown colour which some pupae have), I immediately thought of the gold mentioned by the apostle Peter in his first letter and believed I had the framework of my chapter. After all, are we not told many times in Scripture that to become spiritually mature and to develop a Christlike character, the Lord will, at times, permit us to go through suffering, just as our Lord was made perfect through suffering? (Hebrews 2 : 10)

"These (trials) have come so that your faith of greater worth than gold, which perishes even though refined by fire – may be proved genuine and may result in praise, glory and honour when Jesus Christ is revealed."

1 Peter 1 : 7

Perhaps, many of you would have jumped to the same conclusion as I did. Indeed, possibly for that very reason, the majority of us struggle to surrender ourselves to 'spiritual metamorphosis.' We fear that the redefining process of our character, and of our faith, will automatically mean a "fiery furnace" of tragedy, sacrifice, sickness or suffering of some kind. Blinded, somehow, to the ever-mounting evidence to the contrary in my own life-story, I erroneously assumed that any spiritual transformation or growth would always require being stretched by God through chastisement and trials. However, I have begun to learn that just as this is not true of normal, loving relationships, neither is it true of our walk with the Lord.

# The power of love

We develop as healthy, relational beings, acquiring interests and exercising certain skills, through spending quality time with our parents, family and friends. The presence, encouragement and interest of our loved ones are all paramount to sustaining a relationship of mutual respect, love, obedience and, where appropriate, sacrifice. We mature, and modify our behaviour, as we learn to value those we love. We do not principally grow through testing and punishment. I believe that this also applies to our relationship with the Lord. That is not to say that God just spoils us; a wise Father would never imagine that a strong and loving relationship with his children depended on frequent gifts, or an absence of discipline and challenge. The Lord does allow times of trial and testing in our lives to develop perseverance and to push us onto maturity. However, there is a greater instrument of transformation, that of intimacy with the Lord. The cultivation of a consistent, personal walk with the Lord is foundational to spiritual growth towards maturity. It is often said that we become like those with whom we spend the most time. The Lord's desire is for us to spend such quality time with him that we start to take on his wonderful attributes. These 'golden' times of intimacy with God are the key to genuine change. We shall not be changed at core through stoical duty, gritting our teeth trying to be a nicer person. There needs to be a greater inspiration for change. We need to fall in love with our Saviour and strive for Christlikeness out of passion and devotion. Peace and victory over our old nature are to be found through total fulfilment and satisfaction in him. The Lord has the restorative power to transform us through intimacy with him and for intimacy with him. All praise be to our God that he longs to change us in this way. He bids us to come to him humbly, in faith, entrusting ourselves to the transforming power of unconditional love.

> "Whoever has my commands and obeys them, he is the one who loves me. He who loves me will be loved by my Father, and I too will love him and show myself to him."
>
> John 14 : 21

# My testimony

During the year that the Lord set me aside to write this book, I began to understand the metamorphic qualities of intimacy. I experienced, in the privacy of my own room, the joys and pains of the redefining process of intimacy – a form of spiritual 'histolysis and histogenesis' which entailed being broken down and then built up again. I was not brought to a place of suffering, or to any experience that would normally be considered a trial. Instead, God gave me an opportunity to rest in him, providing an intimacy which broke down my old approach to life and then changed me, just as intimacy within human relationships changes us. Never in all my life had I so much time alone to read, pray, write and listen to the Lord for his message. This may sound idyllic to some of you. I still remember the days when I was a very busy school teacher and, as such, could only wistfully dream of such an opportunity. To the outside world, perhaps it did seem like a time of dormancy but, as with the chrysalis, it was anything but dormancy internally. Yes, it was a great privilege; a time of refreshment and restoration. However, I must also testify that change, even through intimacy, is not easy. In these times of closeness with the Lord, I confronted the reality of my spiritual health, coming face to face with both the cost, and the great gain, of true discipleship. Jesus said that those who love him keep his commands. Obedience is, therefore, key to intimacy with the Lord. Intimacy requires a commitment that challenges our motives and dedication to the relationship. Intimacy also demands that the relationship be exclusive. The Holy Spirit will not abide where sin abides. He is grieved when we set our affections on the things of this world. I found myself challenged to be totally satisfied with "my beloved". The troublesome, oft-arising suggestion that true fulfilment is to be found elsewhere had to be confronted and fought off. Therefore, the initial stages of intimacy with the Lord can be unsettling for, as my title quotation of St. Augustine states, *"Love slays what we have been that we may be what we were not"*. Intimacy beautifies you, stretching you to bring forth your best but, as is often the case with beauty treatments, there must firstly be a stripping away of the old skin!

"Our God is a jealous God."

Exodus 34 : 14

If an intimate relationship with the Lord is to be the necessary spiritual setting for our metamorphosis, let us return to the chrysalis and consider it through the lens of intimacy.

## The beauty and the pain of intimacy
## – the challenges of the chrysalis

The chrysalis stage is a time of miraculous change. No less so is that very special time in our lives when the Lord calls us into a secret place of intimacy with him. There will be a beautiful outcome but the process requires faith through a disturbing period of transformation. This is the bitter-sweet twist to the season in the chrysalis. As such, the time of metamorphosis can be baffling. Intimacy is not a trial, in the commonly understood usage of that word, just as the process of metamorphosis is not a trial in the life of the caterpillar. Developing intimacy, both with the Lord and with others, should be a joyful, life-changing, beautifying and redefining process. However, intimacy also entails exquisite forms of pain and discomfort during the process of dying to our old egocentrism. Intimacy, therefore, can cause fear, demanding a greater step of faith and commitment than we may ever have taken before. If we wish to grow spiritually, there are no other routes to be taken. We must be prepared to be totally changed.

As the Lord calls me into a deeper relationship with him, I am becoming very aware of my hesitancy to be totally changed, to die utterly to myself. Can I really say, with the

Apostle Paul (see Philippians 3 : 8), that I count all other things as rubbish compared to the opportunity to know my Lord intimately and dedicate my life to him? Am I prepared to die to all my self-centred desires in order to take up the Great Commission and work alongside my Lord 'gathering in the harvest'? I feel the pain of disappointing my Lord when my heart clings to other claims on my life and my affections. I wrestle with unsettling thoughts when, at times, I find myself desiring the things of this world to the point of being held back from a genuine surrender of my will in wholehearted commitment to the Lord. I fear that, if I procrastinate, the Lord will even hand me over to these desires that I might experience their emptiness in comparison to the treasure of intimacy with him which I am not yet prizing as I ought.

Nowhere is the call to intimacy more beautifully depicted than in the Song of Songs. The Lover calls his Beloved to come, longing to spend time in secret with her, away from the world, before becoming united and tending together the vineyards, which seem to symbolize the potential fruit of their relationship. *"Arise, my darling, my beautiful one, and come with me."* (Song of Songs 2 : 10)

However, although she recognises his love and devotion to her, her initial speeches reveal an immature and self-seeking love on her part. She seems afraid and not able to commit; she runs off to hide. Once alone, she realises she does long for him and, in calling to him, finds he is right beside her. She becomes his bride but again, at the very moment when he comes to be united with her in physical intimacy, she hesitates and gives excuses to avoid opening the door. It would then seem that the Lover decides to leave for a while to give her time to realise her desire and need for him.

He wanted to be more than someone walking on the periphery of her soul, someone she was convinced would step on her and use her.

'Redeeming Love'- Francine Rivers

Establishing intimacy with the Lord may involve times when the Lord will allow us to go through apparent separation from him. As the lover of our souls withdraws from us, our hunger for his return may seem unbearable, but the appetite being created is only to make the coming feast more delectable! Our problem is our slowness to comprehend how worthy he is of our love and to make our decision to commit the rest of our lives to him.

Do you yearn for the anointing of the Holy Spirit, the Spirit of love, yet remain cynical and afraid of God's motives for intimacy with you? Sometimes, we are afraid to let the Lord change us through intimacy because we find a kind of security in the lifestyle to which we are accustomed. How we need to remind ourselves that God is love and, as such, is utterly trustworthy. Whatever changes he brings into our lives, they will always be for our long-term good and for his greater glory. We are loved and, if we wish, we can choose to embrace it and move forward, putting the past behind us. Developing any intimate relationship requires faith, trusting the other person with your heart and your life. Metamorphosis through spiritual intimacy is by God's design. Becoming more like Christ is the objective of developing a closer relationship with him. As Jesus is the author and perfecter of our faith (Hebrews 12 : 2), so, as the lover of our souls, he initiates the process of our developing intimacy with him and perseveres when we show signs of lukewarmness. I am amazed at the gentleness and patience of the Lord. At times, I give him reason to be offended by doubting his great faithfulness but, in love, he patiently allows me time to resist Satan's lies and embrace the truth.

What will your decision be? Will you trust him and drink deep of his love or will you die of thirst by the side of the fountain? Be not deceived; you will never evade change by avoiding intimacy with God. The Bible warns that those who choose not to walk in an intimate relationship with the Lord become the slaves of the alternatives they choose. Learn a lesson from the caterpillar. If, within the chrysalis, the caterpillar does not become a butterfly, it never becomes anything better. Assuming it does not become a victim of an outside predator or natural accident, it will either bring forth its parasitic host – a wasp or a fly - or it will mutate due to disease, turn dark and die, sometimes spilling out a putrid, black liquid if it is broken open.

> I die of thirst by the fountain.
> 'Charles d'Orleans

Likewise, we are never in a neutral place. Consciously or unconsciously, we are always in the process of being shaped by the priorities and company we choose. Whatever idols we choose, we become like those idols. Intimacy with false gods will change us into their likeness just as intimacy with the true and living God changes us into his likeness!

## No pain, no gain

The butterfly comes forth from the transformation of the caterpillar. Great changes have to occur in the chrysalis to bring such a transformation about. Similarly, you cannot experience intimacy with anyone, much less with God, and expect to remain unchanged. You will be challenged and broken down through intimacy with the Lord. God will be dismantling your old nature as he does that of the caterpillar, in order to bring forth the Christ within you that men may see a reflection of the Creator's glory.

Intimate relationships bring personal faults and weaknesses of character to the surface. Whilst living alone, it is much easier to deceive ourselves that we are good-natured, not given to impatience or selfishness. However, in a close relationship, we are much more likely to see our imperfections. Intimacy ensures that everything matters. Intimate relationships can, therefore, seem like a trial, at times. When we love the person with whom we are building a relationship, the sorrow over our failings troubles us. It should trouble us enough to persuade us to deal with our selfishness or whatever else hurts those we love.

> "If we claim to be without sin, we deceive ourselves and the truth is not in us. If we confess our sins, he is faithful and just and will forgive is our sins and purify us from all unrighteousness."
>
> 1 John 1 : 8,9

A growing intimacy with the Lord heightens the awareness of our un-Christlikeness and the regret over our mistakes. Mercifully, the promptings of the Holy Spirit are not intended to condemn us but to point us to the place of restoration. As we become sensitive to the desires of our loving Saviour we must adjust our behaviour and attitudes accordingly. We must recognize that offending God with our sins blocks our spiritual growth, just as unresolved issues, or indifference to the feelings of others, hinder intimacy. If we stubbornly refuse to repent in any area of our lives, we too will remain unchanged. By contrast, genuine repentance leads to change. Confession is never easy and asking for forgiveness can be even harder but sufficient grace is given when we are obedient to the Lord. What's more, it is the only way to ensure intimacy survives – the kind of intimacy which is a prerequisite of spiritual growth.

J. I. Packer in his book, "A Passion for Holiness," calls this process of spiritual growth through repentance, "growing downward in order to grow upward". This mirrors the truth contained in the chrysalis; as we break down, we are rebuilt. Metamorphosis is only possible through this challenging process of histolysis and histogenesis.

## The new you

It is perhaps all too easy to look at the disadvantages of intimacy, especially in the context of fearing a deeper commitment to the Lord. However, the great hope of the chrysalis is that histogenesis always follows histolysis! The ultimate aim of the disintegration of the old is to bring forth the new creation. In our relationship with the Lord, we do not die to self for the sake of dying but in order to come alive! Similarly, intimate, loving relationships do not show up our weaknesses to crush us but to improve and enrich our lives, and bring forth the best in us. When we are struggling with the thought of being broken down that the indwelling Christ might be manifested, we must constantly remind ourselves of histogenesis! The origin of our fear of commitment needs to be exposed and resisted. Satan will do his utmost to persuade you that total surrender to God will mean giving up so much that life won't be worth living. Far from being impoverished by our surrender to Christ, we enter into the promise of abundant life.

In our human relationships, no matter how loving, we will be adversely affected by the faults of our loved ones. In our relationship with the Lord, however, we are alongside one who loves us perfectly. We will not suffer due to any mistake or weakness of character on his part. He will not manipulate us, nor will he destroy our personality. The God who created the universe "ex-nihilo" refashions the existing components of the caterpillar, rearranging them in an infinitely better way, to bring forth the beautiful butterfly. There are no added components from outside the chrysalis. Indeed, what is broken down is used to create the energy and the matter for the rebuilding process. Most beautifully of all, the heart of the caterpillar is not "broken"; in fact it is enlarged. The heart of the chrysalis is the life source of the

> There is a God-shaped vacuum in the heart of every man which cannot be filled by any created thing but only by God, the Creator, made known through Jesus.
>
> Blaise Pacale- 'Pensées'

metamorphosis process. Similarly, God is taking everything which is already within you, created in his image, and bringing forth from you something of great beauty and purpose, whilst still retaining the very heart of who you are. Your intimate relationship with him is the heartbeat of your spiritual metamorphosis. *"For he chose us in Christ before the creation of the world to be holy and blameless in his sight. In love, he predestined us to be adopted as his sons through Jesus Christ in accordance with his pleasure and will - to the praise of his glorious grace."* (Ephesians 1 : 4-6)

Christlikeness is holiness. God exhorts us to be holy as he is holy. Holiness must, therefore, lead to ultimate fulfilment. Otherwise, we imply that God himself is missing out on something by being holy. Unthinkable! God is supremely majestic in his overflowing joy, beauty and creativity – the God of all hope and peace. God, therefore, does not call us to be holy - through death to self - in order to restrict our enjoyment of life but to bring us into the abundance and enjoyment of his own. *"Man's chief end is to glorify God and enjoy him forever."* (Westminster Shorter Catechism) The opportunity to be transformed through this life-changing, intimate relationship is possible only because *"God made Christ to be sin for us, so that in him we might become the righteousness of God."* (2 Corinthians. 5 : 21) Rather than fear the workings of God in our lives, let us recognise the price paid to enable spiritual metamorphosis and entrust ourselves to its transforming process.

# Facing enemies whilst in the chrysalis

Butterflies are the fruit-bearers so to speak; they pollinate and they lay the eggs for the next generation of caterpillars. However, they must obviously first pass through the chrysalis to reach this stage. Their "enemies" prevent many from ever reaching the chrysalis, but those who survive become even more vulnerable to attack once cocooned in their pupal skin. Apart from camouflage or, in occasional cases, the ability to make a clicking sound to deter predators, the pupa is almost defenceless. Parasites, as we gleaned from Chapter 5, can also hijack the chrysalis from within.

Similarly, Satan attacks us at all stages of our spiritual walk but never more so than at the intimacy stage – the prelude to a fruit-bearing life and ministry. Because the stakes have been raised, he must focus his greatest effort of deception on those who have the potential to do him most harm. Satan will perceive a greater level of vulnerability when our desire for spiritual transformation heightens the challenges of surrendering our self-centred lives. The closer we want to walk with the Lord, the greater the potential for frustrated expectations as our desires and good intentions come against the limitations of our character and faith. There will be some wonderful times of harmony and fulfilment as, standing firm on the promises of God, you successfully keep your spiritual enemies at bay. However, there will also be times when you will have to fight for intimacy. The very decision to commit oneself to a special bond with the Lord can give rise to feelings of vulnerability which are very disturbing. It may seem your relationship is coming unstuck rather than bonding. Challenging circumstances, or inner struggles, can cause doubts, arguments and pretensions to rise up within you, like parasites attacking the heart of the chrysalis. Take courage from the story of the caterpillar. Surely, the initial stages within the pupa seem anything but hopeful. But we know the outcome. Commit yourself to the process – rest in the faithfulness of your Creator-Redeemer – and, in time, you will witness the amazing metamorphic qualities of intimacy, not just in your relationship with God but with others too.

# Bound to be Free

The caterpillar is bound within its pupal skin. Once in the chrysalis, the transforming caterpillar cannot do anything to escape - not even from danger, never mind from transformation!

Intimate relationships can sometimes make us feel trapped. Although, deep in our hearts, we feel a love for the other person, we can sometimes question whether we have done the right thing in committing our lives to that person or whether the relationship will ever be totally fulfilling.

Similarly, at certain stages of our walk with the Lord, we may feel as if we are being hedged in. These negative emotions have to be conquered with truth and fact, just as they do in our human relationships. We have to trust that the Lord's love is an unchanging love and that his ways are always, ultimately, for our good, given that he knows us better than we know ourselves. This is especially true when the relationship seems to be taking us beyond our comfort zone. It can be an anxious time when, having moved deeper into our relationship with the Lord, we realise that the old way of life will never satisfy us again and yet seems to have been replaced only with an uncomfortable sense of isolation from the world around us and uncertainty about the future.

Have you ever felt God has dismantled the structures of independence and security in your life? Has the Lord taken away the desire and the satisfaction of the old way of life, yet apparently left you in the dark, hedged in, waiting to be given a vision and to be set free to find true fulfilment in doing his purposes? I talk to myself as much as to you – do not despair; this is the season of the chrysalis. Let me explain further.

# Hidden for Protection

The miraculous process of metamorphosis, like the development of an embryo, is hidden from the eyes of the world. The chrysalis is opaque until the day before the butterfly emerges. Furthermore, the chrysalis is usually as hidden away as possible, camouflaged against, or on the underside of leaves and stalks. Pupae can also be found covered by leaves on the ground or partially buried underground. Some species hide in dark, undisturbed places such as lofts and roof eaves whilst within the pupa. Secreted away from the world, experiencing great changes hidden in the darkness, the caterpillar undergoes its metamorphosis alone.

Times of spiritual transformation are also usually away from the limelight. Intimacy, by definition, requires a time of being set apart from others. It is not developed in crowds! Your 'spiritual chrysalis' time may also, initially, seem like a dark and lonely place. You may not even be familiar enough with the Lord to be altogether comfortable with this new level of intimacy. Sometimes, he has to draw us away from others, or from the normal confines of our lives, to develop a closer walk with us. This may seem baffling, but it is ultimately for a wonderful purpose. He knows, as he does for the caterpillar, that nothing we may leave behind will compare with that exclusive time with the Lord, the subsequent transformation and the new life ahead.

The book of Hosea holds a wonderful promise for those who are lured into isolation with the Lord: *"Therefore I am now going to allure her; I will lead her into the desert and speak tenderly to her. There I will give her back her vineyards and will make the Valley of Achor a door of HOPE. There she will sing as in the days of her youth as in the days she came up out of Egypt. "In that day," declares the Lord, "you will call me 'my husband'; you will no longer call me 'my master'. I will remove the names of the Baals from her lips; no longer will their name be invoked."* (Hosea 2 : 14-17)

Intimacy and haste are incompatible. A quiet spirit takes time to cultivate. From within what appears to be a place of darkness, a Valley of Achor, there will be a doorway of hope. However, just as the caterpillar does not metamorphose overnight, neither can we expect an immediate transformation. In the book of Hosea, the adulterous wife does not immediately forget her other loves and recognize her desire for her husband. It takes time apart. Intimacy cannot be established through short cuts. There must be a willingness to invest in the relationship consistently over time. Intimacy needs to be kept alive: a strong and loving marriage must be constantly energized through spending quality time together, even when that feels more of a discipline than the natural desire of courting days. The same is true of our relationship with the lover of our souls. The more time we spend with the Lord, the more fresh will be the memory of his presence, and the less attractive competing false promises of fulfilment will become. One of the Jewish customs, established by law in the days of Moses, illustrates beautifully the importance our Creator-God attaches to intimacy and fruitfulness in marriage. The custom provided a very practical measure for ensuring the continuing development of intimacy. Deuteronomy 24 :5 reads –

*"If a man has recently married, he must not be sent to war, or have any other duty laid on him. For one year he is free to stay at home and bring happiness to the wife he has married."*

Surely the Lord attaches no less importance to the intimacy of our relationship with him and will provide special times in our lives for that intimacy to be cultivated. A willingness to devote time sacrificially is the one prerequisite. Those who demonstrate their unwillingness, and their preoccupation with lesser pursuits, automatically disqualify themselves from ever experiencing the all-sufficiency of Christ or finding fulfilment in an intimate relationship with Christ.

# Nurturing Intimacy

A secret of nourishing intimacy lies within the caterpillar. The caterpillar doesn't just pass from its egg stage into the chrysalis stage but passes through five instars where, through its voracious feeding stages, it is preparing for the non-feeding chrysalis stage. During the time as a chrysalis, it is not dependent on outside sources of nourishment - food or drink. It uses its inner store from its days as a caterpillar to provide the energy for change.

The Lord regularly encouraged the Children of Israel to take the time to recall, and celebrate, the Lord's faithfulness to them along their journey. They were to look back and remember the lessons they had learnt along the way. We, too, must recognize the value of commemorating what the Lord has done for us. The ensuing worship and gratitude will provide nourishment and enable us to sense and believe in the regeneration going on in our lives, even in dark and uncertain times.

If we desire to grow into an intimate relationship with the Lord, we must be utterly convinced of the importance of consistently reading and retaining the Word of God in our hearts. Through the Scriptures we come to know the heart of the Lord – what greatly pleases him, and what offends and saddens him. The living force of these scriptures will also come into play as the recreating power of histogenesis. As self is broken down, God's word will speak to us of his promises to rebuild us. We shall be encouraged by his covenant to us as his bride. Just as married couples make vows to each other so the Lord has bound himself into a covenant with us. He is committed never to leave us and never to forsake us (Hebrews 13 : 5). We can be confident that he who began a good work in us will carry it on to completion (Philippians 1 : 6). Recalling these promises will inspire and strengthen our commitment to him.

God's Word is the place of affirmation where he nurtures an intimate relationship with us by speaking of his love for us. In response, by spending time in his presence and in his Word, we affirm our desire for intimacy with the Lord, looking to him to fulfil our need to love and to be loved. This is not to say that a Christian needs nothing and no-one but the Lord. However, intimacy with the Lord will be hampered if we commit "emotional promiscuity" - looking to other means of meeting our emotional needs - especially as a form of compensation when we have allowed our relationship with the Lord to go "stale" through sin or indifference. As in all intimate relationships, there may be times when we feel distant from the Lord. This usually indicates some sort of problem. If, instead of working it through with the Lord, we circumvent these uncomfortable times in our spiritual life by seeking fulfilment elsewhere, we shall never develop intimacy with him.

In my own experience, nurturing intimacy with the Lord has often been a question of self-discipline, rather than of natural and passionate love. I have had to make constant decisions to adjust my natural reactions and go to the Lord for all my needs. It is all too easy to turn instead to a quick, but temporary, relief of the need for fulfilment, whether through other relationships; work; hobbies; food; addictions; daydreaming; or escapism through the media. Having flirted with the world's distractions and attractions, finding our fulfilment in an intimate relationship with Christ, in the routine of our day-to-day lives, may seem like hard work. The "good fare" of his Word may taste bland after the quick "sugar fixes" of the world but, if we persevere, his Word will become sweeter to us than honey and his presence more precious than anything the world can offer.

## Losing one life to find another

A caterpillar has no option but to leave his old life behind as he goes into the chrysalis to develop into a butterfly. Intimacy, too, requires an initial loss. For an intimate relationship to be developed successfully, both parties must be prepared from the outset to sacrifice their independence. There must be a realistic, pragmatic approach to the unavoidable changes and adjustments required by the union of two personalities. Marriage, especially in the early stages of raising a family, is a completely different way of life. Intimacy with God requires no less a change in our priorities and lifestyle. When we consider deepening our commitment to the Lord, Satan will play heavily on what we stand to lose, but we must remember that what we leave behind is as inferior to what we gain as the caterpillar's way of life is to that of the butterfly! In Philippians 3 : 13b - 15, Paul writes, *"Forgetting what is behind, and straining towards what is ahead, I press on towards the goal to win the prize for which God has called me heavenwards in Christ Jesus. All of us who are mature should take such a view of things."*

Spiritual maturity is directly linked to the determination to leave the past behind us and press deeper into God. This will need a time of readjustment. No doubt, some married couples, after the initial honeymoon period, pass through moments of missing their former single way of life, despite knowing in their heart, they desire this change towards greater intimacy! Accepting the loss of an independent, self-centred lifestyle and self-reliance requires a death to self and a commitment to togetherness. Intimacy does not allow for selfish ambition. It requires compromise and sacrifice. This will affect others too. If you choose to spend more time with one person, others will inevitably lose out for a while. Your decision to develop intimacy with the Lord, to minister to him, may be difficult for others to accept. It may challenge their relationship with him. When Mary Magdalene sacrificially anointed Jesus with her precious oils, the disciples looked on very uncomfortably. It was a great act of intimacy; anointing was usually done by the priests (See Exodus 30), not by former prostitutes.

Personal sacrifice is a concept we naturally shrink from but anyone aiming to walk as Jesus walked must come to terms with it. The nineteenth century pioneer missionary, C. T. Studd, famously said, *"If Jesus Christ be God and died for me, then no sacrifice can be too great for me to make for him."* In our relationship with the Lord, it will take sacrifice and discipline to set time aside, away from the world, in the 'chrysalis' - so to speak, in order to continue to mature. Metamorphosis, from caterpillar to butterfly, is a once-in-a-lifetime occurrence but, in our spiritual lives, I believe we shall experience this whole maturing process at different times, in varying areas of our lives, for different reasons.

# Vulnerability

The process of metamorphosis involves a period of great vulnerability in the chrysalis. Vulnerability is also an indispensable part of spiritual growth. We have already looked at vulnerability at the hands of our enemies but, now, in contrast to involuntary exposure, we turn to a deliberate form of vulnerability – opening your heart and learning to trust others. Intimacy, in terms of a closer walk with the Lord, is not compatible with self-sufficiency. We must trust him to protect us as we surrender to his will for our lives, believing he always has the best intentions towards us. In my own life, vulnerability suddenly became far more than a mere concept when I committed myself to develop intimacy with the Lord, living by faith whilst I wrote this book. I was no longer in control. I could not rely on a regular salary to provide my daily needs or meet my financial obligations. I was not even able to distract myself, or meet my needs, through hobbies and new relationships. The Lord, "the altogether lovely one", was asking me to devote myself exclusively to him. I was to learn to trust in him to meet ALL my needs. Not only did he prove himself faithful in this respect but, by using fellow Christians to supply my needs, the Lord transformed my vulnerability into an instrument of blessing as relationship bonds were enhanced.

> Vulnerability is the pathway to intimacy.
>
> Rick Warren

Honesty about ourselves, in our relationship with the Lord and in our relationship with family and friends, is part and parcel of the kind of vulnerability which makes intimacy meaningful. Worship lacking in honesty is self-deception. The Lord requires worship to be offered in spirit and in truth. (John 4 :23,24) Within human relationships, any unwillingness to lay bare the heart and be completely honest with one another, is enough to undermine intimacy.

Over time, I have learnt that I need to express my vulnerability more, to show my need of others and their presence. If I always seek to cope in my own strength, trying not to show my frustration or needs, that is not true intimacy. If we can not acknowledge our weaknesses, doubts and needs, then our loved ones will never feel needed. More likely, they will feel under-valued as if we do not trust them to be able to help us. Our coping mechanisms become a barrier to true intimacy – a barrier to being known and loved for who and what we truly are.

> "An honest answer is like a kiss on the lips."
>
> Proverbs 24 : 26

When in pain, physical or emotional, we often express ourselves, both to God and to our friends, in a way which is more real and honest. This changes our relationships. There is a sense of really knowing someone when you know where they are hurting. Isn't it the case, that when others share their testimonies at church, we usually feel so much closer to them afterwards? When we all wear our masks and handle our lives independently, we wilfully isolate ourselves from one another. If we want to be known, and truly know others, we have to be prepared to be honest about our weaknesses and our doubts. The Lord longs for the same honesty in our relationship with him for the irony is that often, when we are wrestling with God, the depth of our walk with the Lord is unveiled as never before. The heart of our loving Saviour is full of compassion and love towards us, but so often we do not turn to him because of our questioning cynicism. If we would only honestly bring our doubts and fears before the Lord, we would enhance our intimacy with him, not hinder it. Stoicism - putting on a brave face - is often erroneously believed to be evidence of greater faith and, therefore, of a close walk with the Lord. In reality, humble honesty is the most reliable characteristic of genuinely close relationships. The Lord delights when we cry out to him, "Lord, please draw closer to me because I need you!" If we try to suppress our disappointment when we imagine the Lord has withdrawn from us, we are not being honest. Remember, we are his bride, his beloved. Would it be normal, in a loving marriage, to try to keep it all together constantly and never acknowledge weakness or express emotion, for fear that your partner would think less of you? It is no less abnormal to act as though we can cope without the Lord's grace, wisdom and strength. The apostle Paul said in his letter to the believers in Philippi, *"I can do all things through Christ who gives me strength."* (Philippians 4 :13) Can you imagine Paul ever saying, or even giving the impression, that he could do all things in his own strength and without the Lord's enabling?

The Psalmist set us a wonderful example of how to pour out our hearts to the Lord. Sometimes, a cry from the heart may start as an emotional, even angry, accusing outburst. That is better than sentimental platitudes and can be used by the Lord to draw us into a closer relationship with him. The humility to receive as we express our needs is fundamental to the growth of intimacy. There is, of course, no way in which we can repay all that we have received from the Lord. Perhaps the greatest lesson to be learned from our times of extraordinary vulnerability is how to receive the unconditional love of the Lord without feeling we must find a way to reciprocate.

## Beauty shines through

As the newly-formed butterfly comes to its final hours within the pupal skin, the chrysalis becomes transparent and the beautiful colours of its wings begin to shine through. Evidence of an amazing transformation becomes more and more apparent.

The spiritual chrysalis stage is a season of transformation through intimacy with God. Stripped of our old nature and clothed in Christlikeness, we will no more be able to contain the glorious wonder of our metamorphosis than can the newly-formed butterfly. Although for a time the changes may be hidden, the beauty of Christlikeness will begin to shine through our lives. We will be called to break forth and let his glory be unveiled, through the testimony of the changes wrought in our lives.

# Higher Ground

I'm pressing on the upward way,
New heights I'm gaining every day;
Still praying as I'm onward bound,
"Lord, plant my feet on higher ground."

Refrain
Lord, lift me up and let me stand
By faith on heaven's table-land,
A higher plane than I have found:
Lord, plant my feet on higher ground

My heart has no desire to stay
Where doubts arise and fears dismay;
Though some may dwell where these abound,
My prayer, my aim is higher ground.

I want to live above the world,
Though Satan's darts at me are hurled;
For faith has caught the joyful sound,
The song of saints on higher ground

I want to scale the utmost height
And catch a gleam of glory bright;
But still I'll pray, 'til heaven I've found
"Lord, lead me on to higher ground."

Johnson Oatman, Jr
(1856-1922)

# Chapter 9

# Eclosion

## Times of Struggle and Waiting bring Beauty and Strength

*Growing up involves new birth, healthy pain and a gradual autonomy. Philip Yancey*

As the day of eclosion draws ever closer, the chrysalis starts to change in colour as if testifying to the amazing internal changes happening within the opaque pupal skin. The majority of butterflies spend, on average, no more than two weeks within the chrysalis. However, some species do hibernate over winter, hidden away in their pupa. When the day of emergence dawns, the chrysalis finally becomes translucent, revealing the miracle of metamorphosis as the magnificent colours of the butterfly peep through.

The eclosion of the new butterfly is not without struggle. From the first signs of movement as small splits appear in the pupa, the butterfly will wrestle to push open its formerly protective covering and free itself. Finally, the butterfly emerges head first. It is then thought to swallow air in order to inflate its body and push open the splitting pupal skin. As it emerges, it carefully swings itself to hang its wings downwards, usually still clinging onto its now empty pupal shell. When the butterfly first emerges, its wings do not look beautiful but rather somewhat crumpled, wet and stunted. The wings need time to expand. In the case of those species which have pupated on branches, the butterfly must be able to hang high enough that the tips of its wings will not touch the ground whilst, and when, they are fully expanded. If the butterfly does not have enough space for its wings to expand and dry, they will not develop properly and the butterfly will not be able to fly. If the butterfly falls to the ground on eclosion, it may well suffer irreparable damage and, subsequently, die.

Following eclosion, there is a process of preparing for flight. This process may take several hours. Before we consider the important relevance of this preparation, let us first dwell on the lessons we can learn from the struggle to emerge.

## Birth Pains

The struggle out of the chrysalis is the last obstacle which stands between the former caterpillar and its final stage of maturity. The chrysalis has played an important part in its life cycle, but the butterfly must now leave its protective shell; if it does not, it will die. There is only enough food and energy stored within its body for a limited amount of time and for a certain amount of growth. There comes a point where it has outgrown its pupal skin. It must make the struggle into a new stage of life if it is ever to fulfil its potential as the adult butterfly.

Growing up, as Philip Yancey says in his book, "Reaching for the Invisible God", will involve new birth, healthy pain and a gradual autonomy. The process of spiritual maturation is no different. It may involve acquiring new skills, taking on new roles or, indeed, laying a role down and embracing change. It is rarely easy to make such transitions, especially if they mean a new habitat; a new way of living; a new calling to a different role with challenging responsibilities. But the Lord is a God who is always encouraging us to press on to spiritual maturity - to experience both its freedom and fulfilment. He does not want us to stay where we can no longer grow or, worse still, to reach the end of this life without having reached the point of our greatest potential.

> I wonder what an ordinary baby would do if it had the choice. It might prefer to stay in the dark and warmth and safety of the womb. For of course it would think the womb meant safety. That would be just where it was wrong; for if it stays there it will die.
> C. S. Lewis

There is a wonderful objective behind every part of the maturing process - the periods of transformation and the times of transition - in our lives. The Lord is equipping us to carry out his purposes. No less is true of this final transition for the butterfly - the struggle out of the chrysalis. The butterfly does not struggle in vain. The struggle plays an important role in the ultimate stage of bringing forth a healthy and strong butterfly. What a tragedy it would be if the newly-formed butterfly, having survived the dangers of its caterpillar days and the vulnerable process of metamorphosis, failed to complete the struggle through the pupal skin to begin its life on the wing! The maturing process, and the beautiful new attributes of the butterfly, would all be wasted.

## The struggle is beautiful

The butterfly must be left to wrestle its way out of the chrysalis in its own way and in its own time for it is this very struggle which builds up the muscles within the wings to enable the butterfly to fly! If one were to cut the chrysalis open with a pair of scissors, in an attempt to release the butterfly quickly from its struggle, it would lead to a tragic end. The butterfly would more than likely fall to the ground, unprepared for the accelerated release. This would result either in its death or severe damage to the wings, leaving the butterfly vulnerable to its predators. Even if the butterfly survived the unnatural eclosion, it would never be able to fly - its wings now lacking the necessary muscles. Without the capacity to fly, a butterfly is unable to find food in the form of nectar, unable to pollinate flowers effectively and, most importantly, unable to find a mate and reproduce. Therefore, all the God-given purposes for a butterfly's life will have been thwarted by a naively cruel "act of kindness".

The eclosion of the butterfly, therefore, offers us a beautiful piece of wisdom – do not resent, or try to avoid, the struggles of transitional stages in life. The struggle is something of beauty in itself. The struggle to maturity brings strength and splendour. In our impatient, modern world we seem reluctant to accept that struggles are part of the maturing process. Instead, we usually try to circumvent any form of struggle. We justify the alternative quick-fix decisions and solutions with the excuse that God surely wants us to be happy and there's nothing to be gained by delay and struggle. However, in so convincing ourselves, we miss the important role of trials in our lives. Elisabeth Elliot writes in her book, "Passion and Purity": *"If all the struggles and sufferings were eliminated, the spirit would no more reach maturity than would the child. The Heavenly Father wants to see us grow up."*

A misguided prayer for a trouble-free life from God is the equivalent of praying to remain spiritually immature. Scripture confirms that the Lord allows struggles in our lives in order to bring us to maturity, with strength of character and hope. (Romans 5 : 3-5) Struggles often accompany new birth. This is evident not just in the "birth" of the butterfly but in many aspects of creation. God allows us to struggle through the birth of a new season in our lives, or a new ministry, in order to produce perseverance in us to last the lifetime of our work for him. Pushing against great resistance develops strength and a deeper awareness of the spiritual warfare that surrounds our personal walk with the Lord, and our ministry. It also increases our understanding of the greatness of the Lord and what we can achieve with him working through us, especially through challenging circumstances. These outcomes are characteristics of spiritual maturity.

Rather than whinging and pleading with God for a quick remedy to all our problems, let us adjust our perspective and see struggles as opportunities to look for God's purpose. God is not being cruel in allowing us to struggle. Indeed, we have learnt that an untimely, unnaturally quick release from our struggle may land us straight on our heads! God will use every form of struggle, even day-to-day tasks that might seem like mere drudgery, to bring strength to our 'wings'.

"And we know that in all things God works for the good of those who love him, who have been called according to his purpose." Romans 8 : 28

I remember a film from my childhood called "The Karate Kid". It tells the story of a young school boy who finds himself the victim of high school bullies. Determined to stand up for himself, he asks a Japanese man living in his apartment-block to teach him karate. The training begins with the task of washing an old car and then polishing it by hand. At first, the young boy is somewhat resentful, thinking the old man is just using him to do his dirty work. Later, however, his wise teacher reveals to him that this task was all part of building up the necessary muscles for karate, and acquiring a spirit of discipline and diligence.

No-one enjoys times of struggle. However, God shapes us through those struggles. Larry Crabb unfolds the mystery of God allowing struggles and disappointments in his excellent book, "Shattered Dreams - God's unexpected pathway to joy". With candid honesty, he reveals the questions thrown up by his own life experiences. He describes how God has brought him to a place of realisation that the hard seasons in life are all part of God's answer to our deepest need - to know God more, becoming more spiritually mature day by day. I quote a larger than usual passage from his book without apology.

*The exact centre*

*"We will encounter Christ as our best friend when shattered dreams help us become aware of ...*

> *...the strength of our desire to know Him*
> *...how unworthy we are to receive even the smallest expression of kindness from Him*
> *...the intensity of His longing to draw us into satisfying, soul-thrilling intimacy with Him and His Father (which, in His mind, is the greatest blessing He can give, and worth whatever it takes for Him to give it, and for us to receive it.)*
> *...the unparalleled value of intimacy with Him.*

*The evangelical church has made a serious mistake. For years we've presented Christianity as little more than a means of escaping hell. Knowing Jesus has been reduced to a one-time decision that guarantees the chance to live in a perfect, pain-free world forever. Christianity is about going to heaven, but that's not the centre of Jesus' kindness to us. Nor is it the opportunity to lead fulfilled, meaningful lives now. Returning to our Maker's manual and following biblical principles to make our marriages work and our kids turn out well and our bank accounts comfortably bulge is not God's plan for our lives. We've shrunk Christianity into a neat little package full of blessings that, if opened, will empower us to feel good now, and feel even better in the next life. Jesus revealed His highest dream for all his followers when in prayer He defined the true abundant life in these words: "that they may know you, the only true God, and Jesus Christ, whom you have sent." (John 17 : 3)*

# Cruel to be kind

Spiritual maturity can be the miraculous outcome of struggles in our lives if we entrust every situation into God's hands and allow him to teach us. For this reason, it is important to recognise that difficult times will not always arise as consequences of mistakes and misjudgements or always be an indication of a failure on our part. As such, struggles should not be automatically seen as something to be rebuked, either in our own lives or in the lives of others.

Our response to trials will indicate our estimation of intimacy with God. We are told to rejoice in our trials knowing that they can lead to spiritual maturity. Obviously, Scripture is not asking us to wish trials upon ourselves, or upon those we love. Rather, we are given the opportunity to develop the faith to be overcomers! Although trials and difficult transitional times will be an inevitable part of life, we are asked to embrace them, cherishing spiritual maturity over and above a struggle-free and pain-free life.

Admittedly, this is incongruous with the modern-day obsession of avoiding all pain. Some people will spoil their children rotten rather than see them struggle for anything. We grapple with the notion of God allowing us to struggle because we are as loath to see those we love having to struggle, as we are to have to face trials ourselves. But God prizes our spiritual maturity over our care-free "happiness". Would we rather see our family and friends in a closer walk with the Lord, having wrestled through some trials, or would we rather cut them free of the struggle even if this thwarts God's maturing process? Any intervention to release the butterfly from the struggle of eclosion would prove disastrous. Equally, we may well do more harm than good by interfering in the spiritual maturing process of others. With the best of intentions, we may be tempted to cushion others from pain in all sorts of ways. For instance, on seeing a friend go through a time of change, it would be a mistake to do our utmost to keep everything the same for them. Perhaps we know someone who is facing an uncomfortable challenge from God. Instead of speaking the truth in love to encourage them to address the relevant issues in their life, we choose comforting words to give the impression that everything is fine. This is not to say that we are never to help people but, rather, to remind us to pray for wisdom before we presumptuously step in and "help". We need to ask the Lord to show us through his eyes what is happening in the bigger spiritual picture and not to make the assumption that all struggles are to be rebuked. The Lord may well reveal to us his purpose behind the trial.

Hitherto, we may have been baffled by the fact that the closer people are to the Lord, the greater the struggle they seem to face when they want to move into a deeper level of ministry. Perhaps we assumed that the advanced stages of developing spiritual maturity would be easier than the earlier stages of our spiritual lives. We learn from the eclosion of the butterfly that the struggle has the God-ordained purpose of producing the necessary strength for its ultimate role as the mature adult butterfly. God does not want to propel any of his children into a new role without their having first developed the necessary fortitude and attributes. God is not in a hurry.

Accepting the struggles of eclosion is only one part of breaking forth and moving towards maturity. The butterfly, even after emerging from its pupal shell, faces a further time of development and waiting.

## Time to spread your wings

*"Wait for the Lord and keep his way." Psalm 37 : 34a*

When the butterfly first emerges, it has a rather ugly, wet appearance. Its wings appear small and shrivelled. It is not yet ready to fly. To attempt to fly immediately would be to risk falling headlong into the dirt below, back to where it had been crawling in its old form as a caterpillar.

The butterfly must now wait whilst a two-part process takes place. As a butterfly cannot fly until the wings are unfolded to their full size, a newly-emerged butterfly needs to spend some time expanding its wings. This process consists of pumping haemolymph (the blood-like substance of insects) from its abdomen into its wings along the veins. This gives strength and structure to the wings. It must then wait for the expanded wings to dry sufficiently in the sun. During this time, the butterfly is extremely vulnerable to predators. Some butterflies' wings may take hours to dry while others dry relatively quickly.

While its wings are drying, the butterfly expels a reddish, blood-like, nitrogenous fluid called meconium. This occurrence has given rise to fables that it rains blood when many butterflies hatch out simultaneously. Meconium is in fact the waste by-products of the process of metamorphosis. As the butterfly can't defecate during its transformation in the chrysalis, all the waste products accumulate. Consequently, most new butterflies and moths will, therefore, excrete excess dye after hatching. It will not always be red; this fluid may be white, orange, or in rare cases, blue.

During this time, the new adult butterfly can also be seen doing several things to prepare for its new way of life. It will stretch, roll and unroll its long proboscis - a long double straw-like tube for sucking nectar from flowers. It will also exercise the wing muscles, preparing itself for flight. Once the wings have been stretched and dried, the butterfly is ready to take to the air for the first time. If it is cold, windy, or rainy the butterfly will wait for more favourable conditions. From the moment of its emergence from the chrysalis, the butterfly must spend regular periods in the warmth of the sun to acquire the necessary energy for a life of flight and purpose.

# Wait on the LORD

There are many lessons to be drawn from the butterfly's preparation for flight and a new life. It is all too easy to make the mistake, when having once made our commitment to serve the Lord wholeheartedly, of thinking we must be immediately engaged in ministry! We can become stressed about our next steps as if we have to forge our own identity and future. Furthermore, we can be too quick to launch out and do whatever comes along first. Ephesians 2 : 8 makes it clear that the Lord has gone before us and prepared good works for us to walk in. Therefore, it is imperative that we set time aside to listen for the Lord's direction. Beware of launching yourself into ministry too hastily in your own strength. Remember the grim consequences for the butterfly who tries to fly before his wings are adequately prepared.

**Waiting is the hardest work of HOPE.**

*Lewis Smedes*

As we saw in Chapter 7, even at the threshold of our 'Promised Land' - after transforming works of the Holy Spirit in our lives - there may be times of waiting; times of healing; times of gaining the necessary 'wing-span' and strength to go out and use those newly-given gifts. Allow yourself time. Time spent in worship is time well spent. Stay in the Son's presence until you are strong enough to 'fly'. The Lord makes all things beautiful in his time! (Ecclesiastes 3 : 11) Even our Lord Jesus told his mother that he must not begin his ministry until the appointed time. Mary saw the immediate need but did not understand the importance of the Lord's timing in any and every aspect of ministry. Jesus needed to explain that his time had not yet come. (see the story of the wedding at Cana in John 2 ) The disciples, too, were told that they must wait in Jerusalem until they had received the gift of the Holy Spirit, the power that would enable them to fulfil the Great Commission. Acts 1 : 4 and 8 reads, *"Do not leave Jerusalem, but WAIT for the gift my Father promised ........you will receive power when the Holy Spirit comes on you; and you will be my witnesses in Jerusalem, and in all Judea and Samaria, and to the ends of the earth."*

We must not forget that Jerusalem was a place of great fear for them at this stage, and yet, in obedience to the Lord, they waited. They did not go back to their old life; they had made that mistake after the crucifixion. They stayed hidden away in an upper room. It was not idle waiting. They WAITED on the Lord in prayer. They knew their purpose already; they were going to be witnesses, not just to their city and surrounding areas but also to the ends of the earth. But they had no clue as to how this would come about. As mostly uneducated men, they must have felt terribly insignificant and ill-equipped for such a task. They had gone through a dramatic, life-changing three years which culminated in the momentous events of the crucifixion and the resurrection. This emotional rollercoaster must have left them exhausted. Within the space of three days, they were delivered from the depths of despair and stunned by the glorious resurrection appearances of Jesus. For a period of forty days, he continued with them teaching about the Kingdom of God and preparing them for the Great Commission of worldwide evangelisation. However, in order to engage in such a daunting task, the disciples needed something more than teaching. They needed supernatural power – the power of the Holy Spirit. Accordingly, the Lord Jesus insisted that they wait in Jerusalem until they were baptized in the Holy Spirit.

"For by grace you have been saved, through faith; and that not of yourselves, it is the gift of God, not as a result of works so that no one may boast. For we are HIS workmanship, created in Christ Jesus for good works which GOD prepared beforehand for us so that we would walk in them."

Ephesians 2 : 8 (NASB)

Waiting is not an optional, or needless, part of the process of the Lord; it prepares the butterfly for flight. During its time of waiting, it becomes what it needs for its purposes – able to fly! It also has the opportunity to practise rolling and unrolling its new proboscis, which it will use to drink nectar – a process which will result in pollination, a key component of a butterfly's blessing to its environment. It is comforting to note that in the grand scheme of things, the butterfly has to wait only a short time in comparison to its time on the wing - but it still has to WAIT. As Isaiah 40 : 31 explains, strength will rise as we wait upon the Lord.

There are times in our lives when we perceive by the Spirit that the Lord is telling us to wait. At other times, circumstances simply oblige us to wait. Neither situation should be allowed to cause frustration. Faced positively, waiting time can be put to good use. Does it not provide the opportunity to spend more time in prayer, worship, Bible study and scripture memorisation? We all have certain skills which need perfecting by practice if we are to serve the Lord effectively. The same lessons we learn earlier on in our spiritual walk apply now. We must accept the Lord's timing. Even if we know our calling and the destiny promised to us (as we saw in Chapter 2 through the story of Joseph), and even if we feel ready for the new challenge, we must wait for our wings to expand and for God's time for us to 'fly off the branch' and begin that work. John Ortberg in his book, "If you want to walk on water, you've got to get out of the boat", explains that psychological studies of children have proven that the ability to wait well is a test of maturity. The wait for the start of your ministry may well be your first test of spiritual maturity!

Waiting, however, is much easier said than done and many fail to persevere. Even Abram and Sarai were not without fault. (Genesis 16) We ourselves may be severely tested in this realm. The interval between eclosion and flight is very short for the butterfly, but this is not always the case for us in real life. We may have many times where we are required to wait for long periods of time, often with unanswered and difficult questions. God is more interested in who we are becoming as we wait. The discipline of waiting is character-forming. As the butterfly emerges from the chrysalis, it has all the necessary attributes to fly, but it must wait until they are ready to be used. We, too, may have been given all the necessary gifts to fulfil our purpose for the Lord yet still need to wait to be mature enough, or strong enough, to use them. Like the apostles, we may be asked to await the Lord's anointing.

> "May the God of hope fill you with all joy and peace as you trust in him, so that you may overflow with hope by the power of the Holy Spirit."
>
> Romans 15 : 13

Looking at the bigger picture of our earthly lives, our whole spiritual walk with the Lord can be defined as waiting - waiting for the second coming of the Messiah. Jesus tells a parable of ten virgins who take their lamps and go out to wait for the return of the bridegroom. (Matthew 25) They each have oil lamps. But take note – those who are wise are depicted as those who have anticipated and prepared for a long wait! They bring extra oil with them to sustain them.

# Fear of Flying

There are two possible dangers associated with the waiting period in our lives and they are opposites. One is the danger of losing the confidence to launch into a new ministry. The opposite is to give up hope of ever seeing the Lord open the right door of opportunity for ministry. Satan may try to use these times of waiting to taunt us and to undermine any words of prophecy that may have been spoken over our lives. He will cause us to question God's promises in his word. However, my own experience has shown how gracious the Lord is during the waiting season. Just as the butterfly instinctively clings to the empty shell of its former skin, the Lord may well give us something familiar on to which to hold whilst he is preparing us for 'flight'. I certainly found myself needing and appreciating the comfort of familiar surroundings as I wrote this book. Even so, we must remain mentally prepared to let go of such things as soon as 'our wings' are ready. Procrastination at this point would only increase our vulnerability.

Caterpillars are relatively fragile creatures and, as such, may not survive a fall of even quite a short distance. Therefore, for the sake of survival, caterpillars have been known to cling so tightly to a surface that their prolegs have ripped off when forcibly removed. In contrast, the new butterfly learns to do the exact opposite. It lets go of the branch to which it was clinging and takes to the winged life. Having benefited from the waiting time to readjust and to exercise flight muscles, it can now remove itself from harm's way.

Just before a butterfly takes off for the first time, it appears to tremble. It is highly doubtful that this trembling is due to fear but who would blame the newly-emerged butterfly if it were? After all, it has no prior knowledge, or experience, of life on the wing! However, all the God-given instincts for life as a butterfly are already in place, just waiting to be exercised. The butterfly will not have to learn by trial and error how to warm its wings; how to feed on nectar; how to pollinate flowers; how to mate and where to lay its eggs. We, too, may experience a curious trembling of our spirit as we face the uncertainty of letting go. Indeed, the Lord will often ask us, like the butterfly, to let go before we have had any experience of what lies ahead. When the time comes to let go, remember that it is better to trust the Lord than to put our confidence in our previous experience! We are required to trust the same Creator-God who knit us together as wonderfully and as intricately in our mother's womb as he did the butterfly within the chrysalis. He knows our needs. He knows our limitations. He knows the purposes he has for us and he will enable us.

# Don't get grounded

The vulnerability of the butterfly during this period of time between emerging and take-off is of critical importance in our understanding of this season in our spiritual lives. In waiting times, there will be many enemies eager to put a swift end to our new-found maturity. Satan knows the potential of our 'flying ability' and will try to 'ground' us in any way possible.

In his short parable, "The Dream Giver", Bruce Wilkinson tells the story of "Mr. Ordinary" of "Ordinary Land" who receives a dream from the Lord. As he pursues that dream, he has to face the fear of leaving his old way of life behind. He encounters border bullies. We too may encounter border bullies. Obstacles to the ministry the Lord has given us may seem like the terrifying giants of Canaan, reported by the fearful spies to the people of Israel as they stood on the border of the Promised Land. Indeed, border bullies may even take the form of actual people in our lives - some with apparently good intentions - who will try to persuade us to come back to "ordinary" land. Not everyone will perceive the changes in our lives positively, especially if uncomfortably challenged by our decisions. We will be surrounded by many more "land-lovers" than those desiring to rise up and soar with the Lord. This may lead to unexpected areas of discord in our lives which seem to cast doubts on our new way of life, delaying our 'take-off'. In such times, we may need to ask the Lord for his confirmation of our ministry. Above all, we must recall the promises of the Lord and make an active choice to believe that the Lord would not bring us to the edge of the Promised Land – the start of a new life –and then fail us!

If discouragement coming from other people fails to overwhelm us, Satan will try to resurrect old enemies - old desires, or bad habits – to tempt us back to our old nature, away from a new life of service and intimacy with God. We become particularly susceptible to such wiles when we subconsciously fall into discontentment. Perhaps we expected to emerge from the 'chrysalis' ready to 'fly' immediately. Now, looking at 'wet, stunted wings', we question if somehow our growth in the 'chrysalis' went wrong, and if we will ever be able to 'fly'. Did we go through this whole maturing process just to receive useless 'wings' and be left feeling somewhat crumpled and incredibly vulnerable? Discouraged at the wait, and ever aware of our enemies, we may begin to suffer from resentment at the uncertainty of our situation - wondering if we were ever meant to be here in the first place, and whether it wouldn't just be easier to go back to the old way of things!

We look around and see the soil covered with land lovers and believe this is why we were created. God has called us up – up off the ground – and invited us to rise up in His Metamorphosis of Love.

"Teen Street" flyer - "Metamorphosis"

## My testimony

What could be worse when given a dream than finding that one does not have the faith to pursue it? When Moses led the Children of Israel out of Egyptian bondage, they set out on their journey to the Promised Land with great rejoicing and excitement. But, when the time came to trust God to give them the victory over their formidable enemies, their rejoicing and excitement evaporated. They quickly forgot what the Lord had done for them in the past and began to grumble, succumbing to a complaining and critical spirit. Unbelief took possession of them with the result that they spent the rest of their lives wandering aimlessly.

As I write this chapter, I am within sight of completing this book. After leaving the ship, MV Logos 2, the Lord gave me the courage to avoid the search for security in my previous profession. He has provided wonderfully for me over the last twelve months in order for me to realize the vision of this book. Nevertheless, I am aware that a new battle lies ahead of me – that of overcoming negative thoughts such as, "Your writing is not good enough", "Your book will never be published" and "You have wasted a year of your life". Ironically, there is an even darker struggle to overcome my fears of potential success. Am I capable of fulfilling this new ministry, believing the Lord will sustain me, inspire me and help me bring forth fruit for his kingdom? In my insecurity, I am, like the Israelites under Moses - in danger of forgetting what the Lord has already done, and falling prey to two very bitter enemies of mine, self-pity and discontentment.

I have experienced his faithfulness on many occasions, especially when coming out of my comfort zone to travel to other parts of the UK, as well as overseas, to share my message, despite my struggles with loneliness and irritable bowel syndrome. Will I now be paralysed by the fear of 'flight' and the new challenges ahead of me?

In the novel "Redeeming Love" by Francine Rivers, the rescued prostitute, 'Angel', is coming to the point of realisation that she is changing and her life is changing, beyond all recognition. She is falling in love with her rescuer and husband, Michael, as well as getting very close to the neighbouring family. She becomes intensely afraid of this new state of vulnerability. Michael sees her struggle to let go of her old cynicism and to fight off the urge to run back to her old way of life. He tries to offer an explanation of her fear.

*"You're a bird who's been in a cage all your life, and suddenly all the walls are gone, and you're in the wide open. You're so afraid you're looking for any way back into the cage again." He saw the emotions flicker across her pale face. "Whatever you choose to think now, it's not safer there, Amanda. Even if you tried to go back now, I don't think you could survive that way again."*

*He was right. She knew he was. She had reached the end of enduring it even before Michael claimed her. Yet, being here was no assurance. What if she couldn't fly?*

The Lord has brought me so far in my spiritual journey from where I was a few years ago. I, like 'Angel', have also reached a place of vulnerability where I have to lean on him far more and trust that he loves me and will do right by me. For this reason, I, too, often feel as if I am looking back at the "cage" – the "cage" of familiarity, security and 'normality'. I wonder if I should go back to my old career. I look at those who are married with children, have a home of their own and an apparent structure to their lives, and I question whether I have made the right choices in my life thus far. They seem so settled and I seem so rootless. But, as Michael tells 'Angel', even if I tried to go back, I would not be able to "survive" that way again. I, too, had reached the end of enduring it. I had become increasingly aware that I risked becoming far too comfortable and self-reliant, prioritising worldly ambitions over spiritual growth. I longed for a deeper experience of God. Now that the Lord has given me that opportunity, it would be no comfort to turn my back on it for fear of not being able to 'fly'. Rather, I need to surrender myself to his love and keeping and embrace a new way of living.

## Low-level living is over

The life of a butterfly is far superior to that of a caterpillar! In the same way, a spirit-filled, spiritually-mature believer has an enhanced quality of life which is all too absent from the life of a lukewarm, half-hearted believer. Once the caterpillar undergoes metamorphosis, a return to the lifestyle of a crawling wormlike creature is unthinkable. The glorious wings of a butterfly not only transform its appearance but also give it access to a whole new dimension of living. The same is also to be anticipated and experienced by those whose passion for God lifts them above and beyond the realm of spiritual complacency. A spiritual life without vision makes few demands upon us but equally will be lacking in meaningful purpose and satisfaction. However, once we have been given a vision, with corresponding revelation and insight, we have to accept that the days of 'low-level living' are over. We need to ask the Lord to give us the courage to 'fly off the branch' and live according to our new nature, abilities and perspective. Failure to do so will rob the Lord of the glory due to him.

At the aptly-named "New Wine" 2008 conference, Bill Johnson spoke about the disappointment the Lord feels at the slowness of his disciples to understand this concept. Speaking from Mark 6, he showed how the disciples reacted in panic to the storm on the lake because their hearts were hardened regarding the miraculous feeding of the five thousand. Even after Jesus came to them, walking on the water, only Peter dared to believe that as a maturing follower of Christ, and with the Lord's consent, he could cross over the threshold of the supernatural. Having miraculously fed five thousand men, women and children by obedience to Christ, Peter now believed it would also be possible to walk on water. In the light of this understanding, Peter stepped out of the boat to walk on the water to Jesus. Yes, he panicked when he sank to 'low-level' thinking again, seeing the impossible circumstances into which he had taken a step of faith. Nevertheless, he experienced something as miraculous as an earthbound caterpillar becoming a creature capable of flying.

Bill Johnson concluded that one purpose of miracles, and miraculous provision, is to reveal to us the awesome might of God. Miracles also issue a call to us to live as those who believe that the same mighty Christ dwells within us, his wonders to perform. Our spiritual metamorphosis and subsequent empowerment by the Holy Spirit are miracles. If we fail to see this or, like the disciples, harden our hearts to miracles, then Jesus will have to turn to others to be his 'fruit-bearers'. Instead of joining him in his ministry, taking up our new authority and renewed nature to work alongside him, we shall live our lives in a permanent state of vulnerability going from one crisis, or fear, to the next. We will find ourselves constantly calling to the Lord to merely play the role of rescuer in our lives, instead of master. The Lord will provide and protect - just as he did for the Israelites - but we ourselves will miss so much! We will spend our lives 'crawling' when we could be 'flying'.

# Prepare for take-off

What should we do when the struggle to emerge, and the subsequent delay, leaves us paralysed with fear, clinging on to the 'branch'? How should we prepare ourselves for the vulnerability of this season? *"Be self-controlled and alert. Your enemy the devil prowls around like a roaring lion, looking for someone to devour. Resist him, standing firm in the faith, because you know that your brothers throughout the world are undergoing the same kind of sufferings."* (1 Peter 5 : 8 - 9)

We must acknowledge the reality of our vulnerability and take action to defend ourselves by putting on the full armour of God. (Ephesians 6 : 10-18) Praying at all times in the spirit, let us take heart, reminding ourselves of the Lord's promises over our lives.

Waiting on the Lord's timing requires us to keep ourselves as cleansed vessels through which the Holy Spirit can flow to bring glory to God. We must, therefore, be on guard against any temptation which may lead to a break in our communication with the Lord.

Once a butterfly is ready to fly, a simple breath of air will lift it off its leaf. It is that sensitive. Through prayer, and the reading of his Word, we must become as receptive to the Lord's prompting in our lives. With his gift of discernment, we must make the distinction between hesitation and wise caution. It is also advisable to seek the wise counsel of spiritual leaders and trustworthy mentors. There is a clear difference in Scripture between occasions when God tells his people to be still, stand firm and see the deliverance he brings (Exodus 14 : 13, 14) and those occasions when he urges them to press forward into the battle, for the victory has already been granted to them. (Joshua 10 and 11) As clearly demonstrated in the battle of Jericho, sometimes there is a time for prayerful silence, 'encircling the enemy', until the Lord gives the sign to press forward. However, as and when God gives us the authority, we must advance without delay to meet our enemy head on. As David faced Goliath (1 Samuel 17), he immediately went on the offensive. The Lord had prepared him for many years for his future role as protector of the Lord's people. There had been a time to wait – and later, significant times of waiting would test David again - but now was the time to put a swift end to Israel's humiliation by silencing the taunting Philistine. David claimed his victory confidently even before Goliath was dead!

Once the preparation time is complete, it is time to get on with the work the Lord has given. Not all butterflies have the same lifespan. However, none can afford to waste a day and will only delay flight when adverse weather conditions make it impossible. They have very clear objectives to fulfil, not least reproduction, in order to ensure the survival of the species.

## Time to Move On

The Lord does not bring a butterfly out of its chrysalis - after such a process of growth, death and transformation - only to leave it sitting on a leaf, vulnerable to its ever-present enemies! What would be the use of wings, and a new body designed for a new life of beauty and purpose, if the butterfly never left the empty chrysalis shell behind? The butterfly is brought forth to fulfil its unique role in the natural world. Accordingly, at the appropriate time, the wonders of its design and function are displayed for the glory of God. The designer and creator of the butterfly is the Creator-God who also became our Lord and Saviour. Rest assured, he will not bring us through all the challenges of maturation only to leave us powerless, immobilised by fear or lack of direction. Let us pray that he will bring us through the 'eclosion' stage at "such a time as this" in order to fulfil his role for us in these challenging days. In the Lord's timing, and through his sustaining power, may we unveil the glory of the Lord Jesus Christ before a needy world as by faith we 'spread our wings' and 'fly' in the freedom, and responsibility of spiritual maturity.

What a blessing

What a blessing, what a priv'lege!
Called of God a royal priest.
That this glorious, holy office
I should bear, though last and least.

Chorus
All the building of the Body
On the priesthood doth depend;
Ever praying in the spirit
I this office would attend.

If I keep this royal calling
Under Thine authority,
Priestly duty thus fulfilling,
Then the church will builded be.

Now the church is but the priesthood;
Thus the priesthood formed we need;
When the priests are knit together,
Then the church is built indeed.

Through the church's degradation,
Saints this office desolate;
Through the weakness of their spirits
Preaching doth predominate.

Most are leaning on the message
And the preaching emphasize,
Yet neglect the priestly praying
And their spirits' exercise.

Deal with me and make me balanced,
As in preaching, so in prayer;
Leading others oft in praying,
As Thy Word I too declare.

Only serving by our praying
Will our spirits mingled be;
Stressing prayer as much as preaching-
Thus the church is built for Thee.

Witness Lee
(1905 -1997)

# Chapter 10

# Imago
## Butterfly Days: Glory Unveiled

*"Now the Lord is the Spirit, and where the Spirit of the Lord is, there is freedom. And we, who with unveiled faces all reflect the Lord's glory, are being transformed into his likeness with ever-increasing glory, which comes from the Lord, who is the Spirit."*
*2 Corinthians 3 : 17,18*

There is something glorious about butterflies as they flutter busily around our gardens and countryside. Our appreciation of their beauty is surely even greater now as we have learnt of the process through which they have prevailed to be brought to maturity from the immature phase of the caterpillar to the imago – the reproductive adult.

The main aim of this book has been to impart to Christians the aspiration to pursue spiritual maturity. The butterfly stage is not to be seen as one of spiritual perfection but as one of spiritual maturity. We must not excuse immaturity, and its limitations, by equating maturity with perfection and thereby renouncing it as unattainable. Let us refute the notion that we become 'butterflies', so to speak, only as we pass into the next life. We have the opportunity to experience that "Forgetting what is behind and straining towards what is ahead, I press on towards the goal to win the prize for which God has called me heavenwards in Christ Jesus. All of us who are MATURE should take such a view of things."
Philippians 3 :14,15a

transformation on earth. We shall never be sinless here but we are called to maturity - to its capabilities and corresponding responsibilities.

As we consider the life of the butterfly, let us take note of the many attributes that characterize its role as the mature adult and use these as prompts as to how we can live mature spiritual lives.

## Knowing your purpose

Butterflies seem to spend their days aimlessly flitting about, randomly landing on flowers and looking pretty. However, this is far from the truth. Most butterflies have a very short lifespan, averaging about two weeks. Hence they need to use their time wisely if they are to fulfil their role before they die. They live and fly around with one determined purpose; to find a mate and reproduce. The female must then find the appropriate environment and host plant to lay eggs before she dies, if the species is to survive. Living to this end, they unwittingly bless their environment and play their role in sustaining life. As they feed on nectar, they pollinate the flowers, ensuring the reproduction of seeds and fruits. In turn, these will feed animals and humans. Furthermore, butterflies bring much joy to those who observe them on the wing, working hard towards producing the next generation.

What a key lesson for each of us. Our time here on earth is fleeting. (James 4 : 14) Therefore, establishing our purpose and priorities is essential. The Psalms record the wise prayer of Moses: *"Teach us to number our days aright, that we may gain a heart of wisdom."* (Psalm 90 : 12)

We ought to be asking the Lord, with some gravity, to reveal the purpose of our personal lives so as to ensure we fulfil it. God is a God of order, not confusion, and he has a role for every individual. If we seek to order and control our own destiny, we might never discover our part in God's story. But, when we allow him the control of our lives, he delights in revealing that role to us. Clearly, for each one of us, the specific roles, tasks and countries to which the Lord will lead us will all be very different. Just as there are thousands of different butterflies that have unique lifestyles, habitats, colours and lifespans, God has created each of us with different talents to play a unique part in bringing the body of Christ to maturity and to the whole measure of the fullness of Christ. (see Ephesians 4 : 11-13)

However, from Scripture we know that each one of us is anointed with the same general calling: *"But you are a chosen people, a royal priesthood, a holy nation, a people belonging to God, that you may declare the praises of him who called you out of darkness into his wonderful light."* (1 Peter 2 : 9)

My niche - defined in biology as "the role any organism plays within its community"- has already been preordained by God. So has yours. We are called to be royal priests, ministers of the new covenant. Initially, the Lord chose the children of Israel to be a kingdom of priests (Exodus 19) intending for all the tribes of Israel to be represented in the priesthood by the eldest son of every family. However, due to the sinful behaviour of the people, God elected the tribe of the Levites - more specifically, the descendants of Aaron - to serve him as priests. (Numbers 3 : 12

"It was he who gave some to be apostles, some to be prophets, some to be evangelists, and some to be pastors and teachers, to prepare God's people for works of service, so that the body of Christ may be built up until we all reach unity in the faith and in the knowledge of the Son of God and become mature, attaining to the whole measure of the fullness of Christ."

Ephesians 4 : 11-13

and 8 : 18) They were to offer acceptable sacrifices to the Lord to seek atonement on behalf of the people. No other people were to assume this role – in fact, those who tried to perform the role of the priest without the anointing of God suffered the consequences. see the story of Saul (1 Samuel 13) and of Uzziah (2 Chronicles 26).

However, since the establishment of the new covenant, all believers made righteous in

God's sight by the atoning blood of Jesus have the opportunity to minister unto God as his royal priesthood, with Jesus Christ as our High Priest. We have been blessed with many spiritual blessings and attributes for this role and yet the concept of serving as royal priests seems alien to so many believers. One of the greatest obstacles to this calling is ignorance of what it signifies. There are many who know the verse in 1 Peter 2 by heart but cannot even begin to fulfil that role because they have little historical knowledge of the privileges and duties of the biblical priesthood.

At this point, you may well be asking how one of the main characteristics of our spiritual maturity – knowing and understanding our calling to serve as royal priests – can be compared with the life of the butterfly. As I studied the butterfly's life, I saw that there are many parallels to be drawn between the attributes and behaviour of the butterfly and that of the priesthood. As this role is so central to our maturing in our faith, yet so rarely taught, my prayer is that as you watch butterflies in your own gardens, these simple parallels might enlighten you and remind you time and time again how to minister to the Lord and to others as a royal priest.

# Waiting on the Lord

*"Blessed are those who dwell in your house; they are ever praising you. Blessed are those whose strength is in you ..." Psalm 84 : 4,5a*

On emerging from the chrysalis, the butterfly must spend time basking in the sun in order to dry out its wings. This is not a one-off fix for flight; it has to become a habit of a lifetime. They are cold-blooded creatures and so they must bask in the sun in order to gain the strength to fly. They need to be airborne to fulfil their purposes - pollination, mating and laying eggs. Therefore, they will take the time to be still each day and position their wings at the most favourable angle to the incoming light. They then transfer the heat to their thoracic flight-muscles, gently moving their wings up and down. If they are not disturbed, the butterfly may stay in the same spot for quite some time, to gain the maximum strength possible.

The Old Testament priests worked in different areas of the tabernacle and, later, of the temple. However, the principal duty of Aaron's sons and the Levites was to minister to the Lord. Over and over, the Lord reiterated that the priests were set apart to him. Under the old covenant, priests were the only ones who were permitted to enter the inner court. Three roles were given to the priests for this ministry. They portrayed images of constancy and communion. Firstly, they were to tend to the golden lamp stand every morning and evening to ensure that the oil never ran dry, keeping the lamps burning all night. The tabernacle lamp stand is a symbol of the presence of God's Holy Spirit (Revelation 4 : 5) as well as of Christ, the light of the world. Secondly, they were also responsible for the "Bread of the Presence" displayed on the tabernacle table and for the drink offerings – an apparent symbol of the communion service. Thirdly, they were to burn incense before the Lord constantly - a symbol of the prayers of the saints.

(Revelation 5 : 8) Whenever we refer back to the Old Testament tabernacle, we should remind ourselves that in all its intricate detail, it served as a shadow of the reality in heaven. (Hebrews 8 : 5)

From the first chapters of Genesis, we see that God is a relational God wanting to communicate and spend intimate time with his people. When the Lord died on the cross, the veil of the temple was torn in half from top to bottom - a striking display of the Lord's desire and power, through his ultimate atoning sacrifice, to open up the Holy of Holies to us all. And yet, so many of us have little understanding of the value of quiet intimate communion with the Lord, or how to minister to him. We often feel we are called to minister to others but overlook that, first and foremost, we are called to minister to the Lord. (Exodus 28 : 1) As a result, we burn out because we are mainly working amongst the people in 'the outer courts' instead of spending time in 'the inner court' and 'the Holy of Holies'. We need therefore to rediscover the true essence of the priestly role and the wonderful balance the Lord incorporated into their daily duties in order to give them the strength to serve as priests for the rest of their lives.

In fulfilling the roles ordained for them within the inner court, the priests were daily brought into a place of quiet and communion with the Lord. Just as the butterfly needs to gain strength every single day by resting in the light of the sun, so God has determined that we too as his royal priests should daily gain our strength from the privilege of basking in the intimate presence of the "light of the world". Psalm 46 : 10a commands us: *"Be still and know that I am God"*. This does not just signify being physically still but also practising mental and emotional stillness. The tradition of meditation in quietness of spirit is woefully rare in the modern church. Our "quiet times" often miss the very essence of that term as we quickly flick through 'a thought for the day'. Having failed to be still and spread 'our wings' in the Son's presence, we rush into the day in our own strength and then wonder why we feel weak and defeated.

# Son worshippers

If a butterfly falls into shady places, it loses its strength and becomes vulnerable to its enemies, unable to fly away promptly. Ultimately, if a butterfly becomes too cold, it will die. Due to this need of the butterfly to bask in the sun, some describe butterflies as "sun-worshippers". The sun is an unending source of heat and solar energy. On one website, I read the fascinating statement that "the sun is the elixir of life" for the butterfly. An elixir is described in the dictionary as an alchemical preparation alleged to be a sovereign remedy, capable of prolonging life. For us then, we see that the Son is our elixir too. The Son of God is the ultimate sovereign remedy not just for prolonging this life, but for guaranteeing eternal life! Hallelujah!

'For in him we live and move and have our being.'
Acts 17:28a

As his priests, we are called to rejoice in the privilege of knowing and communing with him! We are to declare the praises of the one who brought us from darkness into light. Worship is often mistaken as solely singing and music but, in fact, worship should be a daily expression of our hearts, displayed in everything we do, devoted in loving service to the Lord! The priests' roles in the temple teach us how stay in close fellowship with the Lord - prayer; feeding on the bread of life - the word of God; and remembering in the communion service his sacrifice to make atonement for us. The priests could not even enter the inner court until they had offered sacrifices to make atonement for their

> God's concept of service is what we are becoming. not what we are doing.
>
> Oswald Chambers

own sins and then cleansed themselves in the bronze lather outside the inner court. Although Christ has made the ultimate sacrifice for us, we too must ensure our lives are clean vessels before the Lord, confessing our sins daily so that we can be filled anew each day with the oil of the Holy Spirit.

If, like the butterfly, we remain in the light, we are living worshipfully and obediently before the Lord. If we choose to be disobedient, we move into the shadows, becoming vulnerable to our spiritual enemies. When we read the requirements of 'a life in the light' in Scriptures such as Ephesians chapter 5, we are perhaps tempted to see it as a list of rules – a life of routine and duty. However, the term "walking in the light" already tells us that this is a good place to be. The Lord does not tell us to walk in the light in order to make our lives dull. What a contradiction in terms that would be!

## Finding the right balance

Butterflies do not bask in the sun as a means of self-indulgence like sunbathers desperate to get a suntan! Their time resting in the sun is a necessary means of acquiring energy, but they don't stay there all day!

'Inner court ministry' should always precede, motivate and sustain 'outer court ministry'. If we are not prepared to spend intimate time with the Lord in the 'inner court', we should not be surprised if we do not have the desire, or the energy, to join with him working in the 'outer court' to bring others to a saving knowledge of God, finding atonement for their sins through Christ. However, 'inner court' ministry is not, and was never intended to be, the sole occupation of a royal priest either. We are not to spend so much time "being so heavenly-minded that we are of no earthly use". Quite the opposite! What is the point of becoming spiritually mature if we do not bear fruit - going out into the world to draw others to Christ? Intimacy with the Lord should bring us so to love the Lord that we start to share his passion and want to get out into the 'outer court', seeking to work hard to bless those he loves so much. 1 Corinthians chapter 13 states that we can have any number of spiritual gifts but, if we don't go beyond our inner sanctuaries and love people practically, we are like a clanging cymbal.

## Procreation and Pollination

A butterfly's main purpose is to reproduce. In fulfilling this purpose, it automatically pollinates flowers as it visits them in search of nectar to sustain its flight to find a mate.

The female butterfly knows instinctively that the eggs she lays will be very vulnerable. Therefore a typical female butterfly will lay up to a hundred eggs in the hope that some, or even just one, will survive through to adulthood. It is estimated that only two percent of butterfly eggs survive to become healthy adult butterflies. Therefore, some species will lay whole clusters together, hoping for safety in numbers; others seem to heed the warning not to put all their eggs in one basket (if you'll pardon the pun) and will lay a single egg, carefully hidden under a leaf. Most importantly, the female butterfly will always lay her eggs on the correct food plant for the emerging caterpillar.

As royal priests, we too should be involved in ensuring 'the continuation of the species'. This is the Great Commission, the primary responsibility of the church – to bring people to the Lord and then disciple them to spiritual maturity in order that they will, eventually, do the same for others. As most female butterflies are careful to lay their eggs in the safest place possible on the correct food plant for the new-born caterpillar, so we too should be careful to nurture new believers within the shelter of a caring, prayerful church where the Word of God is revered. Note also that the first instar caterpillar eats only the fresh new leaves at the top of the plant. The older leaves are indigestible at that early stage. Similarly, in the early stages of Christian discipleship, new believers should be directed to the parts of Scripture which are most easily understood, whilst providing the necessary elementary teaching of the Christian faith. Furthermore, as priests of the Lord, we are called to set a godly example for those who are young in the faith. Bearing in mind the subtleties of our spiritual enemies and the persistence of the old nature, spiritual protection should perhaps also be offered in the form of a personal mentor.

For the survival of the butterfly species, reproduction and egg-laying is indispensable. The pollination of flowers is merely incidental as they feed on nectar. Nevertheless, pollination makes a valuable contribution to the world of nature by which our lives are also enriched. This beneficial God-given by-product can be likened to the benefits felt within a community where an evangelical church is faithful to its soul-winning commission. As we live our lives set apart unto the Lord, we will inevitably live a life that blesses others. Indeed, in Matthew, chapter 25, we read that those who refuse to help the least of their fellow men have failed to "see" God. Our spiritual discernment should lead us to bring freedom; justice; healing; comfort; hope; restoration and deliverance as we preach the Gospel. Our order of priorities, however, must be clear. The Bible tells us that it is by our fruit that we shall be known. The laying of eggs is like 'the fruit' of the butterfly. This is a challenge to us all to consider our lives and where we are investing our time and resources. In this twenty-first century, there is a disturbing number of churches and organizations which are in danger of emphasizing 'pollination' instead of 'reproduction'. What is Satan's main objective? Is it not to ensure 'the extinction of the species' – 'fruit-bearing' Christians? If that goal is not attainable through outright destruction (martyrdom) then he will use any deception to hinder 'reproduction'. If the latest generation busy themselves so much with 'pollination' that they forget, or even choose not to 'reproduce', the number of 'plants' they 'pollinate' will cause Satan no concern at all. Obviously, the analogy is not perfect. However, please seriously consider what the butterfly has to teach us. I have reason to believe that there will be many false doctrines based on this very issue rising up to weaken the preaching of the gospel. Christians are to be concerned about the needs of the world's under-privileged, downcast, imprisoned or maltreated people. However, dedicating our lives to improving and blessing the world merely through social action is not in accordance with our role as priests. We are to follow the example of our High Priest, the Lord Jesus Christ, who from the start defined his ministry by publicly reading Isaiah chapter 61 : 1. He was anointed to preach the Good News. In doing so, he also comforted, healed and delivered many people. However, he never allowed the physical needs of the masses to deflect him from his prophetic and priestly calling. We are anointed for the same purposes – to be able to see the needs of those around us and respond accordingly, beginning with man's greatest need to find salvation in Jesus Christ.

# Anointed

*"The Spirit of the Sovereign Lord is on me, because the Lord has anointed me to preach good news to the poor."  Isaiah 61 : 1a*

In nature, scent has many uses. The fragrance of flowers is partly to attract the insects to pollinate them. Scent also has a significant role to play in reproduction. It either attracts the opposite sex or repulses them. Butterflies can identify each other uniquely by their smell. Depending on the concentration of the pheromones released, butterflies of the same species can find each other from up to a mile away in order to mate. When some species mate, the male will even sprinkle the female with his perfume as part of the mating ritual.

The priests were anointed as a symbol of being set apart as holy unto the Lord and granted the special privilege and authority from God to minister to him and to minister on behalf of the people. The fragrant oil used for anointing the priests was unique to the temple. The people were forbidden to recreate it for any other purpose.

Did you know that as the Lord's royal priesthood we too have been anointed with the oil of the Holy Spirit and, therefore, have a unique fragrance? That fragrance has a powerful effect on people and, as in the life of the butterfly, it plays a role in 'reproduction' - attracting others to Christ. *"...wherever we go he uses us to tell others about the Lord and to spread the Good News like a sweet perfume. Our lives are a fragrance presented by Christ to God."* 2 Corinthians 2 : 14, 15a (NLT)

In Ephesians, chapter 5, we are called to live a life surrendered to God, following Christ's example who gave his life up as a fragrant offering to God. Our conduct towards God also produces an aroma, either pleasing or repugnant to God. *"Be imitators of God, therefore, as dearly loved children and live a life of love, just as Christ loved us and gave himself up for us as a fragrant offering and sacrifice to God."* (Ephesians 5 : 1,2)

As we become a living sacrifice (Romans 12 : 1) or, as 2 Corinthians chapter 2 puts it, captives in the Lord's triumphal procession, we too become a fragrant offering and take on the aroma of Christ, spreading the sweet perfume of the knowledge of Christ. It is to be noted that this fragrance will be perceived differently by those who are perishing and by those who are being saved. To one we smell like death and doom but to the other we are a life-giving perfume.

Perfume has often been used to revive the senses. When we are empowered to spread the gospel by the anointing of the Holy Spirit, we not only awaken the lost but stimulate those who are perhaps 'fainting' through discouragement, or even apathy. As we share our experiences and testimonies of how God is working when we spread the Gospel, discouraged Christians are revived by the sweet, life-giving perfume of the Good News.

*"...your name is like perfume poured out."*
Song of Songs 1: 3b

# Royal Robes

*"..for all of you who were baptised into Christ have clothed yourselves with Christ."*
*Galatians 3 : 27*

There is no doubt that it is the beauty of butterflies' wings that make them so breathtaking and eye-catching. Their wings give them a distinct identity, setting them apart from other winged insects. They truly reflect the glory of God with their beautiful 'robes'!

Each butterfly's wing is clothed in thousands of tiny scales laid down almost like tiles on a roof. The wings are so delicate that handling a butterfly can rub off its scales, leaving what seems like coloured dust on your hands. This is due to the fact that a multitude of colours found on the scales of butterflies comes from pigmentation. Each scale cell holds a single colour pigment derived from plants. What they ate as caterpillars determines some of their colours! The colours of a butterfly's wing can also come from sunlight reflecting different colours off the scales depending on how they are positioned. It tends to be the metallic blues and coppers that are visible this way.

*Lepidoptera 'scaled wings'*

The priests' garments were also designed by God intentionally to dignify the priesthood. They set them apart as those who were called to a life of holiness. When they entered the holy inner court, they had to be washed clean and wear linen, as opposed to wool. Wool causes perspiration which symbolises fleshly activity. Linen is a symbol of purity and belonging to the Lord. We see in the book of Revelation that the Bride of Christ (and the armies of the Lord) will be dressed in linen. The linen represents the righteous acts of the saints. (Revelation 19 : 8)

*'Clothe yourselves with the Lord Jesus Christ, and do not think about how to gratify the desires of the sinful nature." Romans 13 : 14*

As royal priests, we too are called to clothe ourselves in such a way as to be distinctive and bring glory to God. We are cleansed and clothed with the Lord Jesus, through baptism, just as the butterfly is adorned in new robes through its watery 'death' in the chrysalis. We symbolically cast aside the old nature and rise up adorned in the robes

148

of righteousness given to us, not through our own merit, but through Christ's sacrifice. However, from then on, as those who seek to be spiritually mature, we must actively clothe ourselves with Christ.

How do we clothe ourselves in Christ? Once again, one answer lies within the colours of the butterfly. Just as the butterfly gains some of its colours from what it ate as a caterpillar, so our 'food' will play a part in determining the colour of our outer garments. If we are 'feeding' on the Word, the wonderful colours of his nature will shine through us.

The butterfly also gains colour from reflecting the light. How do we reflect God's glory? Well, for a start, we must walk in the light; we cannot reflect anything in the dark! We must also understand the importance of refraction. Light appears, at first, to be colourless but we know that, when we see a prism of light through refraction, seven distinct colours become visible. (There are also seven spirits of God so it would seem that the characteristics of light mirror the Light of the World.) The texture of the object refracting light makes all the difference to the colour seen. This observation holds an important lesson for those who wish to bring glory to God by refracting his glorious light. The way we behave and the way our day-to-day lives are arranged is just as important as the way the scales of a butterfly's wing are positioned. Imagine our individual decisions, acts or thoughts to be the scales of a butterfly's wing. The way those 'scales' are positioned will ultimately affect the 'colours' others see in our lives. If we allow God to direct the display of those 'scales', he will take delight in ensuring an arrangement which will 'refract' the beauty of his nature. God's spirit will shine through our lives, his glory unveiled. This may take patience to develop, just as the wings of the butterfly don't have the splendour we expect of a butterfly when they first emerge from the chrysalis

> "This is the message we have heard from him and declare to you: God is light; in him there is no darkness at all. If we claim to have fellowship with him yet walk in darkness, we lie and do not live by the truth. But if we walk in the light, as he is in the light, we have fellowship with one another, and the blood of Jesus, his Son, purifies us from all sin." 1 John 1 : 5-7

# Glory Unveiled

*"Don't hide your light under a basket! Instead put it on a stand and let it shine for all. In the same way, let your good deeds shine out for all to see, so that everyone will praise your heavenly Father." Matthew 5 : 15,16 (NLT)*

Butterfly wing-colours, and thus the very wings themselves, play two key roles. The first is a "fly toward and attract" role. Butterflies need to be airborne to find a mate and use the colours of their wings to attract it. The wings, therefore, play a vital role in ensuring reproduction! As the butterfly attracts admiration, so our good deeds reflect God's glory to the world, causing people to praise the awesome Creator that shines through us.

What 'colours' do people see when God's glory is unveiled? Moses once pleaded with the Lord, "Show me your glory!" He wanted to see God's glory unveiled. The Lord responded with a speech which revealed that God's glory radiates with the 'colours' of love, mercy, compassion, forgiveness, grace, patience and justice. Moses later communed with God, face to face. However, upon leaving God's presence, he had to cover his visage so as not to blind people with God's

"The Lord, the Lord, the compassionate and gracious God, slow to anger, abounding in love, and faithfulness, maintaining love to thousands, and forgiving wickedness, rebellion and sin."

Exodus 34 : 6,7

glory radiating unveiled from his countenance. In a similar vein, after the priests had ministered to God in the inner court, they had to leave their linen robes behind, so as not to consecrate the people in the outer court by means of their sacred garments. (see Ezekiel 44 : 15-20)

Have you ever considered how miraculous it is that, as Christ's royal priests, we are no longer required to 'take off the robes' that might reflect the glory of God to other people? Quite the opposite. The 'linen robes' are to be kept on in 'the outer court' too! We are commanded by Jesus to let our light shine! We are given the awesome and miraculous privilege of reflecting the Lord's glory with unveiled faces as we are being transformed into his likeness with ever-increasing glory which comes from the Lord who is the Spirit." (2 Corinthians 3 : 17,18) What an amazing ministry!

The second function of a butterfly's wings is a "fly away and distract" role. Wherever possible, butterflies will fly away from their enemies. However, when this is not immediately possible, their wings are used for protection, both through concealment and through startling advertisement. Their wing patterns can be elaborate camouflaging or they can be used to scare predators with, for example, large eye markings - known as ocelli - or with bright colours to communicate that they are potentially poisonous to any would-be predator!

Isaiah, chapter 61, records that as priests of the Lord, we are clothed in garments of praise and of salvation, as well as in robes of righteousness. These things are essential to our protection from our spiritual enemies. Robes of righteousness – an upright life – will shield us from many evils, whilst colourful garments of praise, especially when worn in times of trial, will startle our would-be predators away.

"Therefore, as God's chosen people, holy and dearly loved, clothe yourselves with compassion, kindness, humility, gentleness and patience". Colossians 3 : 12

In Ephesians chapter 6 we are also told to proactively clothe ourselves in the armour of God and to take up the shield of faith and the sword of the spirit! We must be on our guard for our enemies can be very sly.

In our world today, our style of dress denotes not just our personality but even our social standing. Spiritually, the way we are 'dressed' is also crucial in declaring our identity. Therefore, our enemies will try to 'dress in the same clothing' as the spiritually mature to deceive even the elect, if that were possible. Be aware. The book of Revelation tells us that in the end times, the "Prostitute", a fierce opponent of God's chosen people, will dress herself in linen and fine jewels, like the High Priest, even using the same colours – scarlet and purple. (Revelation 17) False prophets will come – ferocious wolves in sheep's clothing. There will be those who will either claim to be Christ himself or a prophet coming in the name of the Lord. It is worth remembering that the greatest deception is always the one that is closest to the truth.

As the Lord's priests we have no part in this world's garments of trends, pretence and deception. Our 'garments' must be bestowed on us by the Lord, through his Spirit. We must not allow Satan to deceive us with garments cut from the cloth of good works and religious effort. The children of Israel were forbidden to wear clothing made of a mix of two different fabrics. (Leviticus 19: 19b) We, as royal priests, must be careful not to mix the God-given 'linen' of Christ's righteousness in our lives with the 'wool' of self-effort. As Zinzendorf rightly said, *"Jesus, thy blood and righteousness, my beauty are, my glorious dress, Midst flaming worlds, in these arrayed, with joy shall I lift up my head."*

# New vision

*"The man without the Spirit does not accept the things that come from the Spirit of God, for they are foolishness to him, and he cannot understand them, because they are spiritually discerned."*   1 Corinthians 2 : 14

In order to survive in a hostile world, we as royal priests are given another precious attribute of the mature butterfly - special sight.

The miraculous metamorphosis of the butterfly gives us a picture of this bestowed gift of vision. Called out from the relative darkness of its caterpillar days, through the chrysalis and into the light, the butterfly gains sight. The caterpillar is to all intents and purposes blind, able only to distinguish night and day. In contrast, the butterfly has a pair of compound eyes on its head. Each eye is composed of thousands of image-forming minute eyes called ommatidia, all directed at different angles. The butterfly therefore enjoys a wide field of vision, able to see simultaneously in every direction. This kind of vision is called omni-vision. The image the butterfly sees is in the form of a mosaic. It cannot focus its vision and, therefore, sees a blur in comparison to what we see as humans. However, it can see colour and is also sensitive to movements and, as such, is able to escape from predators more quickly.

We are told in Scripture that we too currently see imperfectly; we know only in part. One day, we shall see the 'greater reality'; we will see our Lord and his kingdom, face to face. We shall know fully even as we are fully known. But for now, as if to compensate for this 'blurred vision', both butterflies and the royal priests of the Lord are given a special gift – vision from the sun/son!

The butterfly is believed to have one of the widest ranges of colour-vision. The butterfly's photoreceptors can perceive colours in a high frequency (frequency is a measuring unit of colour) and can therefore see ultraviolet light. Man cannot detect higher frequency colours beyond violet and so is blind to ultraviolet. For this reason, some of the colours and patterns that a butterfly sees are invisible to man. The patterns of colour on its own wings appear differently to a butterfly. It was formerly believed that UV markings helped the butterfly to identify its own species. However, the current thinking is that the presence, or absence, of these UV markings typically helps to differentiate between males and females and, furthermore, helps a female to choose the best mate by seeking a male with the brightest UV markings!

The colours of flowers also show up differently through UV light. The flower's colours, ultraviolet markings, form, aroma and nectar-guides work in combination as signals and signposts to guide the butterfly efficiently to the source of nectar. The ultraviolet patterns on some flower-petals have been likened to a runway guiding a plane to its desired destination.

A butterfly can also see polarized light. Polarized light (which can be seen even through the clouds) indicates in which direction the sun is actually shining. This, therefore, helps the butterfly with navigation even on dull days.

So, we see how the butterfly uses UV and polarised vision - to help in identifying a healthy mate; to find the best nourishment; and for navigational purposes. But what relevance does this have for us as the Lord's royal priests?

UV light and polarised light and the corresponding vision come from the sun. The photoreceptors which enable this vision are useless in the dark. Spiritual sight - revelation - comes from the Son. All men have the necessary 'receptors'. Unfortunately, there are many who, in refusing to walk in the light, do not have this vision. Instead, they remain in the darkness of spiritual confusion or indifference. They need guidance to be brought into the light and then teaching to continue "walking in the light".

"Now we see things imperfectly as in a poor mirror, but then we will see everything with perfect clarity. All that I know now is partial and incomplete, but then I will know everything completely, just as God knows me now."

I Corinthians 13 : 12 (NLT)

In the Aaronic priesthood, the High Priest was given the privilege of seeking the will of God on behalf of the people. (Exodus 28 : 30) Accordingly, he was equipped with the Urim and Thummin to determine the Lord's response to difficult judgements. The High Priest would then inform the priests on how to instruct the people. The priests were responsible for ensuring that worship unto the Lord was offered reverently in accordance with the Lord's specific teachings. Also they were to protect the people from false teachers, especially those who claimed that the people could make sacrifices by themselves, wherever and whenever they chose.

In the New Covenant priesthood, Jesus is our High Priest. Through the process of 'spiritual metamorphosis', we, his royal priests, have received special insight from God. His Spirit is at work in our hearts and in our minds leading us into all truth and into an understanding of God's will and purposes. The Apostle John refers to this work of the indwelling Holy Spirit as our anointing from the Holy One. In the context of warning about the coming of the Anti-Christ and the many anti-Christs already in the world deceiving people, the apostle John says, *"...the anointing you received from him remains in you, and you do not need anyone to teach you. But as his anointing teaches you about all things, remain in him."* (1 John 2 : 27)

The Apostle John is not contradicting the Apostle Paul who earlier wrote about ministerial gifts given specifically to those called to be prophets, evangelists, pastors and teachers, for the purpose of building up the body of Christ until we reach maturity. Rather, John is writing to build individual confidence in the Holy Spirit's anointing. His anointing not only enables us to discern between truth and error but also enables us, as a New

'I pray also that the eyes of your heart may be enlightened in order that you may know the hope to which he has called you, the riches of his glorious inheritance in the saints and his incomparably great power for us who believe.' Ephesians 1 : 18, 19a

Covenant priesthood, to fulfil our duty to make disciples of all nations and to teach everything that we ourselves have been taught.

Paul's prayer for the Ephesians also shows the importance he attributed to spiritual discernment. He knew the gift of spiritual insight would lead them to inspiring truths which would nourish their souls and empower them - just as the ultraviolet vision leads the butterfly to nectar to gain the energy to fly and to fulfil its purposes – pollination and reproduction. Not only would the glorious message of hope in Christ be unveiled before them but also the power available to those who believe to make an incredible impact on their world.

# The Butterfly Effect– the weight of your glory

"The butterfly effect" was described in a paper by a meteorologist called Lorenz. He theorized that a change in conditions as seemingly insignificant as that provoked by the mere flap of a butterfly's wings may cause a chain of events leading to unexpected large-scale changes in future events. His paper on this "sensitive dependence on initial conditions" was later entitled, "Does the flap of a butterfly's wing set off a tornado in Texas?" Clearly, the butterfly itself does not cause the tornado but the flap of its wings becomes a part of the initial conditions causing a tornado.

Let us consider how sensitive the world, and people around us, may be to the "initial conditions" of which we are all an integral part. Have you ever reflected on the importance of your smallest acts? Maybe you have been impacted by a simple act of kindness or a note of thanks that made everything worthwhile. On the other hand, you may have suffered for years as the result of one sentence carelessly uttered over you by a parent, sibling or friend. There are many people who have injured themselves, or someone else, owing to a momentary lapse of concentration. They now live with the haunting knowledge that the slightest change in events may have made all the difference.

We may be ignorant of the potential of each moment of our lives but Satan is not. He knows even the smallest act of God's love can change lives. Let me give you a true example of a small "beat of a butterfly's wing" that had a dramatic impact on lives right across the world. Imagine the scene with me.

The Tokyo metro was packed; everyone was pushing and shoving. Suddenly a little, old lady fell to the ground. No-one seemed to care. But then a Frenchman stooped to help her gently to her feet. Nicholas looked on, his heart pierced by the kindness of this man to a total stranger. A conversation began. Nicholas was in trouble. For years he had been travelling around the world, involved in all sorts of drug abuse and stealing. Angry at his family and everyone else, he was on self-destruct mode! But his life changed that day in Japan. The Frenchman came to spend ten days with him and led him to know the Lord as his personal Saviour. In time, Nicholas went home and witnessed to his family over many years, desperate for them to experience the same life-change. His mother, Val, after initially hating her son's evangelism, eventually became a Christian, followed by her husband a few years later. Val is now an active member and prayer-warrior in my church. Nicholas, his wife and five children are now working as missionaries in Japan. But the story even goes as far as you holding this book in your hands. Val, in obedience to the Lord, was one of the benefactors who supported me whilst writing it.

Lorenz's example of a butterfly's wing-beat causing a tornado on another continent may be stretching the point beyond credibility. However, it cannot be denied that the choices we make in life, even seemingly insignificant choices, have very far-reaching effects, not only in our own lives, but in the lives of those we touch, either directly or indirectly. From Scripture we know that apparently insignificant decisions, as well as serious life and death decisions, can affect the whole of history! Imagine if Rebecca had not watered the camels of Jacob's servant. What if Ruth had decided to stay in Moab? Where would the Jewish race be now if Esther had not risked her life appealing to the King? What if Mary had declined the opportunity to carry God's son? Do not assume that because these were biblical characters, they were somehow different to us. None of these people was aware at the time of the long-term consequences of their decisions and actions. Many people today struggle to believe that their lives have value. Even as mature Christians, we may look at our day-to-day actions and perhaps think they are so insignificant as to be ineffective. This is untrue. Let us ask God where we need to make changes to our attitudes, to our choices and to our relationships in order to bring glory to him. We can make a difference in our communities. Our presence, as spiritually mature Christians, is highly important, as is the presence of butterflies.

## Spiritual barometer

Because of their sensitivity to ecological change, butterfly numbers can be used as indicators of the health of the eco-system. If butterfly numbers are flourishing, this usually gives evidence of favourable climatic conditions and adequate conservation of the environment. The demise of butterflies indicates the speed and extent of climate change. Butterfly populations can be affected by unusual weather; a change in farming practices; the use of pesticides and urban development, to name but a few. All these changes affect their breeding grounds and therefore, the continuation of the next generation.

If we can think in terms of the butterfly representing the mature spirit-filled Christian serving the Lord as a royal priest, what does the number of 'butterflies' in our churches, and in our communities, tell us about the spiritual health of our environment? Are 'butterflies' dwindling in number? What conditions are causing this and what can be done about it? Or are 'butterflies' flourishing? What can be shared with other churches, and even other countries, to conserve 'butterflies' further afield?

We have seen that 'butterflies' – the spiritually mature - have spiritual insight. By contrast, there is little or no spiritual insight amongst immature believers and people who are unsaved. If there are but few 'butterflies', there will be a serious problem in society for *"Where there is no vision, the people perish."* (Proverbs 29 : 18) How concerned are we to ensure that we pursue spiritual maturity in order to be used by God to fulfil his purposes for his people and the world?

# Conclusion

*"I want to know Christ and the power of his resurrection and the fellowship of sharing in his suffering, becoming like him in his death, and so, somehow, to attain to the resurrection from the dead." Philippians 3 : 10,11*

In the verse above, Paul declares his aspiration for spiritual maturity – to know Christ intimately. Caterpillars know of the process of growth, change, and death which leads to maturity as a butterfly. Metamorphosis can be seen as nature's visual representation of becoming like Christ in his death and then, miraculously, like him in his resurrection, as God's glory is unveiled through the emerging butterfly.

To live for the glory of God is the aim of spiritual maturity. As we have seen, it is a gradual development and not an easy one, but what a life awaits us as we attain it! Spiritual maturity is often erroneously considered to be something that will make life sober and dull but this falsehood is gloriously exposed within the life of the butterfly. Although butterflies live incredibly "We always carry around in our body the death of Jesus, so that the life of Jesus may also be revealed in our body." 2 Corinthians 4 : 10 vulnerable lives, under constant threat from their enemies and exposure to the elements, they are nevertheless a picture of a distinctive life, full of vision, beauty and purpose.

We have been chosen to live our lives in such a way as to reflect the joy, glory and fulfilment of intimacy with God. People should marvel at the transforming work of God in our lives. When we consider butterflies, we marvel that they were once caterpillars. We dwell not so much on the nature of the old caterpillar but rather at the wonder of their transformation. Our transformed lives should prompt the same thought-process in others and inspire a desire for their own metamorphosis. Incredibly, we have the privilege of pointing others to the Creator who is able to fulfil that desire and transform their lives! (See Isaiah 61 or 2 Corinthians 5) We are anointed as his royal priests for this special commission. Living as true priests, our lives will testify to the fact that following God's teachings brings life and peace. (Malachi 2 : 5) This is the privilege and the joy of the abundant life of the spiritually mature – to be a clean channel through which the Holy Spirit can move to touch other people's lives.

"Therefore we do not lose heart. Though outwardly we are wasting away, yet inwardly we are being renewed day by day. For our light and momentary troubles are achieving for us an eternal glory that far outweighs them all. So we fix our eyes not on what is seen, but on what is unseen. For what is seen is temporary, but what is unseen is eternal."

2 Corinthians 4 : 16 -18

Does this seem anything like Satan's portrayal of a life of holiness as dull, dry and religious? Far from it! The life of the spiritually mature is a glorious life – literally. Christ has enabled us to represent his new covenant (2 Corinthians 3 : 6) with unveiled faces, reflecting Christ's likeness with ever-increasing glory as we mature. Furthermore, we are equipped with every spiritual blessing in the heavenly realms in order to help us - just as we have seen the butterfly is equipped with all the skills and beauty it needs to survive and bring about the next generation, whilst simultaneously unveiling the glory of God through its splendour.

This is the story of 'the butterfly-vision'. Everything that happens to us, everything which is invested in our lives, is to bring us forth, through a patient and ordered process, as royal priests whose holy and obedient service will unveil God's glory in a world of spiritual darkness. The tough challenges issued through 'the butterfly-vision' are intended to encourage us to press on to maturity so that we can be used by God to bless, restore and heal other people, bringing them to the start of their own 'caterpillar to butterfly' journey – the walk of faith with our Lord Jesus Christ.

Best of all, the story does not end there, for the amazing process of Christ unveiling his glory in our lives does not finish even as we draw our last breath – it is an eternal process. If he has begun a wonderful transformation in us through intimacy with him in this life, how much more will he continue that miraculous process when we commune with him face to face. His glory is everlasting and so too the unveiling of it. Hallelujah!

*".... Our citizenship is in heaven. And we eagerly await a Saviour from there, the Lord Jesus Christ, who, by the power that enables him to bring everything under his control, will transform our lowly bodies so that they will be like his glorious body. Therefore, my brothers, you whom I love and long for, my joy and crown, that is how you should stand firm in the Lord, dear friends!" Philippians 3 : 20 - 4 : 1*

Common Buckeye (junonia coenia) butterflies

Olive Hairstreaks (Juniper) Callophrys gryneus

©BobMaul 2009

For since the creation of the world God's invisible qualities – his eternal power and his divine nature – have been clearly seen, being understood from what has been made, so that men are without excuse.
Romans 1:20

The Red Spotted Purple
(limenitis arthemis astyanax)

... And we, who with unveiled faces, all reflect the Lord's glory, are being transformed into his likeness with ever-increasing glory

2 Corinthians 3 : 18

© Jay Cossey

# Epilogue

# Glory Unveiled

And so we come to the end of our incredible journey through the life cycle of the butterfly. As I look back to the introduction and to my aim in sharing this vision - to inspire you to press on to maturity - I feel I must end with a word of encouragement.

I wonder if you are reading this book having already reached spiritual maturity and yet feeling disheartened because you currently do not see yourself as a beautiful butterfly radiantly displaying God's glory. Perhaps you are even imagining that in your current circumstances, you are more likely to cause others to question the sanity and value of striving for spiritual maturity. In my experience there are usually two main reasons for discouragement - adverse circumstances or a struggle with our own characters and personalities. Either one, or a combination of both, can cause us to lose faith that the Lord can ever use our lives to bring glory to his name. This then leads us to question the validity of proclaiming a life-changing spiritual metamorphosis through a relationship with Jesus Christ.

Only yesterday I was sitting in a restaurant with a friend, troubled, if not saddened, because I felt so weary through lack of faith. I had just finished writing the last chapter of this book and, as my friend reminded me, that should have been cause for celebration. Instead, I felt overwhelmed by the uncertainty of my future; my financial status, and my loneliness. I was anxious that even if this book leads to further ministry, I would not be able to overcome my personal fears and weaknesses to fulfil God's plans for me. These concerns were robbing me of sleep at night, leaving me wondering, "How can I even begin to contemplate pursuing this apparent madness of publishing a book which claims that spiritual maturity unveils God's glory in your life and draws others to Christ? I don't feel I am radiating his glory. I don't feel victorious. I feel weak and lacking in faith."

Today, after a time of praying and fasting, the Lord lovingly gave me some reassuring words which I leave with you as this epilogue. Can I persuade you to conclude your reading of this book by studying, as I did today, the testimony of the Apostle Paul in his second letter to the Corinthians? No-one would argue that God failed to unveil his glory through the life of the Apostle Paul and yet, as I read through his letter, I realised that Paul did not always feel like an overcomer. He, too, was troubled by these two challenges to faith – adverse circumstances and human weaknesses, not to mention the unnamed thorn in the flesh. (2 Corinthians 12 : 7-10) He admits to sometimes feeling overwhelmed by sorrow, crushed, fearful, broken-hearted, discouraged and lonely.

He talks of crying bitterly, wondering what had become of his ministry, having been betrayed by other Christians. He was criticised for not being a very fine speaker. This wonderful letter to the Corinthians appears to be the culmination of his thoughts and prayers to God about these trials, discouragements, sleepless nights and tears. He

"When we arrived in Macedonia, there was NO REST for us. Outside there was conflict from every direction, and inside there was FEAR."

2 Corinthians 7 : 5 (NLT)

had clearly thought it all through and concluded that his weakness, and failure to impress men did not matter because he had not come to attract glory to himself. His calling was to uplift the Lord Jesus Christ. Although he and his fellow missionaries were often struggling, Paul said in 2 Corinthians chapter 4 : 5 (NLT), *"All we say about ourselves is that we are your servants because of what Jesus has done for us."* He determined that he would go on preaching because he had the same faith as the Psalmist who said, *"I believed in God and so I speak."* (2 Corinthians 4 : 13 NLT)

In the year God called me to serve onboard MV Logos 2, I was staggered to read in George Verwer's book, "No turning back – pursuing the path of Christian discipleship," that he was a "fearful worrier" and suffered "daily from anxiety and fear and a sense of failure." George Verwer is the founder of Operation Mobilisation and, throughout the last fifty years of his life, he has been a pioneer of great vision and faith. God gave him the vision for ocean-going ships bringing literature and the good news of Christ to all nations. This work has changed the lives of thousands upon thousands of people. Imagine if, defeated by circumstances or his personal "sense of failure", George Verwer had decided that he was not qualified or his message was invalid! This "fearful" man, used and empowered by God, and aided by many other imperfect, but dedicated, Christians, was one of the reasons I could embark on the greatest turning-point experience of my life, thus far.

His life demonstrates to me that, in direct opposition to what Satan would have us believe, God is more glorified when, by admitting our own insufficiency, we attribute all we have achieved to God's grace and favour.

George Verwer also stresses that we must be realistic concerning the many discouragements, and even the mental and emotional exhaustion, we shall face as Christ's servants. However, he also reminds us that we are able, day by day, to give our distress over to the Lord and leave it with him. It is the Lord, and the Lord alone, who works through us, enabling us to be ministers of the new covenant. (2 Corinthians 3 : 5,6) He is working HIS purposes out. None of the biblical characters of faith was perfect; they were fearful, impatient, sinful and sometimes lacking in faith. Yet God used them to bring about his plan.

My ministry, or my potential to be used to unveil God's glory, is not negated by a temporary lack of courage or peace. There is no need for any pretence. I am what I am by the grace of God – an open letter for all to read – an imperfect instrument, but available to God. The Lord has, therefore, encouraged me to persevere in sharing this message of the butterfly. I do so

"For God who said, "Let there be light in the darkness," has made us understand that this light is the brightness of the glory of God that is seen in the face of Jesus Christ. But this precious treasure – this light and power that now shine within us – is held in perishable containers, that is, in our weak bodies. So everyone can see that our glorious power is from God and is not our own."

2 Corinthians 4 : 6,7 NLT

willingly because of what Jesus has done for me. Despite my weaknesses and doubts, I affirm, by faith, that he is more than capable of bringing forth from my life what he has promised (2 Corinthians 4 : 14), and to do as much for you and through you. Even to those whose lives have already been blighted by serious mistakes and regrets, Christ offers comfort and hope. All who turn to the Lord in true repentance find mercy and grace in times of need. The Lord will restore you and show you that his power is made perfect in your weakness.

As butterflies draw near to the end of their lives, they become quite faded and rather worn around the edges. You will rarely see such a butterfly without a few war wounds, usually in the shape of a bird beak! Worn out butterflies are only the sign of a life well-lived and a purpose fulfilled – their wounds the evidence of surviving against great odds. Their glory may be faded, but their fruit will live on in the next generation, even though they will not live to see it. Be encouraged as you love and serve the Lord. No matter how you currently feel, or how slow the results of your ministry appear to be, our labour in the Lord is never in vain. The day will come when, as we commune together in heaven, the extent of this glorious miracle will be unveiled to us all.

# End Notes

**Introduction**

Fuchsia Pickett: *The Prophetic Romance* (Lake Mary, Fl.: Charisma House 1996) Chapter 1, p12-13. Used with permission

Heather Gemmen: *Startling Beauty – My journey from rape to restoration.* Chapter 13 p187 Life Journey – imprint of Cook Communication Ministries. (2004) Used with permission of Kingsway Communications.

**Chapter 1**

*Amazing Grace* – John Newton (1725-1807) – Public domain

Brother Andrew: *The Calling.* (Revised and expanded edition) Summit Publishing Ltd (2000) Chapter 4 p.79. Used by permission of Open Doors International, USA

Joyce Meyer: *Beauty for Ashes – Receiving Emotional Healing* (Revised and expanded edition) Warner Books (2003) Testimony used by permission of Joyce Meyer Ministries.

Bernard d'Abrera: *The Concise Atlas of the Butterflies of the World.* Hill House Publishing (2007)

**Chapter 2**

*O Jesus Christ, grow thou in me.* Johann C Lavater (1741-1801) – Public domain

Corrie Ten Boom (with John and Elizabeth Sherrill) : *The Hiding Place.* Hodder and Stoughton. 1971 (This edition 1976) Chapter 13/14

Philip Yancey: *Reaching for the Invisible God.* Zondervan (2000) Chapter 17 p.214, used with permission.

Brother Yun: *The Heavenly Man.* Monarch Books (2002)

Quotations:

* Quotation regarding double-decker bus – http://www.butterflyfarm.co.cr/ed/index.htm

* Quotation regarding cells in waiting: Prof. Lincoln Brower. www.learner.org/jnorth/tm/monarch/ ChrysalisDevelopmentLPB.html Used by permission.

**Chapter 3**

*Remove my covering, Lord* - Witness Lee (1905-1997) Used by kind permission of Living Stream Ministries

Woodrow Kroll: *Struggling with Selfishness (Choosing to look beyond yourself to the heart of the Master)* Back to the Bible (1996)

Philip Yancey: *Reaching for the Invisible God.* Zondervan (2000) Chapter 17 p. 213, used with permission

Rick Warren: *The Purpose Driven Life; What on earth am I here for?* Zondervan (2002) Chapter 22 p.176, used with permission

Collins Pocket English Dictionary, Harper Collins Publishers (1992)

**Chapter 4**

*I asked the Lord that I might grow.* John Newton (1725-1807) – Public Domain

Rick Warren: *The Purpose Driven Life; What on earth am I here for?* Zondervan (2002) Chapter 24 p.191

Elisabeth Elliott: *The Glad Surrender.* Kingsway Publications/ STL Books (1982) Chapter 6 p.37. Used by kind permission of Elisabeth Elliott.

C.S.Lewis: *The Great Divorce.* C.S.Lewis copyright © C. S. Lewis Pte. Ltd 1946 Extracts reprinted by permission.

*How the Ecdysozoan Changed Its Coat.* John Ewer Citation: Ewer J (2005) PLoS Biol 3(10): e349

doi:10.1371/journal.pbio.0030349    Published: October 11, 2005 Copyright: © 2005 John Ewer. (Please see website: http://biology.plosjournals.org)

**Chapter 5**

*Lord, we've seen your purpose.* Henry Thomas Smart. 1813 -1839 – Public Domain

Brother Andrew: *And God changed his mind because his people prayed.* Marshall Pickering (1990) Chapter 6 p.130. Used by permission of Baker Publishing Group.

Brother Yun: *The Heavenly Man.* Monarch Books (2002) Chapter 5 p.50/54 Used by permission of Lion Hudson plc.

Isobel Kuhn: *By Searching:An Autobiography. Vol.1.* (1957). OMF Books, Chapter 6 p. 44

Brother Andrew: *The Calling.* (Revised and expanded edition) Summit Publishing Ltd (2000) Chapter 8 p.145 Used by permission of Open Doors International, USA

* Statistic regarding Peacock butterflies: www.treknature.com/gallery/europe/united_kingdom/photo51629. htm

* Quotation regarding parasites : www.parasitecleanse.com/parasites.htm?src=google

* Story of release of infected butterflies: www.monarchwatch.org/biology/control.htm

**Chapter 6**

*"God knows"* from *"The Desert"* by Minnie Louise Haskins. Copyright © Minnie Louise Haskins,1908. Reproduced by permission of Sheil Land Associates Ltd.

Hannah Hurnard. *Hinds Feet on High Places* –Tyndale House Publishers, 1975 Chapter 18 p.143

Corrie Ten Boom: *The Hiding Place.* Hodder and Stoughton. (1971) (This edition 1976) Chapter 10 p144

Oswald Chambers. *My Utmost for his Highest* 1995 © as quoted in the Dayspring Calendar –Jan 2nd.  Used by permission of the Oswald Chambers Publications Association.

Research papers quoted:

1) The selective advantage of attendant ants for the larvae of a lycaenid butterfly, *Glaucopsyche lygdamus*. Pierce, N.E. and S. Easteal. Journal of Animal Ecology 55: 451-462. 1986.)

2) Assessing Benefits to Both Participants in a Lycaenid-Ant Association J. Hall Cushman,Vanessa K. Rashbrook, Andrew J. Beattie Ecology, Vol. 75, No. 4 (Jun., 1994), pp. 1031-1041 doi:10.2307/1939427

**Chapter 7**

*Lord, may thy blood now cleanse me.* Watchman Nee (1903-1972), used by permission of Living Stream Ministries

Hannah Whitall Smith. *The Christian's Secret of a Happy Life.* Barbour & Co, Inc(1985) chapter 1, p9 (Public Domain)

Oswald Chambers: *My utmost for his highest* 1995 © as quoted in the Dayspring Calendar –Jan 15th and Feb 24th. Used by permission of the Oswald Chambers Publications Association.

CS Lewis: *The Voyage of the Dawn Treader.* Harper Collins  Chapter 7 p.117 C.S.Lewis copyright © C. S. Lewis Pte. Ltd 1952 Extracts reprinted by permission

Quotation from the hymn *Trust and Obey.* John H. Sammis.(1846 - 1919) (Public Domain)

Reference to the teaching of Amanda and Roland Buys of Kanaan Ministries, used with permission. (www. kanaanministries.org)

**Chapter 8**

*Found.* Dave George. ©2002. Hillsong Publishing. Published by kingswaysongs.com for the UK & Eire (tym@kingsway.co.uk)

J. I. Packer: *A Passion for Holiness. Crossway Books (1992) Chapter 5*

Francine Rivers: *Redeeming Love.* Monarch (1997) Chapter 12, p131 Used by permission of Lion Hudson, plc

Rick Warren: *The Purpose Driven Life: What on earth am I here for?* Zondervan (2002) Chapter 35 p.277, used with permission

Jules Poirier: *From Darkness to Light to Flight.* Institution for Creation Research (1995)

\* Quotation regarding cells in waiting: Prof. Lincoln Brower. www.learner.org/jnorth/tm/monarch/ ChrysalisDevelopmentLPB.html Used by permission.

Oswald Chambers : *My Utmost for his Highest* (June 21) "We must get to the point of being sick to death of ourselves, until there is no longer any surprise at anything God might tell us about ourselves." Used by permission of the Oswald Chambers Publications Association.

**Chapter 9**

*Higher Ground.* Johnson Oatman, Jr 1898 (1856-1922 )- Public Domain

Philip Yancey: *Reaching the Invisible God.* Zondervan (2000) Chapter 17 p.217, used with permission.

Larry Crabb: *Shattered Dreams – God's unexpected pathway to joy.* Waterbrook Press (2001) Chapter 20 p.181/2, extract reprinted by permission

Francine Rivers: *Redeeming Love.* Monarch Books. (1997) Chapter 20, p262 Used by Permission of Lion Hudson, plc

CS Lewis: *Mere Christianity.* Fount Paperbacks/Harper Collins (1977) Chapter 10 p.185 C. S. Lewis copyright © C.S.Lewis Pte. Ltd 1942,1943,1944,1952 Extracts reprinted by permission

Elisabeth Elliott: *Passion and Purity.* Revell (1984) Chapter 19.Used by kind permission of Elisabeth Elliott.

John Ortberg: *If you want to walk on water, you've got to get out of the boat.* Zondervan (2001) Chapter 9.

Lewis B. Smedes: *Standing on the Promises.* Thomas Nelson Publishers (1998) Extract used by permission.

Bruce Wilkinson: *The Dream Giver.* Multnomah (2003)

*Teen-street – Metamorphosis* flyer – Quotation used by kind permission of Dan and Suzie Potter. (www. DUZIE.com)

**Chapter 10**

*What a blessing, what a priv'lege.* Witness Lee (1905 -1997). Used by permission of Living Stream Ministries

Oswald Chambers : *My Utmost for his Highest* "God's concept of service is what we are becoming, not what we are doing." Used by permission of the Oswald Chambers Publications Association.

*Jesus, my blood and righteousness.* N L von Zinzendorf (1700 - 1760) tr. John Wesley

**Epilogue**

George Verwer *No turning back – Pursuing the path of Christian discipleship.* OM Publishing.(1983) Used by permission of George Verwer

**Author's note:**

Please note: I have sought by all means possible to seek the permission of the copyright holders of all the quotes / reference material I have used. I am happy to hear from anyone who can give me further information regarding the copyrights of any material used in "Glory Unveiled".

# Website research

www.ukbutterflies.co.uk
www.nettles.org.uk/
http://mamba.bio.uci.edu/~pjbryant/biodiv/lepidopt/GettingIntoButterflies.htm
www.butterflyfarm.co.cr/ed/guide_mod3.htm
www.butterfly-guide.co.uk
www.butterflyschool.org
http://en.wikipedia.org/wiki/Ecdysis
http://en.wikipedia.org/wiki/Apolysis
www.butterflyzone.org/butterfly-articles
www.vncreatures.net/events11.php
www.zi.ku.dk/personal/drnash/atta/Pages/comm.html
www.blackwellpublishing.com/ridley/a-z/Mutualism.asp
http://users.sa.chariot.net.au/~rbg/aurifera_ds.htm
http://news.nationalgeographic.com/news/2008/01/080103-ants-butterflies.html
www.graceperfumes.net
www.kanaanministries.org
http://news.research.ohiou.edu/perspectives/archives/9701/cat2.htm
www.altapassfoundation.org/rearing_monarchs.htm
www.pbase.com/rcm1840/morphing
www.pbase.com/rcm1840/caterpillars
www.learner.org/jnorth/tm/monarch/ChrysalisDevelopmentLPB.html
www.learner.org/jnorth/tm/monarch/ChrysalisFormationLPB.html
http://en.wikipedia.org/wiki/Nectar
www.biology.sbc.edu/faculty/HomePageLPB.html
www.wikipedia.com
www.hilozoo.com/animals/AI_monarch4.htm
www.amnh.org/exhibitions/butterflies/highlights/metamorphosis.php
http://centralamerica.com/cr/butterfly/
www.zoo.org/bflies_blms/basics.html
http://news.bbc.co.uk/1/hi/sci/tech/7363411.stm
http://news.bbc.co.uk/1/hi/scotland/highlands_and_islands/7034039.stm
www.vncreatures.net/events09.php
www.vncreatures.net/events14.php

(All websites correct at time of going to print)

# The Photographers

## Jay Cossey

Jay began chasing butterflies with a net, virtually since the day he could walk. In his late teens, Jay traded his butterfly net for a camera and embarked on a lifelong celebration of Creation. He sees his passion more as nature photo-journalism than art, acknowledging that he had no hand in creating the beauty captured through his lens. Jay's photographs appear in numerous field guides, text books and periodicals, including National Geographic's 2004 Butterfly Calendar. If you wish to see more of his work, please visit www.photographsfromnature.com

Currently, Jay is a field photographer with the Biodiversity Institute of Ontario, at the University of Guelph. He travels throughout North America in "BIObus", a mobile field research vehicle (modified 30 foot motor home), photographing and collecting insects for the International Barcode of Life project - an ambitious initiative whose not-so modest mission is to establish a DNA database of all life on planet Earth. Learn more at www.dnabarcoding.org

## Bob Moul

Bob Moul has been fascinated with nature for as long as he can remember. After retiring he decided to fulfil a long time desire to observe and document as many of "Mother Nature's children" as possible, and to share these special moments with those who are like-minded. It is his hope that as others visit his website, young and old, that their curiosity will stirred or they will be inspired to search for, respect and conserve our natural heritage. Even for those busy with the chores of the day, he hopes that a few moments browsing through his web pages will help them find solace in the beauty of the butterfly. (http://www.pbase.com/rcm1840/profile)

## Dr. William Zittrich

William Zittrich, M.D.is currently a practicing physician in the field of Radiation Oncology in Southern California. Much of his free time is spent in the garden where the wonders of nature are on display. Monarch Butterflies migrate through twice a year, spring and fall. Part of the garden is devoted to Monarch larval plants and each year there is a new "crop" of Monarchs. ( http://www.geocities.com/wyllz)

# Photo Plates

**Plate 1: Egg and First Instar**

**Side 1**: Jay Cossey
Egg of the Red Spotted Purple *(Limenitis arthemis astyanax)* butterfly.
The adult butterfly can be seen in all its glory on Side 3 of Plate 4.

**Side 2:** Jay Cossey
Bronze Copper *(Lycaena hyllus)* egg
Tawny Emperor *(Asterocampa clyton)* eggs
Anglewing Question Mark *(Polygonia interrogationis)* eggs
Giant Swallowtail *(Papilio cresphontes)* egg

**Side 3**: William Zittrich
Sequence of photos showing the first instar caterpillar of the Monarch *(Danaus plexippus)* butterfly eating its way out of the shell

**Side 4**: William Zittrich
Tiny first instar of the Monarch larva *(Danaus plexippus)*

**Plate 2: Caterpillar Days**

**Side 1**: Jay Cossey
Larva of Spicebush Swallowtail *(Papilio troilus)*

**Side 2**: Jay Cossey
This side is to illustrate the amazing variety, and often ugly nature, of the caterpillar in comparison to its adult butterfly.
1.  Giant Swallowtail *(Papilio cresphontes)* larva on Hop tree.
2.  Giant Swallowtail *(Papilio cresphontes)* larva on Hop tree.
3.  Tiger Swallowtail Larva (Brown) *(Papilio glaucus)*
4.  Common Buckeye Larva, *(Junonia coenia)*

**Side 3**: William Zittrich
Larva of the Monarch *(Danaus plexippus)* displaying the appetite which then leads to ecdysis.

**Side 4:** Jay Cossey

This side illustrates the unusual friendship of the ant and the larva of the Blue Azure *(Celastrina Ladon)*.The ant can be seen tending to the larva. However, butterflies face many enemies. Here two orange Northern Crescent *(Phyciodes cocyta)* butterflies can be seen being attacked by a Crab Spider.

## Plate 3: Restless Wandering and Chrysalis Stage

**Side 1**: Jay Cossey
Zebra Swallowtail *(Eurytides marcellus)* Pupa

**Side 2**: William Zittrich
Restless Wandering Stage – Larva of Monarch *(Danaus plexippus)* hanging upside down to shed its skin (ecdysis) through a jerking motion, in order to go into the chrysalis stage.

**Side 3**: William Zittrich
The stages of the Monarch Butterfly *(Danaus plexippus)* chrysalis from the early days through till the point where the chrysalis becomes transparent before eclosion.

**Side 4**: Jay Cossey
Life cycle of the Giant Swallowtail *(Papilio cresphontes)*

## Plate 4: Imago

The last few sides are to show two key aspects of the butterfly's life: mating and feeding/pollination. They also display the wondrous beauty resulting from metamorphosis!

**Side 1**: Jay Cossey
Common Buckeye butterflies mating *(Junonia coenia)*

**Side 2**: Jay Cossey
Olive Hairstreak (juniper) butterflies *(Callophrys gryneus)* mating

**Side 3**: Bob Moul
The Red Spotted Purple butterfly *(Limenitis arthemis astyanax)*
This is the egg from the very start of the photographs. What a wonder!

**Side 4**: Jay Cossey
Monarch butterfly *(Danaus plexippus)*

# Glossary

Chapter 1
**Metamorphosis**: change of character or form / process the caterpillar will undergo to become a butterfly.
**Host plant:** the plant where the butterfly lays her eggs and which subsequently becomes the "host" and food-source for the emerging and growing caterpillars (larvae).

Chapter 2
**Instar:** the name given to each stage of the caterpillar's life. Each time it sheds another skin, it begins a new instar. Most caterpillars have between 4 - 6 instars.
**Diapause:** pause in growth during the egg stage maybe over winter, for example.
Imaginal disks: cells waiting within the caterpillar's body to be later developed into the various appendages of the butterfly, wings, antennae, proboscis, legs, etc

Chapter 3
**Larva (-vae):** insect in an immature stage, often resembling a worm.

Chapter 4
**Ecdysis:** the process whereby the caterpillar sheds its skin.
**Apolysis:** The process whereby the hormones are released into the caterpillar's body to initiate the release of the old skin and the growth of a new skin underneath before the caterpillar sheds the old skin.

Chapter 5
**Pathogen:** disease.
**Predator:** animal which habitually hunts other animals for food.
**Parasite:** animal or plant living in or on another; also person that lives at someone else's expense.
**Protozoan:** Single-celled microscopic organism.

Chapter 6
**Symbiosis:** where one organism helps another to the benefit of both parties.
**Myrmecophily:** ant-loving ( A myrmecophile is an organism that lives in association with ants.)
**Lycaenidae:** butterfly family comprising of the coppers, blues and hairstreaks.

Chapter 7:
**Restless wandering stage:** name given by naturalists to the final instar of the caterpillar as it prepares to go into the chrysalis.

Chapter 8
**Chrysalis:** stage between caterpillar and butterfly inside the pupa.
**Metabolism:** chemical processes of a living body.
**Anabolism ( adj- anabolic):** metabolic process in which body tissues are synthesized from food.
**Catabolism:** the breaking down of complex molecules into simple ones.
**Histolysis:** the catabolic process of breaking down the former caterpillar parts.
**Histogenesis:** the anabolic process of "rebuilding" the butterfly.
**Mitosis:** cell division.

Chapter 9
**Eclosion:** emergence of the butterfly from the chrysalis.
**Haemolymph:** the blood-like substance of insects.
**Meconium:** a nitrogenous substance – the metabolic waste products of birth.

Chapter 10
**Imago:** adult butterfly capable of reproduction.
**Lepidoptera:** (from the Greek for "scaled wings") Order of insects with four scaled wings eg: butterflies /moths.